JENNIE
Lady Randolph Churchill

A Portrait with Letters

JENNIE

Lady Randolph Churchill

A Portrait with Letters

PEREGRINE CHURCHILL

AND

JULIAN MITCHELL

ST. MARTIN'S PRESS

New York

CONTENTS

ILLUSTRATIONS

Mrs. Patrick Campbell (*Paul Popper*)
Electioneering at Oldham (*Peregrine Churchill*)
Jennie at the piano
Jennie and Winston, 1912 (*Press Association*)

Jennie writing letters (*Hulton*)   *between pages* 208–209
Montagu Porch (*Chartwell Trust*)
Jennie with children and grandchildren
Jennie in old age (*Peregrine Churchill*)
Jennie with Peregrine Churchill (*Peregrine Churchill*)

PREFACE

It is hard to believe, in the age of the telephone, how many hours a day an Edwardian society lady spent scribbling notes and letters. First there was the family: husband away shooting or fishing, perhaps, sons at school, daughters being 'finished', mother and father in the country, brothers and sisters married and scattered, in-laws, cousins—all of whom had to be kept informed of what one was doing and where one was dining. Then there were close friends in England, and distant ones in India or South Africa or America, who required regular bulletins from the home country.

There might be one special friend, too, rather closer than close. On top of all that, there was the whole demanding business of issuing and answering invitations and writing thank-you letters, without which the social round could not be kept going. Finally, and very much last, there were tradesmen to be dealt with, and their tiresome bills. One lady's lifetime correspondence would fill a house.

Jennie Jerome, Lady Randolph Churchill, did not keep absolutely everything, but she kept a great deal. She once wrote what a great boon a tell-tale scrap of paper could be for a playwright, novelist or historian, and as a playwright herself, perhaps she had future dramatists in mind as she carefully put away her private correspondence. One of these is extremely grateful that she did, for it is on the papers she left at her death that Julian Mitchell has based his seven scripts for the Thames Television series, *Jennie: Lady Randolph Churchill*. The letters to be found there are a family chronicle in themselves, recording how domestic dramas and public events affected both Jennie and her husband Lord Randolph, and revealing the gradual development of their sons Winston and Jack.

Among Jennie's papers, for instance, are all the letters Randolph ever wrote her, and nearly all hers to him. She kept every ink-blot from her sons, too. And though her second marriage to George Cornwallis-West ended in the divorce court, she never destroyed his love-letters. Then there is a long correspondence from the Prince of Wales, later Edward VII: there are several files about *The Anglo-Saxon Review*, the short-lived literary magazine which Jennie edited: there are some most revealing letters from her mother-in-law, the Duchess of Marlborough. But there are gaps, too, and significant ones. For instance, one of the greatest loves of Jennie's life was the Austrian diplomat Count Kinsky, but only one letter and one telegram from him are to be found among her papers, and those from long after their affair was over. There is nothing whatever about Jennie's not very successful play, *His Borrowed Plumes,* perhaps because George Cornwallis-West went off with the leading lady. And Jennie kept surprisingly few letters from her parents and sisters.

Some of the missing letters may turn up in time, but it has been the material actually available which has dictated the form of this book. It is not a full biography of Jennie: instead, we have tried to draw a portrait with letters, selecting particular moments in her life, and using the documents to throw new light upon them. Jennie's papers contain far more letters than we could possibly hope to publish, and many of them are naturally of little interest to a modern reader. Furthermore, a good many have already been published in the excellent life of Sir Winston Churchill, begun by his son Randolph, and now being completed by Martin Gilbert. We have not felt we need reprint more than a few of these: our subject is Jennie, not her famous son, and we have played down his role in this book deliberately. For the same reason, we have not tried to give more than the outline of Lord Randolph Churchill's political career, a subject of enormous and enduring interest in itself, but going well beyond the scope of an intimate portrait. Nonetheless we believe we have answered some previously puzzling questions and corrected a good many errors, some of them damaging, about Jennie's life. We hope we have shown her as she really was.

We have silently corrected spelling errors, removed insignificant repetitions, expanded obscure contractions, capitalized words according to modern convention, and have sometimes added the punctuation to avoid obscurity. Something very characteristic would be lost from Jennie's letters if we put commas and full stops instead of her almost invariable dashes. French phrases have been left as written: the less obvious ones have been translated in notes at the end of each chapter. The source of each letter or quotation can be found in the references at the end of the book.

We are most grateful to all those who have given us permission to quote from letters in which they hold copyright: the Duke of Marlborough (the Duke and Duchess of Marlborough and the Marquess of Blandford), Lady Mary Grosvenor (Shelagh, Duchess of Westminster), Mr J. H. Pless (Daisy, Princess of Pless), John Farquharson Ltd (Henry James), Baroness Spencer-Churchill (Clementine Churchill), Mrs Bryda Hill-Murray (Montagu Porch), the Earl of Rosebery (Lord Rosebery), Mr Seymour Leslie (Leonie Leslie), the Hon. Mark Bonham Carter (Lady Violet Bonham Carter), Viscount Scarsdale (Lord and

Lady Curzon), Mrs E. J. Spurrier (Lady Warwick), Prince F. U. Kinsky (Count Kinsky), Lady Leslie (Shane Leslie), Miss E. M. Watson (George Cornwallis-West). In some cases it has been impossible to trace the holders of copyright. Will any copyright holders who have not been acknowledged, please accept the authors' apologies? Copyright in the papers of Lord and Lady Randolph Churchill, Major John Churchill and Lady Gwendeline Churchill belongs to Mr Peregrine Churchill. The Chartwell Trust, the Duke of Marlborough, Miss Anita Leslie and Mr Seymour Leslie have kindly allowed us to quote from letters in their possession.

We are also grateful to the following publishers for permission to quote from the works mentioned: William Heinemann Ltd (*Winston S. Churchill* by Randolph S. Churchill and Martin Gilbert), Hutchinson & Co. Ltd (*The Fabulous Leonard Jerome, Jennie* and *Edwardians in Love*, all by Anita Leslie), John Murray Ltd (*Parliamentary Reminiscences* by Lord George Hamilton, *From My Private Diary* by Daisy, Princess of Pless, and *The Jerome Connexion* by Seymour Leslie), the Hamlyn Publishing Group Ltd (*Lord Randolph Churchill* and *My Early Life* by Winston S. Churchill), and the Bodley Head Ltd (*Edwardian Hey-Days* by George Cornwallis-West). All these books have proved extremely useful, as has *Perfect Darling* by Eileen Quelch. Jennie's own books, *The Reminiscences of Lady Randolph Churchill* and *Small Talks on Big Subjects*, and her contributions to *The Anglo-Saxon Review*, were also invaluable.

We are indebted to many people for their help, especially Lady Betty Cartwright, Mrs Peregrine Churchill, Mr Martin Gilbert, Mr David Green, Mr John Hambley, Dr M. A. Hoskin, Miss Anita Leslie, Mr Seymour Leslie, Miss Eileen Quelch, Miss Angela Raspin, Mr Richard Rowson, Professor Peter Stansky, Miss Elizabeth Thomas and Miss Alison Wade, who helped most of all.

INTRODUCTION

Jennie Jerome, christened Jeanette, was born on January 9th, 1854, in Brooklyn, New York. In 1874 she married Lord Randolph Spencer Churchill, the younger son of the Duke of Marlborough. Their eldest son became Sir Winston Churchill.

Randolph came from the old world, Jennie from the new. The Spencers and Churchills had played leading parts in the history of the British Isles over the course of four centuries. The Jeromes had emigrated from England to America in the early eighteenth century, and had, until Jennie's father's generation, made no mark on history at all. Yet it was the combination of these extremely different families which produced the greatest British statesman of the twentieth century.

The Spencers first came to notice under the Tudors, when they were successful sheep-farmers; later they achieved fame when they married into the Sydneys, a more ancient family of soldiers and statesmen. The Churchills were solid West Country folk, rather close to the earth. A link with Sir Francis Drake's family produced John Churchill, the brilliant general whom Queen Anne created first Duke of Marlborough in 1702. The Spencers and Churchills came together through the marriage of the first Duke's daughter to Charles Spencer, Earl of Sunderland. The Duke having no surviving male issue, his titles descended through this female line. The surname Spencer-Churchill was not in fact adopted till 1817.

For a hundred years and more after the death of John Churchill, the Dukes of Marlborough were distinguished mainly for their colossal extravagance. Though the ducal income was vast, they spent it and more. It was not until Randolph's father that a Marlborough again became a national figure of any importance. John Winston, the seventh Duke, was serious and puritanical: he took a passionate interest in Church reform. He was married to Frances Anne Emily Vane, daughter of the Marquess of Londonderry. His mother-in-law was a great political hostess and close friend of Disraeli, and with his wife's encouragement the Duke soon became a political figure in his own right. In 1867 he became Lord President of the Council, and a Cabinet Minister. Thus Randolph grew up in an atmosphere which was as political as it was aristocratic.

Jennie's background was neither. Her father, Leonard Jerome, was born in 1818, one of the large family of a farmer in Syracuse, in upper New York State. The Jeromes were not rich, though they were prosperous. It was Leonard's elder brothers who unselfishly paid for his education at Princeton, and even so there was not enough money for him to complete his degree there. He worked first in his uncle's law office in Palmyra, then bought the local newspaper at Rochester with his younger brother. In 1847 he married Clarissa, or Clara, Hall, one of three orphaned heiresses. Clara's great-grandmother was reputed to be an Iroquois squaw. True or not, the Hall sisters were dark and appeared more Red Indian as they grew old, and Clara was known as 'Sitting Bull' by her impertinent sons-in-law. The Jeromes soon moved to New York, where Leonard rapidly made a fortune on the stock exchange.

The marriage was a triumph—and later a failure—of opposites. Leonard liked racing and yachting, patronized the opera, and had a weakness for female opera singers. He had been passionately fond of music since his boyhood. Clara was rather puritanical, and practically tone-deaf. Her ambitions were social.

Their first daughter, also called Clara, was born in 1851. Shortly after her birth the family went to Europe for nearly two years, for Leonard had been appointed American Consul in Trieste. Europe, Mrs Jerome decided, was where she really wanted to live. But Leonard lost his first fortune and had to make another before they could leave New York again. It did not take him long. In 1858, when Jennie was four, the Jeromes went to live in Paris, where their last daughter, Leonie, was born in 1859. (A fourth girl died in childhood.) The family returned to America in 1860, to a splendid mansion which Leonard built in Madison Square: for the opening ball there were fountains of champagne and eau de Cologne: he liked things to be on a lavish scale. But after the Civil War, when he plunged again into a hurly-burly life of business, sport, and special performances by favoured singers in his private theatre, Mrs Jerome decided she could live a more dignified life in Europe. Although there was nothing the matter with her at all, she announced that her health made it imperative for her to live in Paris; besides, Paris was the only possible place to educate one's daughters. In 1868 she settled there with Clara, Jennie and Leonie: Leonard paid regular visits, but his home remained New York.

Paris was everything Mrs Jerome desired. The Emperor Napoleon III and the Empress Eugénie accepted Americans with none of the haughtiness of other European monarchs, and wealth was a sufficient passport to social success. Mrs Jerome took on a new lease of life: she wrote her name with French accents, Jérôme, and Jennie became Jeannette, with two Ns. Mrs Jerome even began to take an interest in music, and could be heard to hum the simpler leitmotivs of Wagner.

Jennie was fourteen now, and must have peeped with longing from behind the schoolroom door when Princes and Princesses paid their calls, and listened with impatience and envy to her sister Clara's thrilling descriptions of life at the Imperial court. But she must have missed her father, too, for she was his favourite. She loved to ride, like him, and she shared his passion for music: she could play the piano to concert standard. She had a natural eye for the fine arts: in later life she could never resist acquiring things of beauty whether she could afford them or not. But in spite of the close bond between father and daughter, Jennie's ambitions were Parisian ones. In only another year or two she would make her début at that glittering Imperial court.

But, alas, in 1870 came the Franco-Prussian war, with Paris besieged by the Germans. The Jeromes were among the last to flee. Mrs Jerome, hobbling with a sprained ankle, just got her daughters on to the last train to Deauville. Leonard, who was taking part in the first international Atlantic yacht-race, hurried to the rescue, and installed his family in London. But London was not a success. English society was as cold as the climate, and the news from France grew worse and worse. When the Jeromes returned to Paris it was to a very mournful city. The Emperor was deposed, the Tuileries Palace was in ruins. There was no court, no society, nowhere for an ambitious American girl to make her début. All the Jeromes had to look forward to was their annual visit to England, and Cowes regatta. Usually Leonard came too, but in 1873 he was busy in New York, having just lost his fortune again. So he was not there when Jennie was presented to the Prince and Princess of Wales. It wasn't the same as an Imperial presentation, of course, but it was the best she could hope for.

I

COURTSHIP

Cowes, in the Isle of Wight, was in 1873, as it is now, the yacht-racing centre of the world. Led by the Prince of Wales, who took a keen part in the racing itself, fashionable British society came down to the little seaside village to relax after the rigours of the London season. Queen Victoria lived close by at Osborne, the house she had built with her husband, Prince Albert, but the chill formality which her name implied did not extend beyond the walls of her estate. Cowes itself was a delightful place to gossip and flirt and watch the boats and go on picnics. Everyone knew everyone else, and there were no glorified villas or piers or bands or nigger minstrels, and there weren't, Jennie wrote later, too many yachts for too few moorings. It was all very casual and charming. At Cowes the Prince and Princess of Wales could stroll about without ceremony and enjoy themselves like ordinary mortals.

Albert Edward, Prince of Wales, was thirty-two in 1873, and his reputation for fast living was already well established. He was a welcome and regular visitor in the less respectable parts of Paris, and although in that case completely innocent, he had already been summoned to give evidence in a divorce court. He led a thoroughly frivolous life, eating too much, gambling, shooting, fishing, racing, making love—while he waited, and waited, to inherit his kingdom. Excluded from all political life, he needed constant diversion to prevent him becoming bored, and though Princess Alexandra did her best, she was quite unable to keep him amused by herself. Inevitably he became surrounded by people with tastes and morals similar to his own: his friends were known as the Marlborough House Set, after the Prince's London home on the Mall. Marlborough House was no longer anything to do with the Duke of Marlborough, but among the leaders of the Set were his sons—George Charles, Marquess of Blandford and Lord Randolph Churchill. Blandford, as even his family called him, was twenty-nine and unsatisfactorily married. Randolph was twenty-four, and his life had so far been singularly carefree. He had gone to Eton and Oxford, he had been taken on a grand tour of Europe, he had applied himself to nothing except his pack of hounds, the Blenheim Harriers. He was somewhat moody, and had rather poppy eyes, and as he strolled about Cowes that August he had with him a little pugdog called Puggles.

Now they had been presented to the Prince of Wales, Jennie and Clara Jerome were invited to all the fashionable goings-on. Jennie at nineteen was far more beautiful than her elder sister; she was dark, with shining eyes. But the blonde Clara was far more knowing about society: she had spent a weekend with the Emperor Napoleon III at Compiègne. For both girls Cowes was a delight. Their mother's social circle in Paris was dull and snobbish and frowsty: Cowes was all light and air, the sun sparkling on the water, the boom of the starting-gun, dancing. Jennie was an excellent dancer.

That year Cowes received a visit from the future Czar Alexander III of Russia, whose sister Marie had just become engaged to the Prince of Wales's brother, the Duke of Edinburgh. The Czarevitch was a huge man, and his wife was tiny, so they must have made an extraordinary couple when they danced. But they did dance, indeed a special ball was given in their honour on board HMS *Ariadne*, guardship to the regatta, on August 12th. It was an afternoon dance, from 3.30 to 7.30, and the harbour must have been filled with boats carrying the elegant and fashionable across the dancing waves to the flag-bedecked warship.

Jennie had been looking forward to the ball with great excitement—she had never been to such a grand and glittering social occasion, graced not only by the Russian royalties, but by the Prince and Princess of Wales, too. She kept the invitation all her life. But under the words 'To meet', setting him above the Royal and Imperial Highnesses, Jennie later wrote the one word 'Randolph'. For it was on the *Ariadne* that August afternoon that Lord Randolph Churchill was introduced to Miss Jennie Jerome by their mutual friend Mr Frank Bertie. Randolph quickly found himself at a disadvantage: waltzing, he was obliged to confess, made him dizzy. So after a formal quadrille, they sat and talked. It was love at first sight. Before the ball was over, Jennie persuaded her mother to ask Randolph and another friend, Colonel Edgcumbe, back to dinner that night. They were only too delighted to accept. 'We spent a very pleasant evening', Jennie wrote years later, 'my sister and I playing duets at the piano and chatting merrily.' There must have been more to the merriment than music and chat. After dinner, Randolph, immensely struck, told Colonel Edgcumbe half-seriously that he meant to try and marry 'the dark one'. After he'd gone, Jennie asked Clara what she thought of him: he did not, it seems, come up to Clara's exacting Parisian standards. Jennie interrupted her, and told her to say no more: she had a presentiment she would marry him. Clara laughed—it was absurd!

Next day Randolph and Jennie met again 'by accident' and had a walk. The Isle of Wight is very beautiful in summer, but they cannot have spent much time discussing the scenery. On the Friday Randolph came to dinner again. It was a perfect night. The harbour glimmered with reflected lights from the yachts. It was only natural to want to go out into the garden and stand beneath the stars. So Randolph and Jennie went. And Randolph asked her to marry him. And Jennie said yes.

Though swept away by their mutual love, Jennie and Randolph had not altogether lost their senses. They knew very well that there would be aghastness and horror and hands raised in outrage by all those who had forgotten what it was to be young and in love. Mrs Jerome, for instance, would certainly not understand the suddenness of it. So they decided not to tell her. Randolph was supposed to leave Cowes on the Saturday morning, but of course he postponed his departure. The first note he ever wrote to Jennie was carefully unimpassioned, so that Mrs Jerome would not become suspicious:

Marine Hotel

Dear Miss Jeannette   Saturday
   I missed my boat & have not been able to go; so shall not start till early Monday morning Thankyou so very much for the photograph which is much better than the others; shall hope to see you after church tomorrow. You see I keep turning up like a bad shilling
Yrs vy sincerely
Randolph S. Churchill

The letter is in an uncharacteristically neat hand, but for all its artificiality there is something endearingly arrogant—perhaps essentially Churchillian—in the way Randolph ennobled the common penny to a shilling. He valued himself highly.

The weekend was idyllically happy, as the lovers exchanged vows and tokens under the unsuspecting eyes of Jennie's mother. But after he had left on Sunday night, Jennie broke the news to Mrs Jerome. Her reaction was just what they had expected: they were both quite mad, she thought, and she refused to hear of anything so precipitate. Jennie scribbled a first quick note to Randolph that same evening:

   I cannot bear to have you leave Cowes—dearest without a last good-bye—I have told Mama who although she likes you *very* much won't

hear of it But I am sure we shall easily get her on our side later on—
when we see you in London or perhaps here—God bless you darling—

Sunday night

yours

Jeannette

Don't smoke too much——

Randolph received the note next morning:

Steamboat

7.15 a.m.

A thousand thanks dearest Jeannette for your darling little note which
cheered me up wonderfully. I only got it just as I was getting on
board. It is a wet misty morning & I feel wretched. I cannot think
your mother will really not hear of our engagement only I am sure
she thinks we have known each other for too short a time. You and I
do not think so, but it is natural your mother shld. Oh dear how I
hope I may be able to get back to Cowes, but I hardly think I shall be.
Write me some more of those charming notes of yours to Blenheim.
They will be the only gleams of sunshine I shall get for some time. I
will CERTAINLY meet you in London. What a happy evening we had
last night, in fact all yesterday was too happy for me. I have got your
photographs & your dear little pin, to look at, they will keep you every
minute, in my memory Do not you be unhappy at all or low, you have
no need to be so dearest. We shall assuredly meet again before long,
till which happy period may you be protected from every kind of
wrong annoyance or harm. Think of me sometimes & have confidence
& patience.

Goodbye dearest

Love to Clara

Yrs ever devotedly & lovingly

Randolph

And off he steamed into the morning mist, on his way back to the
mainland. Between a Tuesday afternoon and a Friday night a great
Anglo-American alliance had been arranged, with consequences which
no one that August morning could possibly have dreamed.

Mrs Jerome remained, for the moment, firm against the engagement,
and forbade Jennie to write. But Randolph could scarcely keep pen from
paper once he was back home at Blenheim, the enormous palace given to
the first Duke by Queen Anne:

Blenheim
Tuesday

My own darling Jeannette

I cannot let another day pass without writing to you. I do not think I ever had such a day as yesterday; such a melancholy journey away from you. & then to have to listen to the twaddle & gossip of my mother & sisters when my heart & thoughts were elsewhere. It is so curious that my rooms & my things & my occupations here which I used to take interest in are quite hateful to me now, all I can do is to keep reading your letter & looking at your photographs & thinking thinking till I get quite stupid. I do not think dearest you have any idea of how much I love you, or what sacrifices I wld not make to call you my own. My whole life & energies shld be devoted to making you happy & protecting you from harm or wrong, Life shld be to you like one long summer day. Oh dear how few & short were the days we had together, so happy tho; I hope you are passing the time pleasantly. I told my mother everything. Of course she was vy much surprised & cld not understand anything taking place so rapidly. I am going to write to my father in a day or two & when I get his answer I shall then write to your mother & tell her exactly what my position & prospects & means are. The two former are good enough but the latter I must tell you are by no means grand. For myself I am careless, & wld face if necessary even starvation if I had you, but love is selfish as well as blind, I cld not ask you to give up any one of those luxuries & comforts to which you have been all along accustomed; Dearest if you only knew how unhappy & wretched I am away from you. I cannot imagine now however I got myself away from Cowes. Those too few hours we spent together will tell either one way or the other on the future happiness or misery of my whole life. I enclose you a little photograph I had done about 3 years ago at Ischl.[1]* It is not a vy good one but you may like to have it. Dearest Jeannette please do not forget me, I know how much you are *entourée*[2] & admired and feel quite mad sometimes to think that I am not by your side. Goodbye darling.

Believe me ever
Yrs most devotedly & lovingly
Randolph

Randolph's father and brother were both away in Scotland, and with only two of his six sisters married, he may well have felt oppressed by feminine gossip. But it was not twaddle that he would have got from his mother on breaking his unexpected news. The Duchess of Marlborough was a formidable character, who was most ambitious for her younger son, Blandford having proved nothing but trouble since his schooldays. Though he was highly intelligent and took a great interest in scientific inventions, Blandford was also wilful and wayward, violent in temper, and unfaithful to his wife. His parents had abandoned all hope of his ever having a serious political career. Instead they looked to Randolph.

At the gates of Blenheim Palace stands the small Oxfordshire town of Woodstock. In 1873 Woodstock, although it had only eleven hundred and one registered voters, was still a parliamentary constituency. For generations it had been completely under the control of the Dukes of Marlborough. Randolph's father had himself held the seat, before he inherited his title, and when he resigned he handed it over to his brother. Political contrariness ran in the family, however, and the Duke and Lord Alfred Churchill quarrelled over Free Trade: after a still more bitter dispute over Church Rates, a subject on which the Duke held very strong opinions, Lord Alfred had been obliged to resign. For the time being, Blandford being considered unsuitable, and in any case unwilling, the seat was occupied by the Duke's nominee, a Mr Barnett, a banker who was squire of nearby Glympton Park. It was the Duke and Duchess's ambition that Randolph should take over at the next election, which was expected to be soon. Randolph had not yet begun to think for himself, and there was no political disagreement between him and his parents. He rightly, however, anticipated strong parental opposition to his proposed marriage. When he wrote to his father, therefore, the letter was carefully phrased:

> I must not any longer keep you in ignorance of a very important step I have taken—one which will undoubtedly influence very strongly all my future life.
>
> I met, soon after my arrival at Cowes, a Miss Jeannette Jerome, the daughter of an American lady who has lived for some years in Paris and whose husband lives in New York. I passed most of my time at Cowes in her (Jeannette's) society, and before leaving asked her if she loved me well enough to marry me; and she told me she did. I do not think that if I were to write pages I could give you any idea of the strength of my feelings and affections and love for her; all I can say is that I love her better than life itself, and that my one hope and dream now is that matters may be so arranged that soon I may be united to her by ties that nothing but death itself could have the power to sever.
>
> I know, of course, that you will be very much surprised, and find it difficult to understand how an attachment so strong could have arisen

in so short a space of time; and really I feel it quite impossible for me to give any explanation of it that could appear reasonable to anyone practical and dispassionate. I must, however, ask you to believe it as you could the truest and most real statement that could possibly be made to you, and to believe also that upon a subject so important, and I may say so solemn, I could not write one word that was in the smallest degree exaggerated, or that might not be taken at its fullest meaning.

I hope you won't feel any annoyance with me for not having consulted you before saying anything to her. I really meant to have done so; but on the night before I was leaving Cowes (Friday) my feelings of sorrow at parting from her were more than I could restrain, and I told her all. I did not say anything to her mother, but I believe that she did after I was gone; for she wrote to me just as I was starting (I did not, after all, leave Cowes till the Monday), and she said in her letter that her mother could not hear of it. That I am at a loss to understand.

I told Mama when I got here and should have written at once to tell you; but I was so wretched and miserable at leaving thus, I was quite incapable of writing quietly.

I now write to tell you of it all, and to ask you whether you will be able to increase my allowance to some extent to put me in the position to ask Mrs Jerome to let me become her daughter's future husband. I enclose you her photograph, and will only say about her that she is as nice, as lovable, and amiable and charming in every way as she is beautiful, and that by her education and bringing-up she is in every way qualified to fill any position.

She has an elder sister, and one younger, who is not yet out. Mr Jerome is a gentleman who is obliged to live in New York to look after his business. I do not know what it is. He is reputed to be very well off, and his daughters, I believe, have very good fortunes, but I do not know anything for certain. He generally comes over for three or four months every year. Mrs Jerome has lived in Paris for several years and has educated her daughters there. They go out in Society there and are very well known.

I have told you all I know about them at present. You have always been very good to me, and done as much and more for me always than I had any right to expect; and with any arrangement that you may at any time make for me I shall be perfectly contented and happy. I see before me now a very happy future, almost in one's grasp. In the last year or so I feel I have lost a great deal of what energy and ambition I possessed, and an idle and comparatively useless life has at times appeared to me to be the pleasantest; but if I were married to her whom I have told you about, if I had a companion, such as she would be, I feel sure, to take an interest in one's prospects and career, and to encourage me to exertions and to doing something towards making a name for myself, I think I might become, with the help of Providence, all and perhaps more than you had ever wished and hoped for me. On the other hand, if anything should occur to prevent my fondest hopes and wishes being realized (a possibility which I dare not and cannot bring myself to think of), how dreary and uninteresting would life become to me! No one goes through what I have lately gone through without its leaving a strong impress and bias on their character and future. Time might, of course, partially efface the impression and recollection of feelings so strong as those I have tried to describe to you, but in the interval the best years of one's life would be going, and one's energies and hopes would become blunted and deadened.

I will not allude to her. I believe and am convinced that she loves me as fully, and as strongly if possible, as I do her; and when two people feel towards each other what we do, it becomes, I know, a great responsibility for anyone to assist in either bringing about or thwarting a union so closely desired by each.

Good-bye. I have written to you all I have done, all I feel, and all I know.

Anxiously wishing for an answer from you,

I remain

Ever your most affectionate son,
Randolph

Randolph's skill in drafting an awkward political letter had been remarked on by one of his Oxford tutors: 'He made up his own mind; having well reflected, he chose his ground of attack, and then took every pains about the form of expression.' Now he chose to attack his parents where they were weakest; in their love and ambition for him. There was really only one way in which Randolph's phrases about 'an idle and comparatively useless life' and his 'energies and hopes' becoming 'blunted and deadened' could be taken. If the Duke and Duchess refused to let him marry Jennie, then he wouldn't stand for Woodstock at the next election. He did not tell Jennie exactly what tactics he was adopting:

I cannot keep myself from writing any longer to you dearest, although I have not had any answer to either of my two letters. I suppose your mother does not allow you to write to me Perhaps you have not got either of my letters, but still I write on the chance, as I am so dreadfully

afraid that perhaps you may think I am forgetting you. I can assure
you dearest Jeannette you have not been out of my thoughts hardly
for one minute since I left you Monday. I have written to my father
everything, how much I love you how much I long & pray & how
much I wld sacrifice if it were necessary to be married to you and to
live ever after with you never to be parted till death. I shall[not] get
an answer till Monday & whichever way it lies I shall go to Cowes
soon after & tell your mother everything. I am afraid she does not like
me vy much from what I have heard. & yet I feel I cld be so fond of
her *really*. She was so kind to me at Cowes, & so goodnatured that I
wld do anything she wished if she only wld not oppose us. Dearest if
you are as fond of me as I am of you as I like to think you are nothing
human cld keep us long apart. This last week has seemed an eternity
to me; Oh, I wld give my soul for another of those days we had
together not long ago. I daresay the people you see are only too ready
to abuse me. God knows they cannot say with truth any real bad of
me; only I get so mad and distracted when I think that perhaps you
might listen to anybody except me. *Les absents ont toujours tort,*[3] they
say. Oh if I cld only get one line from you to reassure me, but I dare
not ask you to do anything that your mother wld disapprove of or has
perhaps forbidden you to do. If she has kept my letters from you even
I cannot blame her. I can only wish & long that she knew me better
and trusted me more. I do not mind her seeing everything I write as
long as you see it too. Sometimes I doubt so I cannot help it whether
you really like me as you said at Cowes you did. If you do I cannot
fear for the future tho' difficulties may lie in our way only to be sur-
mounted by patience. But remember dearest

There is a love beyond all that the poets have told
When two that are bound by one heavenly tie
with hearts never changing & brows never cold
love on through all ills & love on till they die
One hour of a passion so sacred is worth
Whole ages of heartless & wandering bliss
& oh if there be an elysium on earth
it is this it is this.[4]

Goodbye dearest Jeannette. My first and only love Hoping & pray-
ing that you may get this & longing I can not tell you how much to
see you

Believe me ever to be

Yrs devotedly & lovingly
Randolph S Churchill

While the Duke took his time to reply, Blandford, to whom Randolph had also written, soon gave vent to his feelings. He was unhappily married, and placed his own example before his brother as one to be avoided at all costs. He wrote at length, and in very peculiar though vigorous prose:[5]

Arisaig, Aug. 25/73, N.B.

My Dear Old Chap

I got your letter on Saturday when I arrived but as there is only a post twice a week I could not write before today. I may say that I am not in the least surprised at the contents of your letter as I know you so well that I can easily judge of the effect that impressions such as you describe have on you. You will say when you read this that you expected as much from me. This will be partly because you know my general opinions & partly because you realy feel dowbtful of yourself & your hasty judgement I feel that what I am about to say is like words scattered to the raging gale however! I resemble Samson who tried to slay 1,000ds of men with the jaw bone of an ass (if we are to believe history) only that he succeeded, & that I shall not. I am going to place before you argument & persuasion the two weakest weapons we have in our mental armoury arraid against your combined infatuations! Had you written to me on half a sheet of note paper I should have understood your story as well as if I had been with you & seen you myself wading through that slough of despond which every one in the world is perpetually tumbling into, & from which some get out (perhaps somewhat mudied & begrimed) but where others stick & held fast hopelessly. With a rashness that, I even I, was never capable of you run *tête basse*[6] into the wildest superlative of conceivable folly. This is my Vienna Philosopher, making laws for the nation & following them are widely different are they not? I hold up my hands in silent dismay. You go from impression to impression. Good! *'Mais la suite de cela?'*[7] Listen you will either live to see my predictions fulfilled to the letter *viz*, that before a year you will be painfully aware of your grievous & immutable folly, or you will some day extole my wisdom to the skys, & be careful to avoid like combinations in future. I can say no more without only repeating myself. You are my only brother & what you do affects me far more than anything that can befall to any one else. You know however the weight of your own actions, & with open eyes, not blindfolded, you may chose to throw yourself headlong from a rock, & we can none of us help you or prevent you. It shall not be though without heartfelt counsel from me. It is no use my imploring you, because that adds

nothing to the argument. If you are not quite mad & have yet a glim-
mering of rational ideas about you, Consider once more! Risk anything! *'Même une bassess'*[8] *but dont marry.* [TEAR] nothing teach a
man but [TEAR] experience! Has Destiny [TEAR] powerful a force
over him. [TEAR] no one can deliver him [TEAR]—gnash!! I fear it! I
myself am a specimen of the latter class, & I would therefore place
before you my own example as one to be avoided. Had you been five &
thirty or forty I should have pitied you but at five & twenty, with life
before instead of behind you, I tell you that you are mad simply mad.
I dont care if *la demoiselle* was the incarnation of all moral excellen-
cies & physical beauties on Gods earth, my opinion is the same. Had
you told me that it was a married woman you wanted to go off with, I
should say if you cant live happy without her go! Fate calls you. Had
it been a woman for whom you were ruining yourself, I should say Fa-
tality. But my friend *Le marriage!* It is a delusion & a snare, like all
the rest, only with this disagreeable addition that it is irrevocable.

Will no one believe me!

Have you any solid end in view in this affair No!

Do you marry for a fortune No!

Do you marry to get children No!

Do you marry because you have loved a woman for years No!

Do you marry because you feel you are getting old & played out No!

You realy only want to marry because you are in love with an *idea,
'une phantasie de six jours au bains de mêr'.*[9]

Damnation! here you are a sensible man no longer a child, positively triffling in this manner & here am I a born ass, trying to argue
the matter seriously with you. My dear Randolph for God's sake
listen to me, (though of course you wont) you are bored *desoeuvré*[10]
in fact, *'vous êtes a la recherche des emotions, et vous avez touche
mal,' tres mal!*[11]

'God help your judgement' would say the sectarian, 'use your un-
deniably good wits' is my advice & the inevitable deduction that you
will arrive at as you calm down is that you are a D——d fool. Excuse
my plain speaking old Chap, but seriously I do pity you more than
I can say *'ce sont de ces choses qui font veillir les jeunes têtes.'*[12]
You know what I have often told you but so it must be, I have given
you my opinion once for all, as you ask me, & I do most sincerely
hope & trust that this my answer may assist in persuading you if your
intense misjudgement in this affair Remember old Chap that there
is only you & I, & that when you do marry, it is everything for both
of us that we should all live together, not in the *decousu*[13] sort of

fashion of so many people we know, everything I have is at your service for God's sake dont go & set up a separate existence otherwise, I shall go & camp out abroad for good when England becomes intolerable. I come south the middle of Septer. & will meet you at Blenheim or in London I am going abroad for 3 weeks DO COME. I will listen to all your most *exalté* notions most peaceably so long as you dont set them into operation, & be ever your most affect bro (Damnably anoyed)

Bla (PAGE TORN)

P.S. Love to my mother (PAGE TORN)

Though this letter reveals Blandford's genuine affection for his brother, it made Randolph very angry. But it did not stop him going back to Cowes for two blissful days with Jennie. Mrs Jerome had written to Leonard, and refused to countenance any official engagement till definite permission had been given by both fathers. But she did not frown on the lovers, indeed she seems to have been perfectly happy to let the romance blossom.

The Prince of Wales was still at Cowes, and Randolph took the opportunity to present Jennie to him as the girl he was hoping to marry. The Prince liked her at once, and encouraged the lovers to resist all parental doubts and hesitations. But, alas, Randolph could not stay at Cowes. When he got back to Blenheim he wrote:

Blenheim
Dearest Jeannette   Saturday

I have made up & forwarded to you a few photographs of my father & mother & three of my sisters. I also send one of myself for your sister which I promised her. I daresay you will give it to her. It was dreadful work for me having to leave you, but still not quite so bad as the first time. I feel more hopeful of everything coming right now, and I know for certain now that you do really love me; I wish I was great & very rich in order to be more worthy of you dearest, I cannot help always feeling how much too good you are for me. I hope & trust and pray every day that nothing may ever come between us. If anything ever did I shld not care how soon I died as the world can never contain any attraction for me, if you were kept away from me. I really am afraid I did not half thank your mother for having let us be so much together for those two days, I really am so grateful to her. But I was so *boulversé*[14] at having to go away that I cld hardly say anything. I do not think I half said Goodbye to you even. I hope some day dearest we may never have to say goodbye to each other. Sometimes I get worrying and rather low thinking what your father will say. I hope he wont be very long answering & God grant that he may take the views I shld wish him to.

I go to London on Tuesday to get a locket to put your little bit of hair & your photograph in, & also to go and get photographed myself & try if I can get one done that you will like better than the one you have got. On Monday I am going out to kill some partridges as it is the first of September. I have got some shooting of my own that I rent, & if I can get a good bag I shall venture to send some to Rosetta.[15]

Today I have been driving with my mother. She was rather cross at my not coming back on Thursday but I managed to pacify her. The Prince seems to have spoken on all sides of how much he liked his visit on Thursday afternoon, & how glad he was to have made your acquaintance. My own darling do not be angry with me if I do not write every day or think I am forgetting you. I do not want to make your mother cross by writing too often. Send me back the photographs in a few days dearest if you do not mind as I have taken them out of my book. Remember me most kindly to your sister and that God may ever bless & protect you & soon bring us inseparably together is the constant prayer of

> Yrs devotedly for ever
> Randolph S. Churchill

Jennie replied at once, on paper headed with her name alone:

> Monday

The photographs are charming—& you see dear I have not taken long to send them back—I was more happy than I can say this morning when I received yr letter but dear Randolph I am very angry at yr not telling me the truth I know you are going to London to meet the Standishes[16]—& go to the Play with them—why not say so?—Do you suppose I care? I would never doubt or distrust yr love—if you went with fifty Standishes *Cher ami je suis tellement triste ce matin—encore un petit mot demain n'est ce pas? Seulement pr me réconforter*[17]— The Prince talks to me constantly of you—I am afraid this will be left—

> ever yours
> Jeannette

By now Randolph must have received his father's measured response to the idea of an engagement to an unknown American girl. It was discouraging. The letter began:

It is not likely that at present you can look at anything but from your own point of view but persons from the outside cannot but be struck with the unwisdom of your proceedings, and the uncontrolled state of your feelings, which completely paralyses your judgement; never was there such an illustration of [the] adage *'love is blind'* for you seem blind to all consequences in order that you may pursue your passion. . . .

The Duke had made preliminary enquiries about Leonard Jerome, who sounded 'a sporting, and I should think vulgar kind of man'. Worse, he was 'of the class of speculators' and had already been bankrupt once. It would be a connection 'which no man in his senses could think respectable'. 'I am deeply sorry', wrote the Duke, 'that your feelings are so much engaged; and only for your own sake wish most heartily that you had checked the current before it became so overpowering.'

Randolph remained unperturbed. He went up to London as he said he would, though whether he went to the theatre with the Standishes or not he somehow forgot to say:

Thursday 4
Blenheim

Dearest Jeannette,

I had hoped so to have had a line from you ere this. Do try & persuade your Mother to let you write darling I am sure there is no harm in it and your letters are perfectly SAFE with me. Just a short line every now & then, it is such a comfort to me and I do so love your little notes. I came back from London yesterday. I had a long talk with the Prince on Tuesday afternoon; he spoke much of you & your sister, & said the Princess liked you both so vy much. He said I was a very lucky fellow in which I quite agree with him. For when I am alone here I keep wondering often why you shld like me, as you do, I know; I suppose it is partly because you feel I am so very fond of you & wld do anything or sacrifice anything for you I am sure you must be very dull now at Cowes as most of your friends have I suppose left now. I shall hope to be able to run down the end of next week, only you MUST write & tell me whether your mother will mind, & what she says of me & whether you think of me sometimes. I keep counting the days till yr father's answer can arrive, I get so low & nervous about it sometimes, I feel it depends so much on how your mother has written to him. I went & got photographed the other day in London & shall send you the proofs when they come. I have got your photograph & your little curl in a locket now & am always looking at it. My father comes home tomorrow from the North. Of course we shall have a lot of talk about you my darling, tho I have written to him volumes. I shall write to you again soon. . . .

The Duke's return meant a stiffish interview. Randolph's threats about not standing for Parliament seem to have been ignored, and he was forbidden to return to Cowes. The Duke's orders had to be obeyed: Randolph had no income except what his father gave him. He was not downcast, though. He was too much in love for that:

I am afraid there is no chance of my being able to go to Cowes again dearest. I wrote to your mother yesterday & told her that my father did not wish me to do anything more till your father's answer had arrived. I do not want to cross him just now when there is no absolute necessity for it, tho I wld have given much to have seen you again even if it had only been for an hour or so. I suppose your mother will not let you write to me or else I feel sure you wld have done so. It is very hard I think on both of us, but we must look forward my love to a better time not very far distant I trust. It is very wretched for me here time drags itself along like lead & I am getting quite to hate this place. Another fortnight I suppose at least, to wait before your father's answer comes. I am sure that in these last three weeks I seem to have lived a lifetime. 'Ce sont de ces choses qui font veillir les jeunes têtes'. Dearest I wonder whether you really love me. God knows I do not want to pain you by expressing the least distrust of you, but by love I do not mean the cold ordinary attachment that the world is accustomed to call by that name, but something far higher far deeper seated far more enduring which we often read about, & which does sometimes exist, tho very rarely. A love that is ready to go through any trials to surmount any difficulties to wait if necessary almost a lifetime that looks only to one end & to one goal, that is resolved to look at no other & to be content with no other. Have you that my darling? I feel that I shld be the most conceited emptyheaded creature on this earth if I were to make sure that a love such as I have tried to describe to you cld have sprung up so rapidly in so brief an acquaintance for one so ordinary & commonplace as myself, & yet I like to think it & to dream about it. I know beyond any doubt that it does exist on my side & I cannot help thinking that it must be mutual. God what a cheerless void what an utter blank my existence wld become if the stake that I am playing for shld be lost to me if the dice on which I have set all my hopes of present & future happiness shld turn up adverse. But I cannot think it nor do I allow myself often to dwell on what is to me so melancholy so utterly despairing a view. No I rather fix my thoughts on a happy & bright future shared with you & I incessantly dream & picture to myself the pleasures of an existence which wld be almost divine, the pleasures of having at last found the object to which one can devote what energies and abilities one may possess the pleasures of having an inseparable companion whom it wld be one's highest idea of duty to protect & shield from every harm & worry & on whom one wld continually & untiringly endeavour to heap every source of happiness that this world can afford. Is this only a dream? I cannot think so or at any rate it is a dream which I pray may soon be converted into a reality. Many wld tell you that feelings such as I feebly attempt to describe to you are quite out of date in this practical 19th century, that a love such as this is an anachronism & that what I have written is only the effusions of a too ardent imagination or perhaps the ravings of a lunatic.

God knows with me they are neither one nor the other, but simply the sincere & real description of a true pure love, which I own unhappily for the world is not common, but is not on that account less admirable or less possible. Feelings such as these are not as many wld say from their very strength shortlived, on the contrary they may perhaps from their very strength physically destroy yet they are as enduring as life & I believe fully, last & receive their reward, beyond the grave. The realization of all this will I hope be not long delayed; it is however the one object left to me in this world I have voluntarily with open eyes made it so and it is far from probable that I shall lightly resign the chances of winning so charming so attractive a prize. I wld not weary you dearest by writing more at length on a subject with which I cld fill volumes, I hope I may not have done so already, I feel however that I am writing to one who if unhappily for me cannot reciprocate can at any rate appreciate at its full value a love so deep so great & so true. I asked your mother to let you write to me a few lines from time to time, but if she wld not do so to write herself just to say

Jennie's parents,
Leonard and Clara Jerome

Randolph's father, the 7th Duke of Marlborough

Randolph's mother, the Duchess of Marlborough

The three Jerome sisters,
from left to right, Jennie,
Clara and Leonie

Bertha, Lady Blandford,
daughter of the Duke of
Abercorn

how you all were & what you were doing. Any news of you the smallest & from whatever quarter, Is longed for by

> yr own true & for ever devoted
> Randolph S. Churchill

> Blenheim
> Sunday, Sept. 7th

The Pug I regret to say is still in small health. Like his master ever since he left you, he is down on his luck.

The sincerity of this was unmistakable, but even Randolph felt he had been a little too gloomy. 'A one-sided correspondence is very disheartening I assure you,' he wrote three days later. 'I hope you did not mind my stupid letter of last Sunday but I happened to be particularly in low spirits & I cld not help pouring out all my feelings for you.' Jennie, one can safely assume, did not mind at all. But she was unable to write and say so. Mrs Jerome was no more encouraging than the Duke: perhaps she was determined not to be outdone in correctness by the English aristocracy. At any rate, when she wrote to Randolph, she probably meant her letter to be shown to his father:

> Rosetta Cottage
> Sept. 9th

Dear Lord Randolph

I am very much touched by your kind letter I must acknowledge you have quite won my heart by your frank & honourable manner since our acquaintance and though you may never be more to us we shall always think of you with the kindest remembrance

I hope you will listen to your Fathers advice He can only have your happiness at heart. As a good son your first duty is to him.

I shall probably receive my husband's answer to my letter the first of next month. I will send it to you immediately. We leave Cowes on Monday the 13th.[18] We stop one day in London en route for Paris It is so cold here we are anxious to get away

With kindest regards from us all, believe me dear Lord Randolph

> Ever your sincere friend
> Clara H. Jérôme

While waiting impatiently to see Jennie on her way through London, Randolph's temper was not improved by a new communication from his brother, this time in verse. Though its tone is conciliatory—perhaps in response to Randolph's fury at his original letter—Blandford's message is the same. Nor is his poetry any less peculiar than his prose:

An Elegy on Marriage

1

Undine
rising out of
the waves
1st Act.

T'was yours & not anothers hand that built
the funeral pile near which you tarry
the daggers plunged unto its bleeding hilt
Thy fate is sealed if thou doest marry.

2

*Le Cigne
qui chante
son dernier
chadson!*[19]

Advice & preaching are an idle strain
For madness hath thy mind o'er-took
Delusions snare entraps thy fevered brain
Thy senses hast thou quite forsook

3

Remorse shall seize upon thy stuborn soul
when tinseled charms begin to pall
Thy part is strife, & pitious grief thy whole
If thou doest thus in weakness fall

4

Does marriage then a lovely sea of calm
appear to thy deluded eyes
Times future gifts of Love wilt thou embalm
& all freedom of thy will likewise.

5

Despise them not, those strong mysterious ties
by which the soul is oft-times bound;
Heed not this shaddow that before thee flies,
True love is free as air arround.

6

See thou no future, though still distant light
Some Star, which in thy path may rise
& so with dazzling Rays shall dim thy sight,
and lead thee captive as its prize

7

I know a youth who scarce a year ago
rushed, into the wedded lock
who all his worldly goods would now forgoe
to take his feet from out the stocks

8

The married tie was made for those, my friend!
who revel in lifes worldly good
or would long years of wicked evil mind
& so when old they don the hood*

*Quand
le Diable
se fait
vieux, il
se fait
heremit.20

9

I see thee grumbling oer thy household books,
& adding up thy nurses wage.
Ha! Ha! these trifles must thy spirit brook!
when thou art married, my young Sage!

10

Perambulators & the babies rusks
Shall be among thy chiefest cares
See thou to the bottle that it sucks
Revolt? thy spirit will not dare.*

*If 'rusks'
and 'sucks'
are objected
to, Read!
'See thou to
the cutting
of its tusks.'

11

And when thy better half shall wine & fret
because thou dinest not at home
Perchance the scene shall turn into a pet
Then! wilt thou at thy fortunes moan!

12

Now, think of me in time to come my boy!
All this & more shall thee befall
If, thou doest sell, for this thy pretty toy
thyself, thy Friends, & e'en thy very all.

Dedication

13

Thus pause my brother while there's time
& think not that I wish thy harm
to thee, I dedicate this humble rime
in fond advice & counsel calm.

14

Forgive me then if in my fleeting speech
aught could to thy mind offend
Let loving thoughts still bind us each to each
& let nothing our friendship rend

15

So go you forth on your appointed way
& treat my poor advice with slight
Still will I for a golden future pray,
'May I be wrong', & 'You be right'!

Affectionately addressed
to his brother by the Author
Bd.
Sept 7/73

This remarkable effusion did little to calm Randolph's indignation.
He had shown Blandford's original letter to his father; now he sent it to
the Prince of Wales. The Prince criticized both style and composition,
and said it was one of the most extraordinary productions he'd ever read.
For his encouragement of Randolph he was roundly abused by Blandford, who accused him of not acting the part of a friend. The Prince was
no doubt more amused than cross, and suggested that Blandford must
have been writing to him at a late hour in the evening—that is, probably
drunk. He took the line that Blandford meant well, and that Randolph
shouldn't quarrel with him. He then passed the offending letter to
Francis Knollys, his Private Secretary. Randolph had written to him,
too: Knollys was so close a friend that he was to be his best man. He
gave the same advice as the Prince:

Abergeldie[21]
My dear Randolph　　　　　　　　　　　　　　　　Friday

I was very glad to get a letter from you although sorry to hear that
you think your affairs are not going on well. As however you say the
Duke is kind to you I am sure he will do what he can for you. At the
same time I quite understand how unhappy you must feel until your
suspense is over & how much you must be looking forward to the day
when it will be all over—I cannot help feeling sorry also for Miss
Jerome.

The Prince has shown me Blandford's letter to you—I think you are
perhaps right not to answer him, but to wait to say anything until you
see him—He is I am sure fond of you & what he writes proceeds from
what he considers are good motives however mistaken you yourself
may consider them to be, & were you to reply to his letter just now you
might be tempted to say something which would perhaps create a life
long breach between you & him. Pray forgive me my dear Randolph
for writing all this to you.

I hope you will let me hear from you as soon as you have anything fresh to tell me, & believe me

yrs most sincerely
Francis Knollys

Have you asked H. Lennox[22] to Blenheim.

Meanwhile the Prince replied to Blandford and sent a copy to Randolph, which pleased him so much he wrote and asked permission to show it to the Duke and Duchess. Knollys wrote again:

Private   Abergeldie Castle, Aberdeenshire

My dear Randolph   19 Sept. 1873

The Prince of Wales is very glad to hear that you like his letter to Blandford, & as you are so anxious to show it to the Duke & the Duchess he has no objection to your doing so under of course the understanding that they do not refer to it in any way to Blandford or to any one else. His Royal Highness at first thought of sending to you Blandford's letter to him as well, to enable your Father & mother to judge more properly of his answer, but upon consideration he thinks it would perhaps be hardly fair of him to do this, but you can repeat to them the purport of its contents

I am very sorry that matters do not improve, but we must hope for a favourable report from Sir E. Thornton.[23]

Pray let me hear what it is when it arrives & when you have time to write to me

I quite understand how low you must feel under all this suspense but I trust it will soon be removed.

Ever my dear Randolph

Yours sincerely
Francis Knollys

Meanwhile Jennie and Randolph met briefly in London on Monday September 15th. Randolph then went back to Blenheim to address an agricultural dinner at Woodstock, while the Jeromes went on to Paris. He had reason, he thought, to be cheerful, though Jennie had seemed depressed:

Blenheim
Wednesday

I could not write to you yesterday dearest Jeannette as all my time was taken up with that tiresome agricultural dinner I am happy to say I have got that off my mind now. I think it went off very well upon the whole, but I am sure if I had not had the excessive pleasure & happiness of seeing you again in London I shld never have had the spirits to go to it. We have had a few people staying here this week Lady Wilton[24] by herself & Walter Harbord,[25] both of whom I think you know. & the two county members; a very stupid party Next week thank goodness I shall be quite alone, as my father & mother are going away for two or three days. I never liked being alone before but now I long to be alone if I cannot be with you. I can think of you all day long & have not anything else to take away my attention. Dearest I hope you are in better spirits than when I left you. You appeared so dreadfully low that I tried to be in as good spirits as possible to try & cheer you up. But it made me vy unhappy my darling after I left you to think that I am the cause of making you who ought to be so light-hearted at all worried or annoyed. I hope you keep my poor little bracelet always on your arm. I look upon that as binding you to me irrevocably, & dearest as I have told you often if you and I keep firm & really mean what we have said seriously & solemnly to each other nothing human can keep us apart. I assure you my own love those few short hours we had together in London seem to have given me new life & fresh hope. And now we have persuaded your mother to allow you to write to me, & I hope you will write as often as you can. I shld advise you to tell her whenever you write & if she thinks you are writing too often, why then you must give in a little dearest, & not be cross with her who is so good & kind to you & indeed to me too. There is only one thing I must press you to do as strongly as I can, which is to use all your influence & powers of persuasion which are vy great, together with me to oppose any unnecessary delay. No good can come of it, we cannot be fonder of each other than we are now & there is no reason why we shld lose any portion of our life together, which can only be too happy & like everything else in this world too brief. I feel dearest very strongly about this so you really must beg and entreat of your father to hasten as much as possible his journey to Europe. I mean dearest if you are willing & I know you are to do all that is possible for us to be married in December. There is no legitimate cause or good reason against it, & there are many reasons why it shld be so. Dearest think over all this & write & tell me yr opinion. I never have stood yet any delay in anything I wished vy much for & I never will if I can help it I have always thought that if things are to be the sooner they do take place the better & I will not suffer if I can help it any foolish reasons or empty prejudices to keep me long from one whom I love so dearly & so fondly & whom I cannot exist without. I am going to write to your father & tell him this & I hope you will do so too darling. Our love and affection for each other as I told you in one of my letters has been no ordinary commonplace everyday sort of attachment, there have been all along & are still circumstances connected with it, that I regret to say unless we are both vy firm under the consequences of it doubtful & uncertain & the only one thing certain about it all is that if we are married we shall both be vy vy happy & if we are not (which is a contingency I will not contemplate) well at any rate I for my part, shall be intolerably miserable & unhappy for ever. Dearest I shall hope to get a letter from you in a day or two. I hope you have arrived safely at Paris. & I hope you will amuse yourself there & keep up yr spirits, Darling Jeannette I cannot write more at present, but will write again to-morrow Remember me most kindly to your mother & sister, & tell Clara that I hope when we meet next she wont scold me so much Goodbye & God bless you my love

Yr own devoted & affectionate
Randolph S. Churchill

NOTES

1. In Austria, where Randolph was photographed while on his Grand Tour after leaving Oxford.

2. Surrounded.

3. The absent are always wrong.

4. Randolph is quoting, not entirely accurately, from the then popular *Lalla Rookh*, by Thomas Moore. This verse comes from 'The Light of the Harem', a tale about how a wife wins back the love of her husband: not perhaps a very well-omened choice.

5. Blandford's spelling is so idiosyncratic that it has not been corrected. Nor has his French, which is highly personal.

6. Blindly ahead.

7. But how will it end?

8. Even a dirty trick.

9. A six days' seaside fantasy.

10. At a loose end.

11. You are in search of sensations, and you have found bad ones. Very bad!

12. These are the things which make young heads old.

13. Disorganized.

14. Upset.

15. The Villa Rosetta was the small house in which the Jeromes were staying at Cowes.

16. Henry Standish, an American who lived in Paris and at the Château de Montjoye, and his French wife, daughter of Comte Amédée des Cars.

17. Dear friend I am so sad this morning—another little word tomorrow, please? Just to comfort me.

18. In fact the 15th.

19. The swan who sings his last song!

20. When the Devil becomes old, he becomes a hermit.

21. The Prince's estate near Balmoral in Scotland.

22. Lord Henry Charles George Lennox, 1821–86, son of the 5th Duke of Richmond and Lennox, MP for Chichester 1846–85, First Commissioner of Works, 1874–6. Close friend of Disraeli.

23. British envoy in Washington, being consulted by the Duke about Leonard Jerome.

24. Isabella, second wife of the second Earl of Wilton.

25. Walter Harbord (1834–1913) was a brother of Lord Suffield and an officer in the army.

2

AMOR VINCIT OMNIA

Now that Mrs Jerome had raised her ban on Jennie's letter-writing, Randolph must have been avidly awaiting his first proper letter from his fiancée. But when it came it was a bombshell:

Tuesday Sept. 16th
London

My dear Randolph

I have persuaded Mama to allow me to write these few lines—as they will probably be the last—do not be angry dear—but I have not been able to sleep all night—thinking of all you said—& the more I think the more convinced I am that you are changed—since Cowes— In what way I am at loss to tell but I feel it—& the feeling is sufficient. Sometimes I almost wish I had listened a little more to Mama's advice —from the beginning she asked me not to think of it—& begged me to forget you—as it would only worry & trouble me in the end—not that I mind that—you know I would go through a great deal & sacrifice a great deal for yr sake—if I thought you *really* did care for me—But the truth is Randolph—you are heartily sick & tired of all the ennui it causes you, is it not so? I am sure you think you are bound to me in some way—& that it would be impossible to break off now—even should you desire it. Believe me—I consider you as free—as if nothing had ever passed between us—& as I told you last night if yr father or mother object in the least to our marriage—why cross them? Is it not much wiser to end it all before it is too late?—I suppose of course we should both feel rather badly at first—but with time everything passes —& you might marry some English girl & be much happier than if you married me—I cannot tell you how deeply hurt I felt at the insinuation you gave me—as to yr having heard something against my father —I was unable to answer you or defend him—as you did not choose to confide in me—All I can say is that I love, admire & respect my father more than any man living—& I do not think it possible for him to have an enemy—for a more generous, kind hearted man never lived—the only thing I have ever heard people reproach him for is his decidedly

English taste for horse racing & gambling—Dearest I have no doubt
this letter will pain you—& make me appear in quite a new light—&
perhaps not a very flattering one—but I cannot help it—*Je suis ainsi
faite!*[1]—& I have a bad nature it is difficult to change. My pride always
did get the better of me & it certainly has in this occasion—I had
hoped to leave England without a doubt that it would all come right—
& without a thought of anything else but you—Oh dear why is it??
You told Clara you felt as if a great load had been taken off yr mind—I
think it has fallen upon me—I have just been reading the Court Journal—& I am ashamed to say that after flying into a most violent passion
—I have been crying over those slandering stupid lines, written by a
crazy old man—& not worth being even noticed—I wonder if you are
very angry with this letter?—or will you not care? Forgive me—I really
cannot break quite yet—for I feel that I love you more than anything
or person on earth—& that I am ready to do or say anything you like as
long as you leave my family alone and not abuse it—

Ever yrs

Jeannette Jérôme

If you write please send me those papers with yr speeches. I still take a
slight interest in yr affairs!—6 Rue Presbourg

This dramatic and painful letter is the first in which Jennie shows
some of that American vigour which was to enchant, and in some cases
dismay, English society for almost fifty years. All her life she was someone who went directly to the point: if her pride was hurt, she didn't hesitate to show it. What happened, obviously, is that Randolph let fall
some critical remark about Leonard Jerome—something he'd heard from
one of his father's investigators, perhaps. But Jennie would not tolerate
any slighting remarks about her father, even from the man she loved.
She clearly doesn't really want to break with Randolph: offering him his
freedom with one hand, she takes it back with the other. But she does
want him to know there are some things she won't stand for.

The paragraph in *The Court Journal* over which she raged, then
wept, must rather have clouded the London meeting in any case. Publicity at such a delicate stage of marital negotiations was dreaded by everyone, and Mrs Jerome must have been furious to read under
'Approaching Marriages in High Life':

Miss Jerome, one of the prettiest young ladies that ever hailed from
New York and landed at Cowes, is about to marry Lord R. Churchill,
the third son[2] of the Duke of Marlborough. The young lady, who has

resided for some time in Paris, will receive a splendid dower on her marriage. Mr Jerome is one of the most inveterate of American yachtsmen.

Steps were rapidly taken about this paragraph. The next week's issue of *The Court Journal* was obliged to state: 'There is no truth in the report of a marriage between Lord Randolph Churchill and Miss Jerome.' It looks from her remarks about 'a crazy old man' as if the indiscretion was Jennie's: she certainly seems to have known the author. But Randolph, of course, was concerned with a far more important matter. If Jennie's letter showed some of her true character, so did his reply show some of his. They were an excellent match, these two: they struck sparks from one another:

> Blenheim
> Thursday 18th Sept.
>
> I have just this minute received your letter & cannot rest a moment without telling you what I think of it. This is the first letter I have ever had from you and it certainly is an encouraging one. I can assure you that if I am to receive many like it, I can only say that at any rate I was a good deal happier when the letter writing was only on my side, & when I cld leave your answers to my foolish imagination. I am more pained & hurt than you can imagine, & if that was your object in writing you may congratulate yourself on having fully attained it You are the only person on Earth that has the power to say or do anything to wound my feelings & to vex & worry me for long & certainly you know how to use your power. What in the name of heaven do you mean by saying that I was changed in London from what I was at Cowes. The fact of the matter is (& it is always the way with women when they want to quarrel they take great care to shift the blame off their shoulders) it is you who are changed & who must be changed, if you can write me a letter like your last. How mistaken I was in you & how little you have understood me I thought when I saw you in London blind fool that I was that you loved me as truly as you said you did, & you thought or at any rate persuaded yourself to think, that my feelings for you were less strong. How can you be so cruel so heartless I really may almost say so wicked as to write to me that your impression is that I am heartily sick of the whole affair & only wish myself well out of it. These are your very words & I can hardly bring myself to rewrite them And then in the end of your letter to tell me that you loved me still, why it is the heighth of mockery & nonsense to write in so contradictory a manner. No woman cld ever write so to a man she

really loved. I suppose you think that the affair has gone quite far
enough that it amused you for the moment at Cowes, but that you
never meant to be led into a serious engagement. Well I tell you that if
it is so you have treated me TOO badly. If words mean anything, I consider that we are bound to each other That if you cast me off tho from
your beauty & attractions you will have always admirers at your feet,
but you will have trifled with & spurned, the truest & most honest love
& devotion that man is capable of feeling. I tell you I have placed all
my hopes of future happiness in this world on you I have voluntarily
staked what one may call one's moral fortune on this game, & that if I
lose it, well then I am indeed lost. I have never loved before but I
have loved & do love you as even you will never be loved again;

> Who that knows what love is here
> all its falsehood all its pain
> Wld for half Elysium's sphere
> care to dream that dream again?

> Who that in the desert heat
> Sees the waters fade away
> Wld not rather *die* than meet
> Streams again so false as they!

I thought, nay was confident that you returned my love & with that
confidence was prepared to make any sacrifice & to clear away all obstacles that might separate us. It might have taken time, but at any
rate I shld have been cheered with that idea, & led on by the thought
of how great a treasure wld reward one's toil. Is that confidence to be
taken away from me? Am I to lose that hope. By your letter you have
rudely shaken the one, & you have cast great fears into my mind as
regards the other. How can you thus deliberately & coolly write of
breaking off a solemn & serious engagement for I will not look at it in
any other light. Not that for a moment I wld force you even if I had
the power to marry me against your will & inclinations, but have I
been really so terribly mistaken? Oh No it cannot be, God cld not
allow such utter misery to fall on any one Come write once more & tell
me you do not mean what you wrote, that it was only joking that you
wrote it, & that you regret having written so unkindly. Tell me my
dearest that I am not hopelessly & utterly ruined & left alone. Tell me
that I have not wasted all my affection on one who cld not feel it, that
I have not so deeply loved where there is & where there can be no return. How can you say that I have abused your family, when you

know that I am incapable of doing such a thing? I tell you that as to your mother & sister I am prepared to love them & to be as fond of them as if they were mine, & as to your father I do not know him, but it is quite sufficient to me that he is your father ever to be treated by me with greatest respect & affection. Oh my darling Jeannette pardon me if I have written crossly, but your letter quite took my breath away, & has left me perfectly distracted with grief & worry. I cannot write again to you till I have heard from you that I may, & it will be with the greatest anxiety that I shall wait for & no little fear that I shall open your answer if you care to write one. But I do entreat & implore you to have confidence in me if you really love me & never again to write so cruel & so painful a letter

Yr as ever devoted
but despairing
Randolph S. Churchill

A good quarrel was probably just what Jennie and Randolph needed to establish their love for each other. Jennie seems to have got Randolph's letter the same day. She replied at once:

Paris
Sept. 18th

This must be—& shall be the last misunderstanding between us—my own darling Randolph unless you wish to make it—If my letter pained you & gave you any anxiety—it has caused me a thousand times more—The moment it had gone—I repented & if I could have got it then—you wld never have received it—And yet in [a] way I do not feel sorry—for it has given me a fresh proof of yr love—& has made me discover the strength and depth of mine—I did not know how much I loved you—until I left England & felt that I was leaving all I love most on earth behind me—perhaps for ever—Darling I love yr angry cross letter—it has done me more good—than twenty tender ones—In fact dearest I have been so unhappy, & miserable since Tuesday I was certain it cld not last—Things look brighter now & they *must* come right it is a great comfort to be sure of ourselves. I could leave Father Mother—& the whole world for you—if it were necessary—Now Randolph that I have made this confession you must answer all my questions—& be perfectly frank & confiding in me. I want you to tell me everything—what the 'circumstances are which are doubtful & uncertain' & if there is any particular reason besides the one you gave me—for wishing our marriage to be in December—As I wish this letter to please you—I shall not say what I think it is—you might be angry—But

I agree with you—I hate long engagements & if our parents give their consent—I dont see why it should not be in December—When are you coming? I pray & hope it will be soon—if you know how I long to see you it seems an age since Monday—what will it be—before October?—We did not go to Lord George's[3] to tea—nor to the Play—altho' he had got us the Garners[4] box.

The weather here is quite heavenly—Altho' our apartment commands a charming view & has a dear little garden Mama finds it so big & cold—She has decided to change—We are going back to the Bd Haussmann 146—but you must still address yr letters here—for we shall not be settled before a week—A propos why do you ask me not to write too often Does one letter a week bore you? Shall I make it two? Clara has just given me a very pretty photo: frame with yr favourite monogram—I shall put yr photo: in it I have it in my room where I can see it the first thing in the morning & the last thing at night I have not taken off the bracelet yet I shall not until you come—I do not mind being fettered to you by such a beautiful chain—Please write to me as often as possible yr letters are my only pleasure—I wish I could get ten a day!—*Au revoir, mon seul ami,*

> Ever yours
> Jeannette Jérôme

Randolph and Jennie were both young and of high mettle, and as those who disapproved of their engagement doubtless told them, they hardly knew each other yet. After this little flurry they knew each other better. From it, they emerged strengthened against their opponents. Not that they weren't both a little ashamed of themselves. Even before he received Jennie's letter, Randolph was writing to apologize for the sternness of his own:

> Blenheim
> Friday 19th Sept.

My dearest Jeannette I cannot even if I wld let a day pass without writing to you. The more I read your letter over, altho it makes me vy low & wretched still I cannot bring myself to think that you really doubt me; I feel sure that you really love me, & dearest love & confidence are identical & synonymous. Forgive me my darling if my letter was rather cross yesterday or annoyed you at all. I was so taken aback by yours & wrote on the spur of the moment which one shld never do. I cannot think what shld have made you write to me so. I shall be awfully miserable & wretched till you write to me again & it is indeed you who have made me so. You know dearest you told me in

London that you were angry because you thought I had a great deal of worry & you had none, & that you wld like to share it with me. Well my love it is not the right way to go to work to add to mine. Dearest I love you better than anything on earth & shall *never* love another. Whenever you feel doubts of me, & of course I know that sometimes many horrid thoughts will force themselves unbidden on one's mind when anyone you are vy fond of is away, just read over my letters to you, & I am sure you will feel convinced that no gentleman cld write as I have done to you, without feeling from his heart every word he said. How cld you so calmly write & recommend me to marry some English girl. You have no idea how you pain me when I think you capable of imagining even for a moment that I shld ever look at or speak to again any other girl after you. I mean to marry you my darling & nobody else & I do not intend that anything shall keep us long apart. However dear I have said enough about that letter & shall never refer to it again. I shld like to send it back to you as I cannot help always reading & looking at anything that reminds me of you, & yet it does vex me terribly. I can now assure you dearest that my father & mother will not oppose my marrying you; they will very probably try to insist on some delay in order that their incredulous minds may be fully persuaded that I am as fond of you & that I love you as dearly as I have continually dinned into their heads ever since I saw you that I do. But it wont be for very long. I know them so well, they always pretend to be very stern at first about everything, but they can never hold out long as they are really very kindhearted & vy fond of me (strange to say). And I assure you that when you do marry me they will be as fond of you as of their own daughters & will be vy proud of you indeed & you will never for a moment regret having come into my family. Now dearest I shld not write this to you if I was not certain of it. I had at first I tell you candidly great doubts as to whether they wld consent, & that was what worried me so & made me so wretched, & that was why I tried to persuade you that perhaps we might have to do without their consent. You see dearest, they do not know you & they think I am very young, & being very practical unsentimental sort of people they will not yet quite believe in so strong an attachment having arisen in so short a time But I am happy to say that since yesterday all my doubts as to their consent have disappeared, & tho they may still try to make difficulties in order to satisfy themselves they are doing their duty. Still ultimately & before very long too it will all come right. Of that I am now confident. I was not quite so before, & perhaps that was what made me appear to you a little changed, when I saw you in London. For it cld not but make me a little wretched, when I saw how nice how good you were & what an angel you were to care about me, to think that perhaps my own father & mother wld be the people to step between me and my only chance of happiness, & I felt & they knew that I shld never never speak to them again if they did, & that convinced them of the reality of what I told them & when once they come to know you they will understand why. However as I told you I know it will all come right now although there may still be little 'tracasserie's',[5] difficulties & annoyances. But dearest what do you and I care if there are? 'The course of true love never did run quite smooth.' When people just have an ordinary liking for each other as happens in 999 cases out of a 1000, they always seem to marry without the least bother but when as in our case it is no ordinary liking or inclination but a strong deep enduring & I think I may say mutual love, then there seems to be always some malignant power at work to keep those two apart. But my darling true love must always win the day, & when God has made two people for each other, as I am sure he has you & I, intending that we shall lead a happy life on this earth together, never is anything permitted to come permanently between them. Dearest I cld write to you for ever, if I was not afraid of wearying you with such long letters. You MUST now write me an answer not only to my letter of yesterday but to this one. Things are now coming to a crisis; your father's formal answer will soon be arriving & I must then finally speak out all my mind to my father & get a formal answer from him, & I must feel convinced & certain & sure of your sympathy approval & consent, so my darling I not only implore and entreat but I call upon you most solemnly & seriously to write to me words of affection and encouragement such as you know so well how to write. I know you well enough to feel certain that you never wld have spoken to me & talked to me as you have done without feeling every thing you said or without being prepared to abide by it all. Talk of my giving you up!! Why as long as I feel sure of your affection as I do now, thank God, you might just as well expect the earth to stop still from ever moving or the sun to cease to shine. I shall expect a letter from you about Wednesday next, & mind dearest it is this one I want answered, & if you have answered yesterdays you must write another in answer to this. I enclose you two of the small photographs perhaps you may like them better than the others. I will send you the papers tomorrow in which will be the account of our dinner. & now dearest darling Jeannette Goodbye & God bless you & keep you ever true to me; I have written perhaps at too great length, but you have not your equal on this earth, & never will have & there is nothing I will not do say or write to win you & to call you my own.

Ys lovingly & ever devoted
Randolph S. Churchill

It is a magnificent letter, wonderfully written, with touches of the humour which was to make him such a popular political figure, and a sense of confidence in himself, his love, his future, that recent events hardly bore out. It is also very revealing of his relations with his parents: everything he says of them is true: they *were* very fond of him, they *would* make difficulties in order to satisfy themselves they were doing their duty, their sternness *would* give way to acquiescence. He knew them, perhaps, better than they knew him. But for all the confidence the letter exudes, Randolph had had his qualms, as he admitted in his next letter, written after he had received Jennie's one making it all up:

Blenheim
Saturday 20th
Evening

You dear little darling Jeannette Your kind loving reassuring little letter just arrived as I had finished my letter of this morning. I did not expect to hear from you in any case till Monday or Tuesday, so you may fancy how delighted I was. But I assure you when I first got it I was so nervous & frightened I did not dare open it for some minutes. And then oh how glad & relieved I was. I feel quite happy again now & I have been so wretched. However it is all passed. You need not think I shld ever quarrel with you or be angry really. You might treat me as badly as you liked, (I know you never wld) & I shld never do anything but love you all the more. I am very glad you have got back safe to Paris after all we are not much farther apart than we were before, & now dearest I do beg & entreat of you to be careful about riding that horse before it has been properly exercised. I know what those nasty hot fiery brutes are after a long rest. I shall be so nervous & worried about you unless you promise me to be careful. How nice & good of Clara to give you that photograph frame it must be awfully nice to have a sister like her. You quite misunderstand me when I wrote to you not to write too much. I was only afraid perhaps you might make your mother angry & she might forbid you to write at all. Dearest I do implore you to write as much as ever you can to me. Your letters, (like your last) give me new life. You will have got my letter of yesterday by this time. I think perhaps you will like one of the photographs I sent you better for your bracelet than the one I put in. You must tell me all you do at Paris, I have literally nothing in the way of news to write to you from here. I am all alone now here with my two sisters in this enormous house but I had rather be here than anywhere else except with you I have been asked to go to one or two places, but I hate the idea of parties now. I potter about all day thinking of you. The pleasantest time is taken up writing to you & I always make that last as long as possible. The pug has been very ill with distemper, I hope he is getting over it now, He is fed on nothing but beeftea The poor thing had a fit yesterday but I do not think he has got it badly. If he is all right I shall bring him to Paris with me and ask you to take care of him, I am sure he will be happier with you. The man who is taking care of him has just come in to say he has had two more fits, & I feel rather alarmed & have sent for the doctor from Oxford. I am sure you will be sorry for the poor pug. Tell Clara about him. Dearest I cannot write more now as it is just dinner time, thankyou a million times for your letter I feel quite a different being to what I did this morning. Please remember me to your mother & Clara & with a thousand kisses to yourself. Believe me my darling Jeannette

yr most loving & devoted
Randolph S. Churchill

One of the troubles with correspondence is that it is very difficult for the writers to co-ordinate their moods. As one's spirit climbs, the other's sinks. Now Randolph was happy, Jennie was glum:

Friday evening

I have just received yr letter my dear Randolph & I feel so happy that you are in better spirits if you knew the influence yr letters have over mine perhaps you wld write differently—If I get a gloomy, melancholy letter from you in the morning I am unfit for anything the rest of the day—All I can do is to wander about & wait impatiently for the next mail—My darling if things are as you say—I do not see any cause to be either low or in the least cross—I am sure everything will come right with time. Of course what does worry & torment us—is being apart from each other—but parents forget those things—& we must make the best of it—What I am afraid of is that if we do not see each other for a year—& are not allowed to write—it must necessarily fall through—Do not be angry dearest Randolph but you know few people stand the test—even if they write to each other & see each other occasionally. Oh my darling I wish things might be arranged that is, our engagement settled—as for the date of our marriage that is quite secondary & may remain for a long time yet *dans les nuages*[6]—without its worrying us

much for the present—You see dearest I know Mama well enough to
know that she will not allow you to come to see us here—under these
circumstances—Unfortunately people have associated our names
together—& she wld think it very compromising for me to have you
seen with us & yet to deny that there is anything in it—as we have
done so far—In fact I am more than blue tonight altho' I pretended in
the beginning of this letter to be cheery—I do not care what anyone
says or does—or what happens! if I can only see you again if only for a
day—It is really cruel of you to remain at that Blenheim! Forgive me—
I know you wld come if you cld & I am sure you wish it as much as I
do—I am ashamed of this letter—instead of giving you advice—& trying
to console you—I do nothing but complain—You must try & pacify yr
father & after you receive my mother's letter—try & get his consent to
our engagement—& then I shld certainly wait until *after* the election
to say anything more—Now darling I must say goodbye—it is very late
—& I hope you will forgive this very untidy letter—How did you hurt
yr finger—do take care—Don't smoke so much & write *every day*—it is
my only pleasure—Ever yrs

Jeannette Jerome[7]

Randolph did write every day, and his spirits remained high:

Blenheim
Monday

Your two darling letters arrived this morning my own dearest Jeannette I was so happy to see yr handwriting again it is the next best
thing to seeing you. Well my dearest as you will have seen from my
letter of Friday which when you wrote you had not received, we have
no cause now to despond or be in bad spirits, everything goes on as
favourably as we cld expect, & my father does not wish for a moment
to prevent my seeing you as often as I can, & has promised to give his
consent to our marriage when he is sure we are fond of each other.
As to the year I have every right to say that I do not think they will
insist on it, & I enclose you a letter I received from my eldest sister
Cornelia[8] who is of the same opinion. It may comfort you. I assure
you my dearest I only require to be with you now to be as happy as a
lark. I am only waiting to hear from Mdme Jerome to fly over to Paris.
As you in the beginning of yr letter freely scolded me, I am going to
do the same to you. & I want to know how you can write such a sentence as the following 'What I am afraid of is that if we do not see
each other for a year and are not allowed to write it must NECESSAR-
ILY!!!!! fall through'. & then you add 'don't be angry'. My dearest the

idea is too absurd to be angry about, as I know you are only joking, but all I wld say is that I think jokes of that sort vy bad ones. What a word 'necessarily'. What in heaven's name can you mean? It nearly made me ill. Why my own darling do you mean to confess that you cld not keep true to me for a year even if we did not see each other; you cannot mean that, or else you cannot care about me vy much. Or do you mean that you doubt my keeping true to you. I swear by everything that ten centuries wld make no difference to me, & I thought you felt it & knew it. I do not think you have any idea how those little sentences of yrs which you write quickly & carelessly sometimes give me pain, or I am sure you wld not write them. Thank God there is now no necessity in our being separated at all, or any reason why there shld be any concealment about our marriage and I am sure yr mother will see it in the same light. The clouds have all cleared away & the sky is bluer than I have ever known it since I first saw you at Cowes. It is exactly six weeks to-morrow since I first saw you on board the *Ariadne*. I am sure I seem to have lived 6 years. Oh how I do bless that day, in spite of all the worry & bother that has come since. For it has been bad for me at times my love, more so I think than you can fancy. I am so glad yr father has written kindly about me, it is entirely owing to you & your dear mother writing as you have done. Well I am sure you will never regret it. I have not had any further conversation with my father since I wrote to you as I think it is best to leave things for the present as they are. Our early golden dreams of being married in December wont quite become realities but still it wont be very long to wait & I shall be able to see you from time to time & write as often as I like & in fact we can be regularly engaged and all the world may know it. That is dearest if you like. Well it is a great deal better than I expected at one time, & I feel a great deal happier. What has kept me up all along has been the conviction I had that you darling loved me, & feeling that, I cld have gone through anything.

I have just come back from shooting with my father. They all go away to-morrow & I shall go to London. I cannot stay in this big house quite alone as even my sisters will be gone. Henry Lennox tells me he will be going through Paris sometime next week & that you promised to give him a dinner. He had a long conversation with my mother about you and me & he told me she spoke very nicely & kindly about us. He is a good friend of yours I think, much better than that old fool G.P. I am very glad to hear you do not ride or go out into the world. I am sorry to say dear that I am afraid I smoke more than ever, & that it will require all yr influence and authority to make me give it up at all. Oh dear how I do long to be with you I hope I shall hear from you again to-morrow in answer to my letter of Friday & I hope you will write in better spirits. I wonder what made you feel so *'blue'*. I like yr good advice & yr scolding & yr cheery letters, so much better than your last; they do me so much good & make me feel quite a different creature. It is curious what an effect books have on me. I have two old favourites & when I feel very cross & angry I read Gibbon, whose profound philosophy & easy tho majestic writing soon quiets me down & after an hour I feel at peace with all the world; when I feel vy low & desponding I read Horace; whose thorough epicurianism & quiet maxims & beautiful verse, is most tranquillising. Of late I have had to have frequent recourse to my two friends, & they have never failed to have their usual effect. I strongly recommend you to read some great works or histories, they pass the time & prevent you from worrying, or thinking too much about the future. I wonder whether you will understand all this, or only think me rather odd. Novels and even travels are rather unsatisfactory & do one no good except to create an unhealthy excitement which is bad for anyone. There are three new elections to come off owing to death vacancies, & if they go against the government, as they very probably will do we are sure to have a dissolution, & then I shall become member for Woodstock. But after all, a public life has not great charms for me, as I am naturally very quiet & hate bother & publicity, which after all is full of vanity & vexation of spirit. Still it will have greater attractions for me if I think it will please you, & that you take an interest in it, & will encourage me & keep me up to the mark. I hope your mother wont delay writing to me, as I cannot keep away from you much longer I hope Clara is quite well & comforts you & sticks up for me, when you abuse me to her, or doubt me. Please give her my love & remember me vy kindly to yr mother. Dearest Jeannette Goodbye.

Ever yrs devotedly
Randolph S. Churchill

Years later, Winston was to find much solace in Gibbon, too. Jennie found hers in playing the piano, and the Jeromes' Paris apartment must have rung with some very passionate playing that September, as she waited for her father's letter. Randolph's mercurial ups and downs alarmed her considerably, and she felt he did not always tell her the whole truth about things when he ought to. She wrote and told him so:

Paris Sept. 22

I am afraid I shall not be allowed to write again in a long time my dearest Randolph as Mama seemed quite annoyed this morning when I asked if I might—I suppose you expected a cross letter like yrs *méchant!* & that is the reason you wished me to answer the last one— Your letters astonish me dearest—I am afraid you are too confident of success—too easily moved by a word—One moment you are in the depths of despair—thinking that if you marry me it must be without yr father's consent & the next seeing every thing *couleur de rose* & writing to me that there will be no opposition—Now darling you must not be angry I assure you I am not blaming you in the least—for I am that way myself—but you must not try & cheer me with hopes which are not to become realities—I have been reading a letter you wrote me in Cowes—saying the same thing & after all you confess that the last time I saw you in London you had great doubts 'as to whether yr father & mother would consent or not'—What has made them disappear??—is it quite true that they *have* disappeared or is it only to cheer me that you say so—& to make me think you are not worried & troubled as I know you are—Dearest that is bad policy—for if I am to share all yr troubles for the rest of my life—I had better be a little initiated beforehand— Not that I think we shall have many—on the contrary—when two people love each other as we do—nothing can annoy them much the most matter of fact stupid, dull life on Earth can be made happy by love— And I see no reason why ours should be an exception—After all then— I was right as to yr being changed in London—why not have told me dear?—you must have a very poor opinion of my affection for you—if you think anything your father & mother can say—can change it in the least—Of course they can prevent our marriage—but that is all—& whether I marry you or not I shall always think of you as the only man I could have married & the only man I ever really loved—I hope & pray dear Randolph you will come soon—Paris wld be charming with you—Tomorrow we go to 146 Bd Haussmann do not forget to address yr letters there—I shall be very glad to begin my music & studies I think any town a bore unless one is well occupied—I rather like those last photographs *les 6 boutons sont resplendissants!*[9] Clara sends her best love—

Ever Yours—
Jeannette Jerome

How is Puggles?—I found yr paper very interesting—but what a bore such a dinner must be!—

In response, Randolph told Jennie exactly what he had in mind:

> Blenheim
> Tuesday 23rd

Dearest, I got your letter out shooting today. My sister Annie[10] brought it out with my luncheon. I cannot tell you what pleasure & happiness yr letters give me they make me feel quite a different being, so you really must not threaten me with a long silence never mind if yr mother is a little cross, but DO keep on writing as OFTEN as you can if you at all care to prevent my being worried & '*triste*'. I have often told you that all my bother & worry & sadness is chiefly owing to being away from you, & so if I hear from you from time to time I am much happier. You certainly my dearest Jeannette have great powers of perception, & I cannot but own, that there is a good deal of truth in what you say about my being one moment vy despairing & another moment vy sanguine; I can't help it, I was made so. & you say you are a little bit the same. My father has been away for a few days & yesterday I got a '*piece*' from him on the subject of his consent. After a good deal of unnecessary rigmarole & verbosity he says. 'The great question is still unsolved; whether you & the young lady who has gained your affections, are or can be after a few days acquaintance, sufficiently aware of your own minds to venture upon a step which is to bind you together for life. To marry in haste & repent at leisure is a trite saying but not less trite than true; What I have now to say is that if I am to believe that yr happiness is really bound up in yr marriage with Miss Jerome you must really shew me proof of it by bringing it to the test of time; I will say no more to you on this subject for the present but if this time next year you come & tell me you are both of the same mind we will receive Miss Jerome as a daughter & I need not say in the affection you cld desire for your wife.' Now my darling these are his words but I do not mind telling you that it is all humbug, (at least if I know him at all) about waiting a year. I cld & wld wait a good deal more than a year for you, & I am sure you wld do the same for me, but I do not mean to, & it is not the least necessary & no good can come of it. Tho' we have only known each other a short time, I know we both know our own minds well enough. & I wrote a vy long & diplomatic letter to my father yesterday, doing what I have never done before, contradicting him and arguing with him & I hope persuading him that he is got a vy wrong & foolish idea into his head. You see my darling I have to a great extent got him in my power & I will tell you why. Both he & my mother have set their heart on my being member for Woodstock. It is a family borough & for years & years a member of the family has sat for it. The present member is a stranger[11] tho a conservative, & is so unpopular that he is almost sure to be beaten if he were to stand, & the fact of a radical sitting for Woodstock is an idea perfectly insupportable to my family. It is for this that they have kept me idle ever since I left Oxford; waiting for a dissolution. Well as I told you the other day a dissolution is sure to come almost before the end of the year. Well I have two courses open to me, either to refuse to stand altogether, unless they consent to my being married to you immediately afterwards or else, & this is still more Machiavellian and deep, to stand, but at the last moment, threaten to withdraw & leave the radical to walk over. This may all appear vy strange to you but you have no idea how much they think of this borough & how much they have set their hearts on it & I am so certain of the success of one or other of these plans that that is why (having obtained their conditional consent) I am in comparatively good spirits as to my being able to obviate any long delay. All tricks are fair in love as well as in war & if I am crossed, I can plot & intrigue like a second Machiavelli. However I really do not think any of this will be necessary. I hope to be able to write to you in a day or two that my letter to my father yesterday, which I wish you cld have seen as it was a sort of 'ultimatum' has had the effect of considerably modifying his resolutions. Now please dont you go and tell yr mother about this idea of a year's delay as I think it is an idea which has already got much too much into her head as it is, & I do not mean to stand it if I can help it, which I know I can, if I am quite sure of yr entire approval & concurrence. Now my dearest you know really everything I really must make one remark on yr letter & scold you a little & that is upon the apparently calm way in which you continually envisage the fact of our not being married after all. Now my darling this does really rather annoy me I have never suffered such a thought to enter into my head for a moment since I have been quite sure & confident of your dear love & I really must most solemnly protest against yr ever thinking such a thing again. I have told you times & times, yet you will not seem to trust me, that nothing whatever, no circumstances & no people shall ever keep you from me, & that sooner or later if we both live, we will [marry]. I am sure you will not mind my remarking upon this. Dearest you must write vy soon. As soon as I have got one letter from you I never am happy till I get another, & you do write so charmingly & so lovingly you dear that it wld have been better never to have begun than to stop. I know you cant refuse what I beg of you so shall confidently expect letters from you. I have been out shooting today, & it has been terribly hot & *je suis*

ereinté.[12] The poor dear pug is in a most critical state. He has
frequent fits, & never seems to know me or anyone now. However I
have still some hopes of his recovery tho vy slight. I am sure Clara will
be sorry about this, she always used to tell me she liked the pug better
than his master. Please give her my love, she says I never send her a
message but the fact is you dont give them. I shall certainly go to Paris
when I hear from yr mother. It wont be long now, your father's final
answer must come vy soon. Do tell me what you have already heard
from him, as I know you must have heard. The fact is you tell me
nothing really altho you are always accusing me of not telling you
things & I do tell you everything. Dearest I am afraid my letters are far
from amusing & will not give you a very high idea of my abilities, but
my life here is a perfect blank as far as excitement or amusement of
any sort goes. I hope you really will work hard at your music when
anyone plays as beautifully as you do it is well worth working at it.
Please do not ride that vicious horse. I have formed the worst opinion
of him. Remember me vy kindly to your mother & tell her from me
she is not to be cross with you for writing, but only with me for I have
told you to. Dearest you may really cheer up & be in good spirits now,
as things are looking much brighter, & I begin to see my way quite
clear.

   With fondest love to you

                              Yrs ever devotedly
                              Randolph S. Churchill

Emotional blackmail is permitted within one's own family, perhaps,
but even so, Randolph's plan was Machiavellian indeed. His lack of
scruple as to the means by which he attained his ends was to prove disastrous within eighteen months. Jennie, however, was shocked less by the
unscrupulousness itself than by Randolph's rashness in exposing it to
prying eyes:

                                                  September 26th
Randolph my dear I think I shall have to put a black faveur on that
last letter of yours to mark it from the others—you are really very
wicked to *write* such things about your father & mother—it is bad
enough to say them—but write them is really dreadful—After all
dearest—it is not so very long to wait—& you must have a little patience—I am also angry with you dear for saying you would like 'a
peaceful happy life with no particular occupation' indeed I cannot
believe you would be contented to sit and fold yr hands for the rest of
yr life. I shld like you to be as ambitious as you are clever—& I am cer-

tain you would accomplish great things—We might have a nice little
home of our own as you say—whatever yr family is to you I know
mine will always be kind & loving to both of us—I received two letters
from my father yesterday—I wish you were here to read them—I cannot tell you how kind they are—of course he thinks it all rather sudden & *surtout* rather hurried he is afraid I do not realize how important such a step is etc—but on the whole I can see he gives his consent
& I am sure will do everything he can for us—he says he wld have
preferred an American for me—but that there is not much difference
au fond between English & Americans. He adds—'I am as confident
that all you say of him is true as though I knew him myself.' You see
dear, Papa & I are the greatest of friends as I have told you—& he has
always done everything on Earth he can to please—Mama also
received a letter from him, a very long & serious one full of stupid
affairs—& I believe she will write to you in a day or two. I hope you
have not quarreled with yr father & that you will come to us very soon
—I am getting *so* tired waiting. *Croyez vous que vous êtes le seul?*[13]
People are so curious & annoy me so with questions that I have quite
retired from the world—I have quite a hermit's life & remain all day
in my little salon—only emerging for a walk before dinner I have not
been able to ride yet—*malheuresement*—as I have for the present no
available chaperon—I am afraid I shall have to wait until Papa
comes. . . .

Leonard Jerome's letters were written on different dates, though they
arrived in Paris on the same day. In the first he was alarmed:

My dear Jennie,
    You quite startle me. I shall feel very anxious about you till I hear
more. If it has come to that—that *he* only 'waits to consult his family'
you must be pretty far gone. You must like him well enough to accept
for yourself which for you is a great deal. I fear if anything goes
wrong you will make a dreadful shipwreck of your affections. I always
thought if you ever did fall in love it would be a dangerous affair. You
were never born to love lightly. It must be *way down* or nothing.
Something like your mother. Not so Clara—happily not so. . . .

He went on to say he wouldn't object as long as his wife didn't—
'Provided always he is not a Frenchman or any other of those continental cusses,' a remark which goes some way to explaining why he
preferred to live alone in New York rather than with his family in Paris.
His next letter was written when he had more details. 'I must say I have

been very happy all day,' he wrote. 'I have thought of nothing else.' He promised to give her £2000 a year, and went on:

> I cannot imagine any engagement that would please me more. I am as confident that all you say of him is true as though I knew him. Young, ambitious, uncorrupted. And best of all you think and I believe he loves you. He must. You are no heiress and it must have taken heaps of love to overcome an Englishman's prejudice against 'those horrid Americans'. I like it in every way. He is English. You will live in England. I shall see much of him and you. And my dear Jennie the very best of it is—*a love match*. Like your mother & me. Did you ever know a couple to get on better than we do? There is nothing that compensates for love rank wealth all the honours that all the world can heap upon you are nothing compared wtih genuine love . . .

Mrs Jerome wrote to Randolph, announcing Leonard's formal consent. But she had serious doubts about the Duke's attitude, in spite of what Randolph had told her:

Septer 29, 1873
146 Bd Haussmann

My dear Ld. Randolph

I have just received a letter from my husband which I do not send you as there are many things in it which would not interest you. Of course dear Ld. Randolph he knows nothing about you except what I have written which I need not say was most favourable. Taking for granted that what I said must be true & listening to his daughters earnest appeal who thinks all her happiness in life depends on her marrying you, he gives his formal consent. I must however say that my husband has not the slightest idea of any opposition from your Father as I wrote him very particularly what you told me at Cowes that there would be none. I can only repeat that both Mr Jérôme and myself have too high an opinion of our daughter too much love ever to permit her to marry any Man without the cordial consent of his family.

My husband also writes. 'If the settlement of £2,000 a year & the assurance of one third of all my fortune later is satisfactory this can all be easily arranged.'

If yr Father gives his consent I shall wish you to see more of each other before taking such an important step & if there is any engagement at all it must be a long one

Pray believe dear Ld. Randolph in my sincere affection for you.

Clara H. Jérôme

Randolph replied to this effusively, thanking Mrs Jerome for having spoken well of him, admitting that his father felt as she did that a long engagement was desirable, and saying how very much he loved Jennie. Jennie's next letter must have reached him the following day:

> Monday evening
>
> My darling I can only write a line otherwise this letter will not go to-night as it is late—But I must tell you how happy I feel now that things are coming right—& that I may see you soon—I hope you will never know what a worthless & idle life I have been leading since we came here—& all owing to you *Monsieur!* Really I have not had the heart to do [the] slightest thing—I have felt so anxious about it all indeed I have grown quite thin & I am afraid you will think me so ugly when you come—you wont care for me any more I was glad to see by yr Friday letter that you had not quarrelled with yr father, as I was afraid you wld—I think him quite in the right—& understand perfectly that he thinks as he does—altho' I think it rather tedious—I am not astonished as I expected it if not from yr father—from my mother —who does nothing but sermonize me on the subject—Dearest you must not come to Paris—until you have written to Mama—I know she wrote you yesterday & you must answer before coming—for it is in vain that I have told her all you said & even read her yr letters she does not seem to be quite convinced—& I think it will need all yr elo-quence to persuade her to allow you to come—I am afraid she does not quite believe all you say yr father said—I am sure you wont mind my speaking frankly—you must try & get yr father to write—or let Mama know in some way what his decision is—on receiving yr let-ter this evening I went & had a long talk with her—which resulted in my feeling *fameusement* again—She says she cannot have you come here & be seen with us until things are entirely settled & the engage-ment an understood thing in both our families & by everyone—darling I hope you are not angry at my telling you this—you know how difficult it is to manage parents indeed I am tired of trying to do it—I shall expect a letter on Wednesday in answer to this—why did you not write Saturday? I cannot do without one *everyday* you have spoilt me too much to stop now—I am *so sorry* about poor dear Puggy—I had hoped we wld have him in our little house—when we are married—it wld remind us of Cowes, Rosetta, & those happy days—How short & few they were—If we love each other so much now—fancy what it will be later! I have a great quantity of photos: taken all sizes & poses—I

think I shall wait until you come (which I hope will be next week) to give them to you—I really must stop—good night my own darling Randolph—

> Ever yours
> Jeannette Jerome

Randolph was furious at the suggestion that he was not telling the truth, and at once wrote and told Mrs Jerome so, and announced his imminent arrival in Paris. Jennie was aghast—not at his arrival, but at his letter. Many of the confusions of the engagement might never have arisen if people had not replied so swiftly to their letters. This was a case in point. Another misunderstanding now was more than Jennie could bear to contemplate:

> Friday morning

How could you write such a letter to Mama my darling *stupid* Randolph? Did you not see that when I wrote that wretched letter—neither Mama or I had received either of yours—& I wrote mine on the spur of the moment ('a thing one ought never do') after a discussion with her which made me feel very cross—altho' she did not say half I wrote—but in my stupid anger I wrote whatever came in my head—that she did not *believe* you—words she *never did say*—I did not know I had written them myself—I shall explain it all to you when you come—& darling for Heaven sake don't spoil this meeting by misunderstandings & quarrels—I have been so longing for it—& looking forward to it—I cld not be so cruelly disappointed—You wld have a perfect right to be furious & feel very much injured if things were as you thought them—but they *are not*—Pray believe what I say that it is all my fault & I beg you to forgive me if you love me & not be angry & come to me as soon as you arrive—We shall expect you to dinner—& I shall be quite greying with disappointment if you do not come—oh my darling don't ever write such a letter again—when shall we have finished with all these misunderstandings & distrusts?—

> Ever yrs most lovingly
> Jeannette

I am so very sorry Mr Livingstone & another American gentleman are dining with us—I hope it won't annoy you Mama asked them long ago—

DO COME[14]

Randolph came—to the Hotel France et de Bath, in the Rue St Honoré. Misunderstandings seem to have melted away. Even Leonard, weeks behind the events in New York, had his last scruples removed and announced 'Between you & I and the post—and your mother etc. *I am delighted* more than I can tell It is magnificent. The greatest match any American has made since the Dutchess of Leeds.' And so it was—though Leonard would have to learn to spell Duchess. (The Duchess of Leeds, who died one week before Jennie's wedding to Randolph, was the daughter of a Baltimore merchant, Richard Caton.) Bliss seems to have become general. Jennie and Randolph dawdled about Paris, pretending to look at furniture for the 'parrot's perch' they planned to live in, but no doubt much more interested in each other. The wedding, it had been agreed, must wait on the election. Meanwhile Randolph could visit Paris as often as he wished, though he must nurse his constituency as well.

He was planning to come over for Jennie's birthday, on January 9th 1874, but his mother's sister, Lady Portarlington, was taken mortally ill in Ireland, and the Duchess insisted that the family, including Randolph, should attend the death-bed. Jennie and the Duchess had not yet met, and it boded little good for relations between them that the Duchess's first letter to her future daughter-in-law should have indicated quite so plainly her authority over Randolph. On matters of duty, the Duchess rarely had doubts:

Emo Park
Portarlington

Dear Miss Jerome　　　　　　　　　　　　　　　　Jan. 7

Although in great anxiety & affliction I write a line for dear Randolph to enclose as I feel grieved for his disappointment in not being able to start so as to spend your birthday with you. He was on the point of starting when my poor sister had a relapse to the state of fearful gasping for breath which is so anxious & so painful. It was almost impossible for him to go while she was in such a state for if the worst had happened he would have blamed himself & I feel sure you would not have wished it. I therefore urged him to remain & I telegraphed myself to you. He felt much the disappointment not only to himself but to you. I hope he will be rewarded for his self denial in a few days.

I am sorry my first communication with you should be of such a sad nature but the Duke & I hope please God to make your acquaintance under happier Circumstances ere long.

I remain dear Miss Jerome

Yrs Sincerely
F. Marlborough

The hope was not immediately realized. Lady Portarlington kept gasping for some time, then had to be decently buried before Randolph could get away. And when he did, he was half-way to France when he heard that Gladstone had dissolved Parliament and there was to be a General Election. Randolph went straight to Woodstock where 'the stranger' obligingly made way for him (not that he had much choice). Then he threw himself vigorously into the election.

Randolph was inexperienced (he hid the notes for a speech in his hat, much to the merriment of his audience), but he fought the campaign with enthusiasm, knowing that his victory would remove all obstacles to an early marriage. And in fact he won by 165 votes, then sped to Paris, where he was shortly followed by the Duke and Duchess, come to inspect their future daughter-in-law. Their conclusion was apparently satisfactory, though they did not find themselves able to attend the wedding, fixed for April the 15th. This was not the snub it would be today; the cult of weddings had not yet begun. But it was a snub of a sort, and the Duchess found herself unable to spare Randolph's sister Rosamond for the occasion, either. Anglo-American relations were not helped by the negotiations for Jennie's wedding settlement, which dragged on for several weeks. It was agreed by everyone except Leonard Jerome himself that he had behaved disgracefully, mainly, perhaps, because he thought it quite wrong that an English husband should have control of an American wife's money. The Duke was extremely sensitive on such points. All was settled in time, however, and Randolph arrived again in Paris in early April. Jennie wrote to him just before he left:

. . . I think it will be very nice to give Clara & Leonie a locket—but why not get them here? Mme Henry has charming things—much nicer than in London—besides dont you think it wld be better to get them together?—*Pourtant que ce soit comme vs le desirez cher ami—vs êtes le maître*[15]—You really must let me ride I am so strong now I assure you I have grown quite fat,—& it will be so charming to go out in the morning—I wont marry you if you dont let (me) do *exactly* as I like—*il faut vs preparer a une vie de sacrifices*[16] with me my dear. . . .

Women are supposed to be contrary, but to say almost in the same breath that Randolph was master, and that she wouldn't marry him unless he let her do exactly as she liked, was going too far. In his reply Randolph ignored the provocation and told her about a dinner party he'd been to with the Prince of Wales. 'I am so glad to hear you have got so strong again', he added, '& that I shant find you such a little bag of bones as I left you.' He ended with an order, perhaps hoping to go on the way he was starting: 'Don't forget to order my apartment at the hotel d'Albe. I shall be furious if I don't find one quite ready.'

The wedding took place in the chapel of the British Embassy on April 15th. Jennie wore white satin with a long train and flounces of Alençon lace. Blandford was there, and three of Randolph's sisters and an aunt. The best man was Francis Knollys. For her going away the bride wore a dark blue dress with white stripes, and a white hat with a white feather. The dress was one of the twenty-five with which Lady Randolph Churchill began her married life.

NOTES

1. That is how I am made!
2. Strictly speaking this was true: a brother between Blandford and Randolph had died in infancy.
3. If this is the same as 'that old fool G.P.' of Randolph's letter of September 22nd, it may perhaps have been Admiral Lord George Paulet (1807–79), ADC to the Queen, CB, and officier de la Légion d'Honneur.
4. William Garner was an extremely rich American cotton manufacturer. He and his wife were drowned in 1876, leaving three daughters: Florence married Sir William Gordon-Cumming in 1891, the moment after his disgrace for cheating at cards in the Tranby Croft affair: Edith became Countess Leon Von Moltke Huitfeldt: and Marcelite the wife of the Marquis de Breteuil.
5. Vexations.
6. Unsettled.
7. Perhaps as a mark of Anglophilia, Jennie now dropped the French accents from her surname.
8. Lady Cornelia Henrietta Maria (1847–1927), married to Sir Ivor Bertie Guest, 2nd Bart, created first Baron Wimborne in 1880.
9. The six buttons are dazzling!
10. Lady Anne Emily, Randolph's third sister (1854–1928), married James Innes-Kerr, Marquess of Bowmont and later 7th Duke of Roxburghe in June 1874, after a much shorter engagement than Randolph's to Jennie.
11. Barnett was hardly a stranger. Glympton Park, where he lived, is precisely four miles from Blenheim Palace.
12. I am exhausted.
13. Do you think you are the only one?
14. Underlined five times.
15. However it shall be as you wish dear friend—you are the master.
16. You must prepare yourself for a life of sacrifices.

The Jeromes' invitation to the ball
at which Jennie first met Randolph

'The Ball on Shipboard'
painted at Cowes by
J. J. Tissot in about 1873

To meet
Their Royal Highnesses the Prince and Princess of Wales
and
Their Imperial Russian Highnesses the
Grand Duke Cesarewitch and Grand Duchess Cesarevna.
Captain Carpenter and the Officers of H.M.S. "Ariadne"
request the honour of the Company of
Mrs & Misses Jerome
On board, on Tuesday, August 12th, from 3.30 to 7.30, p.m.
DANCING.
Boats will be in attendance at the R.Y.C. Landing Place.
R.S.V.P.

Randolph's first letter to Jennie (right)

Part of Jennie's letter to Randolph suggesting they break off their engagement (below)

Jennie and Randolph in 1874 (opposite)

Winston aged ten with his younger brother Jack

The Marquess of Blandford,
Randolph's elder brother,
later to become 8th Duke
of Marlborough

Jennie hunting in Ireland, 1877

Edward VII when Prince of Wales

Blenheim Palace, a contemporary painting (above)

A political rally at Blenheim (below)

3

CHURCHILL QUARRELS

Blenheim Palace has been the home of the Dukes of Marlborough since 1715. The Royal Manor of Woodstock was granted by Queen Anne to the first Duke, and ever since, on the anniversary of the battle of Blenheim, his heirs have presented to hers a standard of France, in commemoration of the great victory which finally checked the pretensions of the Bourbons and the power of France.

The history of Woodstock begins with the history of Britain. A Roman road, still visible, paved with cobble-stones, passes through the park. In Saxon times the Kingdoms of Wessex and Mercia met nearby. The country was heavily wooded, and there was probably a royal hunting lodge in the valley of the little river Glyme, where the forest began. The neighbouring kings could meet there to discuss their affairs.

A visitors book of the Royal Manor would contain all the great names of the succeeding thousand years of British history. Alfred the Great and Ethelred the Unready hunted the forest. The first great quarrel between Henry II and Thomas à Becket occurred here. Henry I had enclosed the park in a continuous wall, still standing, some twelve miles in circumference. Inside it he kept lions, bears and camels, and other wild animals from the east: there was no such extensive menagerie in the whole of Europe until modern times. Henry II also used the Manor to support a mistress: the fair Rosamond lived in a 'bower' here, till Queen Eleanor found out. Legend says that Eleanor poisoned the well, and Rosamond went to an early grave in nearby Godstow Nunnery. The Latin inscription on her tomb puns on her name and implies 'The rose was fair but not pure', but pure water now bubbles out of Rosamond's well, and is piped across the valley to play in the fountains around the palace.

Richard Coeur de Lion, King John and the Black Prince were all born at Woodstock. Chaucer lived in the village, and his son became a ranger in the park. Queen Elizabeth I, as a young princess, was imprisoned in the gatehouse of the Manor by her sister Bloody Mary. James I hunted the deer every year: there is a tradition that his son Charles I was himself hunted through the park by Oliver Cromwell and the Roundheads.

But after the Restoration in 1660, the Royal Manor fell into disuse until it was granted to John Churchill, first Duke of Marlborough.

Marlborough had returned from his victories on the continent in triumph, but criticism and frustration met him at home, and complex political intrigue soon lost him royal favour. He turned therefore to planning the construction of his great palace in the old royal park. Blenheim was to be his silent answer to his critics, his monument, and his epitaph. For his architect he chose John Vanbrugh, an old comrade in arms. Flemish by descent (the Flemish were one of the peoples liberated by Marlborough's victories), Vanbrugh was a soldier by profession, but also a playwright of distinction. The dramatic scale of the site suited him, and the grandeur of the building he conceived was symbolic of the momentous events it commemorated. The Duke wanted an English Versailles, combining the arts of England and Europe. Vanbrugh created a setting whose theatrical impact is strikingly revealed as one passes the entrance gatehouse of the park and first sees the lake in the valley, the bridge, and then on the slope of the hill, silhouetted against the sky, the encircling arms of the palace, with its fantastic roofline. (The impact would be still more striking if Capability Brown had not later flooded the valley far more than Vanbrugh designed.)

Inside, the palace was a treasure-house. The Duke had been presented with gifts from all over Europe, and was in any case a great collector of works of art. Splendid tapestries celebrating his victories were specially woven at Brussels, famous pictures were acquired, statues were bought or seized as spoils of war: among the gifts was a scale model of Bernini's famous fountain in the Piazza Navona in Rome. There were silks, marbles, gems, Sèvres china, gold plate, Boulle furniture, Vandyke portraits, to say nothing of the diamond-studded sword presented to Marlborough by the Emperor. To all this splendour his descendants added: if they squandered their money, they often squandered it well. The fourth Duke, for instance, was a connoisseur, and collected the celebrated Marlborough gems. The Sunderland Library was one of the finest in the world. There were magnificent collections, too, of Limoges enamels, Oriental china and eighteenth-century French furniture. Blenheim Palace was altogether magnificent, inside and out.

Randolph brought Jennie to Blenheim on a beautiful spring day in May 1874. Some of the Duke's tenants (who were, of course, also Randolph's constituents) met them at the station, took the horses out of the carriage, and dragged them through the town to the palace. As they entered the park, Randolph turned to Jennie with pardonable pride and said 'This is the finest view in England.' She was deeply impressed, and when they reached the palace itself, awed. But life inside the treasure-house struck her as very strange, stiff and formal. Everything went on with the regularity of clockwork, and there was very little to do. Jennie practised her piano, read and painted, till she began to imagine herself back in the schoolroom. Everyone read the newspapers avidly, and the conversation was largely political. There were afternoon calls to be paid, social and charitable, otherwise there was only the garden to walk in. Dinner was a solemn full-dress affair. Afterwards everyone sat in the Vandyke room: the only excitement was a mild game of whist, played strictly for love, not money. People grew so bored that they sometimes surreptitiously advanced the clock so they could go to bed: no one dared suggest moving till eleven had struck. Then everyone would rise, fetch his candle, kiss the Duke and Duchess good night, and depart, with great relief, to his own room. Jennie was used to a considerably gayer life than that, and was not amused by the Duchess's instruction in the correct ways of behaviour for an aristocrat's wife. If Blenheim was like a schoolroom, there was no question as to who was the mistress. The Duke was kind, but the Duchess, Jennie wrote, 'ruled Blenheim and nearly all those in it with a firm hand'. *Nearly* all, yes. The household trembled at the rustle of her silk dress, but not Jennie. Her American pride rebelled. Though she acknowledged that the Duchess was a very remarkable and intelligent woman, she never got on with her, and there was continual sniping and criticism between the two.

Though Jennie and Randolph had their own house in London, they spent a good deal of time at Blenheim. Jennie could not go out much in the social world, for she was immediately pregnant. And it was at Blenheim, during one of her many visits, that her first child was born on November 30th, 1874, six weeks premature. Winston caught everyone by surprise. The Duchess reported to Mrs Jerome in Paris that 'we had neither cradle nor baby linen nor anything ready'. Randolph sent a full account:

I have just time to write a line, to send by the London Dr to tell you that all has up to now thank God gone off very well with my darling Jennie. She had a fall on Tuesday walking with the shooters, & a rather imprudent & rough drive in a pony carriage brought on the pains on Saturday night. We tried to stop them, but it was no use. They went on all Sunday. Of course the Oxford physician cld not come. We telegraphed for the London man Dr Hope but he did not arrive till this morning. The country Dr is however a clever man, & the baby was safely born at 1.30 this morning after about 8 hrs labour.

She suffered a good deal poor darling, but was vy plucky & had no chloroform. The boy is wonderful pretty so everybody says dark eyes and hair & vy healthy considering its prematureness. My mother and Clementine[1] have been everything to Jennie, & she cld not be more comfortable. We have just got a most excellent nurse & wet nurse coming down this afternoon, & please God all will go vy well with both. I telegraphed to Mr Jerome; I thought he wld like to hear. I am sure you will be delighted at this good news and dear Clara also. I will write again tonight. Love to Clara.   Yrs affty

Randolph S.C.

I hope the baby things will come with all speed. We have to borrow some from the Woodstock Solicitor's wife.

While it would be idle to pretend that Jennie was a doting mother, it would be quite wrong to suggest that she did not love her children. Both her letters and Randolph's are full of references to Winston as a baby, and though no woman of her position spent very much time with her children, Jennie spent quite as much as most. In an aristocratic household a wife was expected to produce her babies, then hand them over to wet nurses,[2] nannies and nursemaids, till they were old enough to go to school. The nursery was an establishment within an establishment, with its own specially cooked meals served by its own staff, and its own hierarchical structure. Meanwhile the father and mother got on with their own lives, looking in occasionally to make sure all was well. Jennie's relations with her two sons were usually very good, but it was not a system which led to invariable accord between parents and children, as was amply demonstrated in the family into which she had married.

Blandford, as we have seen, was a man whose experience of marriage was so bitter that he seriously upset his brother by the way he inveighed against it. His wife was called Bertha. She was a daughter of the Duke of Abercorn, and much given to practical jokes. It was the great age of such jokes, but hers were of the simplest: inkpots on doors and the substitution of soap for cheese. But she was amiable, and did not seem to notice that Blandford was, at this time, in love with someone else. He had also warmed to Jennie, and came to like her so much that he gave her a ring to demonstrate his affection: perhaps she had expressed sympathy for him in his plight. While Randolph and Jennie were staying at Blenheim in October 1875, Jennie showed this ring to the Duchess and Randolph's sister Rosamond. There was immediate trouble. Next morning Randolph wrote to his brother:

My dear Blandford

My mother & Rosamond who appeared strangely annoyed last night about the ring you gave Jennie inform me this morning that it was one of Bertha's rings. I dont believe this for a moment, but as they have permitted themselves several vicious looks and insinuations concerning it, please write me a line to say that they are mistaken. Jennie wishes me to thank you for it immensely. If by any chance the ring ever did belong to Bertha, you wont mind I am sure if Jennie asks you not to press it on her. She knows quite well that you like her very much without any rings, tho' it was most kind of you to wish her to have it. I am sure you will understand this.

Ever yr. affly

Sunday 31st Randolph S. Churchill

Since his parents found ceaseless fault with him, Blandford was no doubt delighted to have an excuse to find fault now with his mother. His response to Randolph's letter was to send it straight to the Duchess with the following note:

My Dear Mama 36 Piccadilly

Well acquainted as I am with the intense jealousy that you often display in your actions & the mischief which you so often make in speach I should not have thought you would have allowed yourself to be so far carried away, as to descend to untruth to substantiate an assertion or give color to a fact. I am therefore compelled to write to you to inform you that if in future you condescend to make such statements as the enclosed letter contains you need not expect to hear very often from Your very affec son

Blandford

The Duchess received the two letters as she was just setting off from Blenheim to go to London. She was dreadfully upset, and passed them straight to the Duke. As soon as they arrived in London, the Duke wrote to Randolph in indignation so high that it affected his spelling:

London

Randolph Nov. 4

Your mother has received today the enclosed correspondence.

I have only three words to say to you upon it.

1st you have grossly misrepresented facts to Blandford.

2nd you have while being received with kindness, yourself, wife, and child dishonorably and treacherously abused the confidence, which you yourself pretended you shared with yr mother abt Blandford while you were well aware that she never entertained any motives but those of the truest affection for you both.

3rd you have thus induced your brother to pen to his mother an unparalelled letter, which I do not trust myself to characterize in words You are the best interpreter of these things and their natural results and I leave you to form yr own conclusions; further communications upon the subject are needless I am yrs

Marlborough

Randolph replied the same day:

Dearest Papa

I most respectfully remark with regard to yr letter of this afternoon that I think you have formed a hasty judgement of the enclosed correspondence. I venture to think that expressions such as 'dishonourable' 'treacherous' 'liar', are hardly applicable to me. As long as these expressions remain in force further communications between us, are not only as you remark useless but impossible.

Yr affte son
Randolph

It took no time at all for the Spencer-Churchills to put each other into the most terrible rages, rages which seem literally to have 'blinded'. For instance, the Duke did not call Randolph a 'liar', he said he had grossly misrepresented facts to Blandford, which is not at all the same thing.

Doubtless appalled by the violence of the storm which had broken about her innocent finger, Jennie wrote next day to the Duchess:

Almond's Private Hotel,
6 & 7, Clifford St,
Bond St. W.

Dearest Duchess   Friday

I feel I cannot let you go away without saying at least how deeply I regret this unfortunate quarrel of which I am most unhappy at being the unintentional cause—I am sure that at present a discussion on the subject would be more than useless. But I must say that as much as Randolph is to blame in having used expressions in his letter to Blandford that no son ought to use about his mother—still the spirit of the letter was neither 'treacherous', 'dishonorable,' or untrue—& was written moreover in anger & haste—& never intended for your eye—The

Duke's letter to Randolph is such as no man should write to another—not even a father to a son—All I can do is to repeat how dreadfully sorry I am—& that whatever happens I hope you will believe that I am most grateful—both to you & the Duke—for all yr past kindness to me—& that I shall ever remain Yrs most affectly

J Spencer Churchill

This could be considered quite a tactful letter, under the circumstances. Jennie admitted Randolph's fault, pointed out the Duke's intemperance, and said how sorry she was. A loyal wife could hardly do more. That was not, however, how the Duchess saw it. Her outburst in reply is extremely revealing about the tensions and suppressed emotions within the Marlborough family:

Dearest Jennie   Nov. 5

I thank you for writing to me & am very sorry for the annoyance which this must cause you—You talk of it as a quarrel but it is much too serious for that. It is a bitter sorrow to find both our sons turn against us & reward our affection & kindness by insult & abuse. I fear Randolph's words are but an instance of the way he has got into with Blandford of abusing & ridiculing us. I cannot trust myself to write all I could abt. it for I do not wish to be harsh but I cannot think that his Father's Language though strong was not deserved—Randolph did misrepresent what I said abt the ring & the way I said it & it was not true to say Rosamond expressed annoyance when she never mentioned it at all—Randolph also spoke of 'our pretended views, looks & insinuations' which was perfectly untrue & he did this knowing it would rouse Blandford's angry temper. It was treacherous & dishonourable towards us but indeed he has got himself so into the habit of abusing People that I think he hardly knows how far he goes, & he will surely get himself into trouble. I never was so upset as when these dreadful Letters were put into my hands as we were leaving Home & it was such a blow to me that I cld not control my emotions and the Duke was naturally indignant. I will not argue abt it for I feel too cut up. I believed Randolph to be loyal & true & to find him otherwise cuts me to the heart. Nothing can change it. Randolph has trampled on my affections & God forgive him for it. As for you dearest Jennie Time will prove to you that I have treated you as a daughter in word & deed. I love you & your dear little child & I shall never cease to take a loving interest in you. Nor can I accuse myself of anything but kind intentions respecting you since I have known you. It is not in me to be false & though I may at times have thought you unwise I have not intended to offend or pass judgement on you. I wished to be more a mother than a mother in law to you & perhaps I was wrong—When you are away you will think kindly of me. I quite feel that it is not in our Power to make our sons love & respect us & to change their hearts towards us & yet I have been brought up to think *strongly* of Duty to Parents.

Sadly I admit therefore that it is perhaps well that Randolph should see less of us for a time & perhaps he may get to value more our affection & confidence.

Yrs most affly. F Marlborough

The bitterness of this letter seems out of all proportion to Randolph's offence—which was, after all, unintentional, unless we accept the Duchess's highly improbable notion that Randolph was deliberately stirring up Blandford's temper. Randolph, in fact, had found himself in an extremely awkward position, caught between an upset wife and an insinuating mother—a situation whose millions of historical precedents only showed how unlikely it was that the husband and son would emerge unscathed. The fact that he chose to defend Jennie against the Duchess was, surely, what caused the real offence. The Duchess thought he was 'loyal and true' to her; but he was more loyal and truer to his wife. Otherwise why should the Duchess have felt it necessary to defend her role as 'more a Mother than a Mother in law'? What else could have made her feel that her affections had been trampled on so badly that only God could forgive it? The Duchess had abandoned hope of Blandford: her maternal ambitions were all for Randolph. Now she was desperately hurt, and showed it.

She also showed that she knew her son. Randolph had got himself into the habit of abusing people, and didn't realize quite how far he went: when he and Blandford ganged up together, they could get into serious trouble. Now, though, all that happened was that Randolph passed the Duke's letter on to his brother. There is irony in Blandford's suggestion that his father must have been writing after dinner: it was precisely the Prince of Wales's explanation for Blandford's own outburst against Randolph's marriage.

Oak Dene
Holmwood, Dorking

My dear R.   Friday

His graces admirable composition is a disgrace to his intelligence as well as being 'eminently ungentlemanlike'. He contradicts himself flatly in his first and second points: 'misrepresentation of facts' &

'abuse of confidence' are two ideas in direct contradistinction to one another. I fear he must have written his letter after dinner judging from the haziness of the phraseology & the utter incongruity of all the nonsense he has endeavoured to string together. I think your reply quite sufficient, & if he does not see what a fool he makes of himself by entering into my mothers mischief I am only sorry for his intelligence & I leave him to his worst enemy 'himself'. If he expects respect from his sons he should learn how to treat them as gentlemen & not suppose that the overbearing manner & assumption of superiority which for years he displayed to us in our youth is going to be quietly submitted to when we have attained maturer years, & I for one am determined to make a start against it. / / I sent you a wire today I shall not come to town tomorrow but shall expect you by the 4.55 from Victoria

Yours affly
Bd.

P.S. I return you his graces composition herewith

This letter brings the sad state of family feelings out into the open. Blandford thought his father overbearing, and bitterly resented it; the Duchess, whom he seems to have hated, believed *strongly* in Duty to Parents; the inevitable result was a disturbed, rebellious son, for whom maturer years had not tempered an early sense of injustice and maltreatment. Unfortunately, he seems to have had a strong influence over Randolph at this time, and to have encouraged him to rebel, too. The quarrel continued. It was still not over the following January. Randolph wrote to Jennie, who was skating in Paris:

Marlborough Club,
Pall Mall. S.W.

My darling

I am staying at Almond's Hotel. Fanny[3] & I had a row & I considered that she was vy impertinent so I left. She informed me that she wld rather I did leave her house than listen to a word against the Duke & Duchess, so I took her at her word. I am quite decided to stand no impudence of that sort from any of the family, & the sooner they find it out the better we shall get on.

I have the same rooms we had the last time we were here together. I thought of you so much last night; I wish I was back with you, it seems an age since I saw you. I am sure I cannot get away till Saturday Pawle tells me he cannot conclude the business sooner. It is vy tiresome as I have nothing to do in London. The only thing is that

Clayton[4] says he wants to see me 2 or 3 times more, to put me quite right.

I had a letter from Henri Standish this morning who tells me that he arrives Tuesday morning. I shall try & get him to wait for me that we may go back together. I think we will be off to Nice vy soon. Clayton says it will be vy good for me to go there. If you like we will arrange to go Saturday week, & I will write to Saraceveski to get us rooms. Say in yr next if you approve. I am vy anxious to settle about Cook's lodgings for next season. I feel sure that it will suit us better than an hotel & will be *much* cheaper than a house. I think I can get the rooms, virtually the whole house for 20gs a week. & I am sure we shld be vy comfortable. If I take them I shall engage them from the 21st of April. Write me what you think. The frost has set in harder than ever. Do be moderate my darling in skating & dont overdo it. I am dying to get back to you. & Skinny[5]

Sunday 16th

Ever yrs
Randolph

Randolph consulted Dr Clayton, then the family doctor, for everything, including rheumatism. Presumably it was something more serious to require so much attention. With Mr Pawle, Randolph was arranging a loan, as we can see from his letter of the next day:

St James' Club,
Piccadilly, W.

My darling

I have to thank you for two letters received this morning. I enclose you one from Fanny to me, from which you will see that our little difference is made up. I expect Henri Standish tomorrow morning & have ordered him a room at Almonds. I think I may decide upon Saturday for my return to you. I shall know for certain tomorrow. I hope to sign the necessary papers for the loan & *'toucher le magot'*[6] Thursday morning. I saw Clayton this morning who said I was much better. & I am to see him again Wednesday & Friday. . . . I forgot to tell you that Bill Cumming[7] paid me a visit the other day. He asked most affectionately after you, & expressed his intention of coming to Nice later. . . .

My mother wrote to Blandford the other day a sort of grandly forgiving letter which drove him wild. He had previously written to her a vy questionable sort of apology.

Cook has yr cloak ready & I am to bring it back. I have no news darling with ever so much love to you & the baby

Ever yrs
Monday, Jan 17th   Randolph

Jennie thought the row had gone on quite long enough, and said so.

Dearest R. On awaking this morning Marie brought me yr letter of the 16th also one from Fanny—I was so distressed at hearing of yr new quarrel—that I was on the point of writing you a very cross letter—When luckily for me (as you no doubt wld have been furious) I received yr other telling me that it was all over—Really darling forgive me for saying it—but if you want to *éviter* discussions & quarrels on *that* disagreeable subject why dont you drop it—Why talk about or occupy yourself with it? I should like very much to go to Nice—but I am afraid it will be very expensive—& in this cold weather a long journey for Baby might be imprudent. . . .

It certainly needed saying, though alas, Jennie was not to succeed in persuading Randolph to avoid quarrels. However, he seems to have become rather apprehensive over the possible effects of this one. If his father had made his own brother resign the Woodstock seat over Church Rates, Randolph might well wonder about the consequences of being rude to his mother. The Duke's power over the majority of the constituents of Woodstock was great, but they still would not vote for his nominee without encouragement of a kind which was to be made illegal by the 1883 Corrupt Practices Act. A constituency was nursed with money, not love. Randolph feared that his father might withdraw his financial support. Since they were still not on speaking terms, he got the electoral agent to speak for him. The agent's report on his conversation with the Duke throws fascinating light on what was and what was not considered fair play in 1875:

Woodstock,
Oxon
Dear Lord Randolph Churchill   22 December 1875
    I have seen the Duke upon the subject of your letter, and stated what you wished me to represent.
    It is clear from the Duke's reply, that there is no intention whatever on his part, to recede from the offer which he made to you with reference to donations to Local Charities, and the necessary expences of maintaining the Registration.

But, with regard to the former, the Duke appears to feel, that the subscriptions which have been given by your Predecessors in the Borough, and which have been generally received as adequate, and liberal, are not likely to be regarded, less favorably when offered by you, my Lord; and therefore that a scale of appropriate subscriptions should be submitted for approval, as a guide for future years: and with this view, I am directed to ascertain what has been the usual amount of subscriptions throughout the Borough for some time past.

Upon the subject of Game I had better state to you specifically what the Duke's views are.

The Duke holds, in the first place, that presents of Game in a Parliamentary Constituency are generally injudicious, and more likely to create enemies, than Friends, to a Representative.

The Duke's own practice, he assures me, has always been consistent with the opinion which He thus expresses: and the presents of Game which have been given from Blenheim, have been given entirely for non-political objects—objects in connection either with the Landed Estates, or with the Duke's own personal position, but never with a view to political favor.

The Tenants, the Duke says, and many of the Neighbours, usually receive presents, and the list may probably be elastic enough to include the Friends whom you have mentioned at Tackley and Wootton, as well as a few more at Bladon and Handborough: but the Duke maintains that it is absolutely necessary, on the ground of supply, as well as for other reasons, to draw the line somewhere: and if the line is not drawn in a most distinguishable manner, quite irrespective of the Register of Voters, the result will probably be the reverse of what is intended, producing instead of favor, jealousy, and dis-content!

With respect to the arrangement which you allude to for the sale and purchase of Blenheim Game at cost price last year, it seems, though I don't know whether it was made clear to you, that no special prohibition was intended to be made upon a similar arrangement this year: but the circumstances were altered, and a local Dealer was not the Purchaser this year.

Now, my Lord, may I make you a report as to your own kind gifts to the Poor. When the cold set in, with a deep snow, at the beginning of this Month, I sent £10 to Tackley, £10 to Kidlington, £5 to Wootton, £5 for Thrupp, and Shipton; and £3 for Begbroke—The gifts were very opportune, and could not fail to be acceptable—The Recipients best speak for themselves, and I enclose their own replies —You know what I have in hand, to be applied according to your suggestion to urgent cases, (if any appear) as they may arise. But I shall be happy to fulfil any further direction you may like to give with respect to the amount, or any part of it—

I beg to offer my best wishes to yourself & Lady Randolph Churchill—

I have the honour to be
yours very faithfully
R. B. B. Hawkins

Lord Randolph Churchill M.P.
The Rector of Wootton acknowledged the Gifts in person.

The Duke, then, continued to give his necessary support to Randolph as a Member of Parliament, and this trivial family quarrel blew over. But almost at once Blandford and Randolph were involved in a far more serious affair, a full-blown Victorian scandal which was to have disastrous consequences. Once again, it was Blandford who started it.

NOTES

1. Lady Camden, Randolph's aunt.

2. The Duchess wrote to Mrs Jerome on December 3rd that 'the Milk is subsiding satisfactorily'.

3. Randolph's sister, married to Edward Marjoribanks, later 2nd Baron Tweedmouth. He became a prominent Liberal politician.

4. Dr Oscar Clayton, F.R.C.S., had a consulting-room in Harley Street. He was Ext. Surg. in Ord. to the Prince of Wales. He was knighted in 1882.

5. Winny.

6. Get my hands on the money.

7. Sir William Gordon-Cumming. His affectionate wishes may not have been very welcome: he was notorious for pouncing on newly married women.

4

THE AYLESFORD AFFAIR

Three weeks before the Churchill family raged at each other over a ring, the Prince of Wales had set off for a grand tour of India. It was an impressive expedition, for which the House of Commons provided £112,000, and the Indian government another £100,000, but though the Prince had three chefs, a studgroom, a chaplain and the Duke of Sutherland's piper among his retinue, he was much disappointed not to be able to take a detachment of Life Guards, too. Queen Victoria said that would be too much. She also disapproved of most of the Prince's personal guests on the tour, but they went all the same. Shooting elephants and tigers, presiding over state banquets, exchanging presents with Maharajahs and sticking pigs, the Prince led his party in triumph all over India. On February 20th 1876 they camped on the border of Nepal, where they were greeted by Sir Jung Bahadur with a turn-out of 1000 elephants and 10,000 soldiers to assist less than twenty sportsmen. It should have been a particularly splendid day. But in his diary the Prince wrote: 'Letters!!!'

The letters were about Blandford. Among the Prince's personal guests was Lord Aylesford, popularly known as 'Sporting Joe'. His wife Edith had not wanted him to go to India, but in the end she had given in. Shortly after he'd gone, Blandford had moved himself and his horses to an inn near Packington Hall, the Aylesford's house near Coventry. Ostensibly he was there to hunt. But after a day in the saddle, he would make his way under cover of darkness to a side-door of the Hall. He had his own key. The affair was extremely serious. In February, deeply in love, Blandford and Edith decided to elope together. They would seek divorces, defy society, and marry.

It is very difficult for us, a hundred years later, with divorce made easier year by year, to understand the horror its very mention sent through the upper classes in the 1870s. An anonymous French diplomat wrote that the dominating idea of English society was not the cultivation of virtue, but the prevention of scandal, and he explained it as due to 'the extreme sensitiveness of the ladies and gentlemen prominent in London

society to the public opinion of their inferiors'. But why were they so
sensitive? Surely because they were fully aware that they belonged to an
incredibly privileged class, and ever since the French Revolution
privileged classes had looked anxiously over their shoulders. The only
justification for their privileges was that they did, and were seen to do,
their social duty; and that was to lead the nation not only politically but
morally. Unfortunately, official Victorian morality, established by the
Queen herself, and followed, at least in theory, by the respectable middle class, bore no relation whatever to upper class practice. Hence hypoc-
risy and cant now seem to be the chief characteristics of the period. Fashionable people were not in the least prudish or puritanical; they hardly
could be with the Prince of Wales as their leader. Affairs were common
and gossip was rife: known lovers were assigned neighbouring bedrooms
on weekend parties: but it was felt, and passionately, that nonetheless a
pretence of disciplined, loyal, married life must be kept up. A far worse
sin than adultery was its advertisement. 'Society', wrote the same
Frenchman, 'regards as, in some sort, an enemy and a traitor to itself, the
man or woman who puts it openly to the blush.' A public scandal—or
Public Scandal, as the Aylesford affair was to be capitalized by one of
the courtiers who kept it quiet—was thought literally to betray the whole
social class. Hence the extreme punishments inflicted on those who let
down the side by allowing their indiscretions to reach the courts and
newspapers. Any divorced woman, innocent or guilty, was ostracized for
life. The careers of such men as Charles Stewart Parnell, Sir Charles
Dilke, and Oscar Wilde were ruined not so much by what they did—but
by their failure to keep it out of the public eye. It is only by trying to understand the horror and fear attached to publicity rather than to sexual
misdemeanour itself that one can see why Blandford's intended divorce
caused such a hubbub. A divorce meant the Divorce Court, and the
Divorce Court meant publicity. The Prince of Wales felt particularly
strongly on the subject because he had been dragged into court himself
in the Mordaunt divorce case of 1870. Though quite innocent, he had
been strongly censured. Scandal must be avoided at all costs.

Thus the news of Blandford and Edith Aylesford's intentions caused
consternation everywhere. In Nepal the Prince denounced Blandford as
the greatest blackguard alive, and Aylesford set off home on the back of
an elephant. In London counsels were held by both families, and eminent men were called in for advice. Edith's brother, Hwfa Williams,
wanted to challenge Blandford to a duel. (Some years later he was shot,
much to his own amazement, by a demented Post Office clerk as he was
strolling through St James's Park.) Randolph, rushing to prevent his
brother doing anything stupid, put detectives on Williams till it was

agreed that the only person who had a real right to challenge Blandford was Aylesford himself. Aided by his brother-in-law, Edward Marjoribanks, Randolph succeeded in persuading Blandford not to proceed with his plans at least for the time being. It was not easy. Blandford was even more excitable than usual. But Randolph, Marjoribanks informed the Duke, 'is doing and has done all he can to influence' him. It was mainly due to Randolph's influence that Blandford had not taken any irrevocable step. But now Randolph took one himself.

Whether or not the Prince had himself had an affair with Edith Aylesford is not established. But he had certainly written her some indiscreet letters, which Edith had shown to Blandford who had passed them on to Randolph. They made Randolph very angry, for it is clear that he already believed that the Prince had deliberately encouraged Blandford's affair, and had insisted on taking Aylesford to India so that it could be carried on with greater freedom. He even thought that Aylesford connived at it, that there was collusion between him and the Prince; since the Prince was therefore in a large measure responsible for the impending disaster, he must do everything in his power to prevent it. Randolph had already telegraphed to the Prince in India to persuade Aylesford not to seek a divorce. Now, with the hotheadedness his mother had deplored in the affair of the ring, and the unscrupulousness with which he had intended to treat his father if his plans to marry Jennie were thwarted, Randolph went to Princess Alexandra and told her that, if Aylesford did sue Edith for divorce, the Prince's letters would be produced as evidence in court. He told her that it was the Solicitor General's opinion that if that happened, the Prince would never sit on the throne of England. It was blackmail.

It was a bad enough business already. Now it took on even more serious proportions. The Prime Minister, Disraeli, was called in. Queen Victoria was outraged—especially on Princess Alexandra's behalf. (The Princess herself seems to have behaved with exemplary calm throughout.) The Prince, still shooting tigers in India, sent the Master of the Buckhounds to convey to Randolph his 'just indignation'. The Master of the Buckhounds was Lord Hardwicke, and his chief claim to fame is that he invented the shiny top hat which was to become an essential prop for envoys all over the world. As an inner member of the Prince's set, and a friend of Randolph's and Jennie's, he would seem to have been a very suitable choice for ambassador in such an awkward affair. But it turned out he wasn't. A new element of unpleasantness now entered the dispute. Randolph and Hardwicke seemed to have some personal feeling quite apart from the official business at hand.

They met early in April. The Prince wanted an apology, or a duel.

Randolph was prepared to apologize to Princess Alexandra, but not to the Prince, whom he virtually accused of cowardice for issuing a challenge he knew Randolph could not take up. (A subject may not fight his prince.) This was highly insulting, and no doubt angry words were exchanged. Later Randolph accused Hardwicke of 'having exaggerated much and invented more, and altogether done his best to embitter the quarrel'.

Meanwhile Aylesford had returned from India, and Blandford went over to Holland to avoid him, though he wrote to Randolph that 'if it is a question of having it out with him someday, I would 1000 times sooner it was now when H.R.H. can be nicely compromised than later when he has managed to slip out of it'. Though the Prince denied that there was anything scandalous in his letters to Edith Aylesford, it certainly looks as though Randolph and Blandford thought otherwise, and the gossip was that H.R.H. was staying away as long as possible. When Randolph went to see Blandford, Jennie stayed behind in London, apparently to supervise spring cleaning. Randolph found his brother a great bore. 'Blandford's eternal lectures & harangues always about himself are awfully wearying', he wrote to Jennie. *'Dieu! comme il m'ennuie.* I shall be so glad to get back to you darling & I am always thinking of you & the baby & wondering what you are doing.' He had a heavy cold, and felt quite sorry for himself.

On April 19th Jennie wrote with the latest news:

London
April 19th

Dearest—I dined with Fanny last night & Edward did not arrive till quite late—so I cld not gather much from him—particularly as Fanny's presence seems to silence him—However I found out that yr father & mother will not return before the end of next week.[1] Edward took rooms for them at the Westminster for this Saturday—so I suppose they intend remaining in Paris—The Duke it seems is in a fright for fear you shld show his letter to Blandford he received B's lengthy epistle & was much disgusted so E. said nothing but ravings & appealing to him as a friend to help him to get a divorce from Bertha—At first the Duke thought of not answering it but he has changed his mind—E. advised me to write to the Duchess—& when I told him I had—he said that she thought I ought to have written all along—fancy!—However I think she will like my letter & I hope it will put all things straight between us—Edward enjoyed himself very much in Paris went to the play with T. Trafford[2] and Rosebery[3] the former has gone to Bordeaux to taste wines—& from thence proceeds to Corsica This letter came for you this morning I send it as perhaps you wld like to answer it—there came also one from Henri Standish nothing particular so I keep it—I think I shall write to Mr S.—I feel so ill *'souffrante'* today that I haven't the strength of a cat & feel all doubled up with cramps so you will not be angry at this stupid erratic letter. I shan't stir out today besides it is cold & nasty—I believe Bertha is coming to stay with Fanny for a few days. Fanny is the most 'bottled up' creature I have *ever* met—Standish says he [is] coming here next month in order to look for a house or lodgings as they intend coming in June for the Season. E. says he has heard that the Prince has been going on in an extraordinary manner in India so he has heard—& that it is very evident he wants to stay away as long as he can—going to Spain etc—Of course he will stay with Mme Murrieta[4] at Seville I suppose—She has a house there I know & is there now—I have no doubt Hardwicke will abuse us to H. Hatzfeldt[5] as most likely she will talk about us—Goodbye darling I hope you dont mean to stay away long—I am so lonely

Yrs ever

J.

Next day Jennie had even more important news:

April 20th

10 p.m.

My dearest darling R.

I have just received yr letter of yesterday—You ask me what I think of yr fathers 2d epistle. I think it very bad—He is quite willing that you shld do all in your power to prevent Blandford from disgracing himself & his family—but is not at all willing to take upon himself any of the responsibility—or share any of the *désagrément* which must arise from being at open war with H.R.H. But my dearest there are few as generous as you & not many brothers wld risk what you are risking for one so worthless as B. tho he be yr only brother. A letter came for you tonight from Hardwicke. I do not send it to you—as you might miss it—besides you told me not to forward any letters—I can hardly bring myself to write calmly about it—so insolent & *disgusting* it is—It is just a repetition of what he said to you in yr last conversation together—the only important part being that he has heard from the Prince who wishes him to acquaint you that he H.R.H. has sent yr letter to the Queen—Hardwicke adds that he seems very much annoyed at the tone of yr letter & that he (H) is not astonished. The letter will keep till yr return I think but it made me boil with rage—If you want it immediately telegraph I have it locked up safely—*Au premier moment* I thought of writing to him telling him that you had asked me not to forward any letters—but that if *he* thought his letter important enough or worth sending on to you to let me know—However I thought better of it *'le silence est d'or'*. Nasty hateful creature! Oh! I'm *so* angry—that a man of that kind shld *dare* to write to you in the way he has! *C'est trop fort*—My own darling dear Randolph I wld give anything to have you here tonight I feel so wretchedly—if we are to have all these ennuis—do for Heaven sake lets go through them together—As long as I have you I dont care what happens—Now dont say 'oh yes that is all very well but you are weeping over yr Marlboro' House balls—& yr O.M's F.K's & Hardwickes gone for ever' No darling I assure you it is not so—how can I help feeling sick at heart when you are away from me—in difficulties *et pardessus le marché, avec un 'rhume accablant'*[6] of which I'm sure you take no care—Shall you return Sunday? I hope so *cher mari de mon coeur—de ce pauvre coeur qui est si gros ce soir*—[7] I shall write again tomorrow—

> Ever yrs
>
> J.

Jennie's loyalty to Randolph in this crisis was unswerving. Randolph was running, she knew, appalling social risks. But she was prepared to go without the Marlborough House set, without Oliver Montagu, Princess Alexandra's devoted admirer, and Francis Knollys, who had been Randolph's best man; and above all, without Hardwicke. If any evidence were needed that Jennie was not simply a social butterfly, this letter provides it. Randolph had not received it when he answered her earlier letter from The Hague:

> The Hague
> April 20th
>
> My darling I have just recd yr two long interesting & dear letters You seem to have been most industrious, & to have found occupations for yrself in a wonderful manner. I shall be awfully glad to get back to you; first because I love you & dont like to be away from you & 2nd because Blandford is a horrid bore. He came raving to me just now because Lady Aylesford had been told by Bircham[8] that she had much better make it up with her husband. I told him to go the devil, so he is rather angry. Really the heartless selfish way in which he talks is too much for me. He really is very bad. I am glad you wrote to my mother. I hope she dont intend to make herself disagreeable or give herself airs when she comes back
>
> We have been to Amsterdam today, & seen a vy curious town, & some vy nice quaint pictures of the Dutch school. I bought there at a

curio shop for 40 frcs, 4 oriental plates which hold hot water; vy nice for a mutton chop or Kidney. You will get them Saturday Please pay for them. I went into two or 3 curio shops but saw nothing which tempted me.

Tomorrow morning we go to Brussels & Sunday morning I hope to be en route for England. Please go to Carreras Princes St Leicester Sqr. & order me several boxes of cigarettes large & small sizes. Good-bye my own darling Kiss to the baby

Yrs ever
Randolph S.C.

Unfortunately Randolph does not seem to have answered Jennie's second letter, and by the time he got her next he must have been on his way home. She was having second thoughts, but was still furious about Hardwicke:

April 21st
London

Dearest,

I half regret my letter of last night I wrote it on the spur of the moment & I was dreadfully angry—I hope it wont influence you in any way—*if* you answer H's letter I am sure it ought to be in the most calm & dignified manner—Dont be angry with me for offering my advice it is really very presumptuous of me particularly as you are such a capital writer but notwithstanding I am glad you will have a day or 2 to think over it—for if you answered it immediately you might write something rash—Do you think the Queen will have an interview with Disraeli? if so perhaps you will have one with him in which case he wld be sure to see the clever way you have managed the whole thing—& you may get him on yr side (in a way) before H.R.H. returns—Am I talking nonsense? Yr letter to H. which the Prince has sent to the Queen—if I remember rightly was a very dignified firm one—& she certainly cant find fault with it if she is enlightened as to the whole matter—& if she shld—*Après!* what harm can she do? That does not prevent my feeling horribly anxious—& I feel so restless & worried I cant sit 2 *mts de suite*[9] in a chair & I have done nothing but read that nasty hateful letter all day—I am glad I am not going to spend the evening by myself I'm to dine with Fanny & Edward & go to the opera afterwards I have had such a *'démangeaison'*[10] all day to send word to Hardwicke to come & see me & then to *délivré* myself of a *pièce 'à la Blandford'* but discretion is the better part of valour I am only afraid I shall never have the opportunity—The idea of his talking about yr animosity to the Prince when his to you is a 1000 times stronger—I shall be so happy when you return darling—I daresay after all, things will turn out for the best *mais c'est une mauvaise cause*[11]—& not worth all the energy & brain you have spent on it. . . .

What was it that made Jennie so particularly angry with Hardwicke? Why did she call him 'a man of that kind' and a 'nasty hateful creature'? That does not emerge from her letters till later on. Meanwhile the Prince returned to England, had a private meeting with Princess Alexandra, in which he no doubt explained as best he could his own part in the business, then went to the opera with her, and was loudly cheered. There was nothing in the papers as yet, but there was a great deal of gossip, most of it in the Prince's favour. He had refused to intervene personally, as requested by Randolph at the beginning—that is, to ask Aylesford not to give Edith a divorce. But Randolph's blackmail had, indirectly, worked. Aylesford could not seek a divorce now, knowing that the Prince's name would be involved. The day after the Prince's return to London Aylesford asked Hardwicke to call on him. Hardwicke reported, to everyone's relief, that no Public Scandal would now take place. The Queen congratulated Hardwicke on his conduct, and asked him to urge the Prince to keep clear of all doubtful people in future; not a request that was to be granted. But the Aylesford affair was over in the sense that publicity had been avoided.

In another sense it had only just begun. Punishment for not sticking to the rules was ferocious. None of the principals was ever forgiven. Aylesford—an innocent party, at least in this business—was obliged to go to America, where he took up ranching. Outdrinking the Texan cowboys, he seems to have drunk himself to death at the early age of 36. The guilty Edith and Blandford lived together on the continent for some years, and had a child. But even after Aylesford was dead, and Bertha had (in 1883, when the scandal was stale) divorced Blandford, he did not marry her. Instead, not long before his own early death in 1892, he married a rich American widow. Leonard Jerome was a witness at their wedding in New York.

It was nearly ten years before Randolph was readmitted to the Prince's favour. For the time being, his social ostracism was almost complete. Albert Edward might not have any political power, but socially he was an absolute monarch, and he made it clear that he would not go where Randolph and Jennie were received. His honour had been impugned.

Randolph had never been to America, and Jennie had not been back since she was a girl. They decided that now might be a good time to pay a visit. The Duke of Marlborough was doing his best to arrange a reconciliation, and requested an interview with the Prince. On the day he was going to see him, Jennie went over to Paris for a few days to say goodbye to her mother and sisters. By mistake she took a bottle of Randolph's medicine with her:

Friday morning

Dearest—I have just received yr letter & cheque—I hope darling you didn't get my telegram too late last night—it was rather late before I cld send it—I got on all right till we came to Calais—& then we had to get into a tug before landing—& it was really very dangerous because the 2 boats made a tremendous swell & it was most difficult to get on board & it was *so* crowded that one cld hardly stand—I saw Schouvaloff[12] who made himself most useful—old Robert got me a coupé & I found the whole family drawn up at the *gare*—delighted to see me—I am so sorry about yr medicine it was Thompson's[13] fault *et par comble de malheur*[14] my own bottle was broken in her bag—luckily I have the prescription & am going to have it made up—You must write me all about the interview between yr Father & H.R.H.—of course I shall feel the greatest interest to know *ce qui s'est passé* mind you let me know—if you see Clemmy[15] please tell how sorry I was not to go with her yesterday—& that I hadn't time to write perhaps I had better do so now—I shall write to you again tonight & tell you what I've been doing Goodbye darling I feel homesick after you. Kiss the Baby they all send their love to you—
I send back the prescription yours.

God bless you
Yours J.

Randolph seems to have taken this with him to some perhaps tactical conference, for on the back he drew what seem to be stumps and bails, and wrote the addresses of Disraeli and Delane, the editor of *The Times*, and the names of some of those involved. The interview between his father and the Prince had been a success, according to the Duchess: the Prince was peaceable and 'I believe that everybody in the Set are sick of the whole Fight and the unpleasantness it makes in society generally.' Randolph was to send an apology. The Duke advised him to remember that a soft answer turneth away wrath. Randolph was gloomy, and gave a very different account of the interview to Jennie:

June 30th
8, Clifford Street,
Bond Street,
London, W.

My dearest

I was very glad to get yr letter this morning. I had no time to write to you yesterday. Yr telegram was delivered here at 2 A.M. Friday morning;

The interview between my father & HRH came off yesterday evening. It led to no satisfactory result. The Prince seems to have expressed the greatest animosity agst me, but I believe my father stuck up to him well, & told him that if he intended to remain so highly displeased with me, he had better extend his displeasure to himself & my mother.

Hardwicke's account of his interview with me written to the Prince was read to my father. Hardwicke appears to have exaggerated much & invented more, & altogether done his best to embitter the quarrel. I have written my father an account of what really passed between Hardwicke & myself a copy of which I will show you when you return. It is a vy good letter, & my father will send it to H.R.H.

I have no particular news. HRH has declined Ivor's[16] ball Fancy Ivor going a 2nd time to see Francis Knollys to ask if he was coming. F.K. shewed him all the correspondence, relating to late events & also the letters & Ivor seems to have quite chimed in with F.K. He had the impudence last night to tell me that he thought I had been completely wrong all thro. & when I said that whatever he thought I hoped he wld keep his opinions to himself, he replied that he shld do nothing of the kind He must be mad.

Blandford has been going on in an extraordinary manner. But it is much too long to write. He has been expelled from the Blues mess by the committee dont tell this to yr people.

The baby is vy flourishing. If you wld like to remain in Paris till next Saturday or Monday I dont mind vy much, as I think I shall go down to Broxmouth[17] on Wednesday or Thursday. I dine & lunch & breakfast at St James's Sqre.[18] I hope you are happy & enjoying yrself. What news do you hear of yr father, & when is he (PAGE TORN) I saw a most charming little house in Hertford strt. yesterday. A freehold. $\frac{1}{2}$ the size of Charles Str[19] but wld hold us well. 16000£ they want for it. Which I think I see my way to managing. We must go & have a look at it when you come back. I took my father to see it & he liked it vy much. Give my best love to yr mother & Clara

Yours
R.

Jennie had not expected anything from the interview, as she wrote on July 2nd:

Sunday
Paris

Dearest R. Yr letter this morning did not surprise me as to the result of the interview with HRH. The fact is I am sure it is too soon to attempt any kind of reconciliation. I own I am rather astonished at Ivor's conduct—I suppose he is furious with you for being—(probably to him) the cause of the Prince's refusal to his ball—Hardwicke I've no doubt was only too delighted to give an exaggerated account in order to give himself more importance in the whole affair—

Has Disraeli done anything? I hope darling you dont worry over all this tiresome business. If you go to Broxmouth I will stay here a few days longer but if you don't I wld rather return Thursday as our stay in London will be very short & I want to see as much of Winston as possible besides having several things to do—It is very pleasant here & I am delighted to be with them all—yet I cannot help worrying a little at what is going on in London—& then you know I can never be quite happy away from you—& so Blandford has been going on in an extraordinary way—he must be mad. . . .

Randolph was feeling lonely in London. 'I don't like this house without you it is awfully dull,' he wrote. 'The baby is vy well. He came in to see me this afternoon & carried off the paper basket in triumph. Blandford came up to town last night, I did not see him. My mother tells me he is vy unhappy & desperate agst everybody.' On July 4th he wrote again, enclosing a copy of his letter to his father about Hardwicke which had been forwarded to the Prince of Wales. The Prince 'returned it, merely saying that he wld again see my father about it on my father's return to town'. The Duchess thought the house in Hertford Street was *much* too big. 'Dont you go and spend too much money,' Randolph said, more in hope than expectation, perhaps. Winston was flourishing. Next day he wrote again:

8, Clifford Street,
Bond Street,
London. W.

My dearest

I am off to Broxmouth tomorrow morning at 10.35. There is a dinner at St James's Square tonight for the Prince Imperial[20] also a Mr Blake Minister of Justice in Canada dines & I mean to pump him as to the attractions of Canada in the fishing line, as I hear he is a grt. fisherman.

Your letters are awfully short & tell me nothing what you are about. I am really vy disappointed about yr father after all his promises as to what he wld do for us if we went to America, he now will hardly see us there at all. I dont believe yr mother wants him to be there with us. Do you think the gentle Clara wld like to accompany us? ask her.

I think we have *remporté*[21] a victory over Hardwicke. I met him the other day. I was in a cab in a block in Bond Strt, & 'fixed' him from a long way off. I gave him such a prolonged look one of my worst scowls right at him. I fully expected a row, & indeed hoped for one, but he turned down his eyes after a second or two. He told Rosamond[22] last night that he had been vy badly treated that the family distrusted him, & that he had seen my letter to my father, which was most unfair & unkind to him. What a snake!! Knollys has written to my father that HRH wishes to see him tomorrow. I think it looks like peace. Cornelia's ball is tonight but I am not going. Do write me longer letters darling. You had better start Tuesday morning, & *nous arriverons ici tous les deux à la même heure.*[23] Love to Clara

Yrs ever

July 5th Randolph S. Churchill

Jennie replied promptly, and at length; and at last giving us the clue to the personal feeling between Hardwicke and Randolph:

Thursday
Paris

Dearest R—You must not think that I write short letters—the fact is there is so little to tell you—& I am so little left alone that it is most difficult to write anything '*en suite*'—I have written for my cabin for Monday so I think I had better stick to that day—Can't you manage to meet me Monday night?—How delicious it will be—to be together again. I hope you have missed me & feel that you can't do without little J——?

It is no use talking to you in a letter—about Papa—but I believe he intends to be in America the end of August so we shall see something of him. I am glad you glared at Hardwicke—but do be careful—for I wldn't have him for *worlds*—think that you know what I told you—& if you are not discreet, it will somehow get about. Don't be angry darling but I am *so* afraid of my name being mixed up in it—& you must remember that last year people saw us a great deal together & thought he made up to me & so of course you must be extra careful not to let him or anyone else think that yr *brouille*[24] is about anything else but Blandford's affair. You've not written to me anything about Disraeli, *c'est-il passé quelque chose?*[25]—I wrote to yr Mother yesterday The Duc de Guiche called here today—& I made his acquaintance. He is very good looking only 23 & a widower with one little girl his wife was a Mlle de Beauman whom he married 2 years ago He is supposed to be a great *parti* here & all the Mama's run after him—I can't understand what his attraction can be here unless it is Clara—He has been here several times this week & today immediately proposed that we shld go to the Circus Saturday & I believe he is dreadfully afraid of compromising himself—& he treats Clara just like a *Jeune fille française* & she naturally '*posée's*' tremendously—He is the eldest son of the Duc de Grammont & his grandfather was the celebrated Count d'Orsay—he has now 80,000 frcs a year which is *beaucoup ici*—& will have more Mama & I both agree that *he* wld do admirably but of course it is ridiculous to think of it—

R de Fitzjames[26] came also this afternoon & amused me very much he *raffolléed* about '*cette petite horreur*'[27] & naturally I did not abuse her—*car cela serait de très mauvais gout*[28]—

Has Tommy Trafford answered yr letter?—I went over to the Bon Marché this morning with Mama & got some gloves—& I frittered to the extent of 6 francs in some rich silk nets which are *la grande mode* & which I think look very pretty *sur mes cheveux noirs—ne te moques pas?*[29]. . .

I hope darling *petit* R. that you will come back Monday. It will be so jolly—I have no news to tell you we potter about all day playing the piano reading & driving—& pass the evenings quite alone so I can't have much to say except that I love you & am longing to see you. Have you quarrelled with Cornelia?—Good night dearest I shld like to kiss you *grand comme Ça*——

Ever yrs

J.

It is impossible to say for sure what Jennie wouldn't for worlds have Hardwicke know she'd told Randolph, but it is not hard to guess. If people thought Hardwicke had been making up to her, they may also have thought he'd done more. Jennie's letter certainly suggests he probably tried. Given Randolph's quickness to anger, he may well have taken the choice of Hardwicke as envoy, and Hardwicke's overbearing manner, as especially insulting under the circumstances. He may even have suspected the Prince of knowing of Hardwicke's attempt (if that's what it was) on Jennie, of sending him deliberately: Randolph's mind had its dark suspicious corners, and he already thought the worst of the Prince's behaviour over Edith Aylesford. If the Prince *had* deliberately taken Aylesford to India against Edith's wishes, so that Blandford should be able the more easily to carry on his affair—then he'd be perfectly capable of choosing as envoy to Randolph a man who'd tried to seduce his wife. Furthermore, knowing what Randolph did of Hardwicke, but unable to reveal it to him—because Jennie had at all costs to be kept out of the *brouille*—must have made him seethe with even greater anger as he listened to Hardwicke's lectures on his own behaviour. So much is speculation, of course. But Jennie's letter makes it clear that something of the sort had happened.

Whatever the truth about Hardwicke and Jennie, the whole unhappy business left Randolph very bitter about high society: the bitterness was an important element in his later political radicalism. He continued to lead the privileged life, of course; but there is more than a suspicion that he would have gladly sold the whole social world down the river.

The Prince was bitter, too. He would not accept the apology Randolph made, in spite of the Duke's second intervention. Negotiations went on for several weeks, through the Lord Chancellor. Meanwhile Jennie and Randolph were in America, and it was not till August 26th that the agreed text of the apology reached them. Randolph signed, but added a post-script which still further annoyed the Prince. The Lord Chancellor considered the Duke and Randolph had made their submission in the most ungracious and undignified way possible. The fact that Randolph signed at Saratoga, where General Burgoyne had surrendered to the Americans in 1777, was doubtless not lost on anyone. Randolph obviously considered his apology a defeat for British honour in 1876.

Meanwhile, the Duke, deeply mortified by his sons' dreadful behaviour, agreed to accept the post of Viceroy of Ireland as a way of withdrawing from English social life with some dignity. Even this disappointment was not without embarrassment, however, as the retiring Viceroy was Bertha Blandford's father. But it had one great advantage: Randolph could be given useful work as his father's private secretary. And as for Jennie—well, Jennie could look after Winston, and she could —well, in Ireland the one thing everyone could do was hunt. So she hunted.

Before the Marlboroughs left England, the Queen invited them to spend a night at Windsor Castle, on the strict understanding that there were to be no references to the 'domestic circumstances' which had caused Victoria 'anxiety and deep regret'. 'Its all most unpleasant & humiliating', wrote the Duchess. 'Oh dear—when will all this annoyance be at an end?' The visit went off very well, though the Queen was 'much grieved to see the alteration in both of them since she saw them at Osborne a year & 4 months ago. They looked so *distressed, wretched* & the poor Dss especially, who cd scarcely restrain her tears.'

On 10 January 1877 the new Viceroy, accompanied by his Duchess, Randolph and Jennie, the guests, and his three unmarried daughters, made his public entry into Dublin. Winston was one of the party, too. His earliest memories were to be of his time in Ireland. He wrote of his mother in a famous passage:

> My picture of her in Ireland is in a riding habit, fitting like a skin and often beautifully spotted with mud. She and my father hunted continually on their large horses; and sometimes there were great scares because one or the other did not come back for many hours after they were expected.
>
> My mother always seemed to me a fairy princess: a radiant being possessed of limitless riches and power. . . .

But Jennie had neither riches nor power. She was the wife of a disgraced second son. While Randolph was in London, attending Parliament, she often felt 'blue'. 'I don't find it dull', she wrote to him, 'except when I think of London and its amusements.' She must have thought of them a good deal. The Vice-Regal court was hardly lively, and though Clara often came over, there wasn't much to do. She painted and played the piano and rode. She saw more of the Duchess than perhaps she liked. When she took singing lessons, the Duchess seemed surprised: 'Have you any voice?' she asked. Jennie had married for better or worse, and this was definitely the worse. But for all that, she still shone for Winston 'like the Evening Star'.

NOTES

1. The Duke and Duchess had been cruising in the Aegean. They did not feel tempted to hurry home.
2. Tommy Trafford was a close friend of Randolph's, and frequently travelled with him. He had a Parisian mistress whom he later married.
3. Lord Rosebery, a friend of Randolph's from Eton, later Prime Minister.
4. The Murrietas, Spanish nobles, took a lavish part in English social life, in London and at Wadhurst, in Sussex.
5. Helen Hatzfeldt, wife of the German Ambassador in Madrid and, in 1885, London. The Hatzfeldts were friends of the Jeromes in Paris.
6. And into the bargain! with a 'dreadful cold'.
7. Dear husband of my heart—of this poor heart which is so heavy this evening.
8. Lady Aylesford's solicitor.
9. Two minutes on end.
10. Longing.
11. But it is a bad cause.
12. Russian Ambassador to Great Britain.
13. Jennie's maid.
14. As a crowning misfortune.
15. Lady Camden.
16. Sir Ivor Bertie Guest, later Lord Wimborne. He was married to Randolph's eldest sister, Cornelia.
17. Broxmouth Park, Dunbar, was the home of the Marquess of Bowmont, eldest son of the Duke of Roxburghe. Bowmont was married to Randolph's sister Annie.
18. Where the Duke and Duchess lived in London.
19. Randolph and Jennie's house in Mayfair.
20. The son of the Emperor Napoleon III, killed by the Zulus while fighting for the British in 1879.
21. Won.
22. Randolph's sister.
23. We will both arrive here at the same time.
24. Estrangement.
25. Has anything happened?
26. Charles Robert, Comte de Fitzjames, was a descendent of James II's illegitimate son by Arabella Churchill, sister to John, first Duke of Marlborough, and thus a very, very distant relation of Randolph's.
27. Was infatuated with that little horror.
28. For that would have been very bad taste.
29. On my black locks—don't mock me?

5

THE FOURTH PARTY

The Churchills were over three years in Ireland, and easily the most important thing that happened, as far as Jennie was concerned, was the birth of her second son, Jack, in February 1880. But if these were dull years for her, for Randolph they were a time of important personal development. Before he went to Dublin, he had been an MP for three years but made little mark: he had not begun to take either himself or politics seriously. But now, with Society closed to him, he began to think about society in a larger sense. Ireland could not have been a better place to be exiled to, for then, as now, the Irish question was the most intractable in British politics. Randolph took the opportunity to examine it in the greatest detail. He explored the country from end to end. He met the politicians of all parties and religions. Famine, as so often, loomed over the land, and the Duchess dutifully organized a charitable fund. It was Randolph, though, who administered it, who learned at first hand what poverty and starvation were. As a result, he became one of the few English MPs who had any real understanding of Irish conditions. (It is scarcely credible, but Disraeli never visited Ireland at all, and Gladstone only did so once.) Almost inevitably, Randolph began to think for himself about Irish matters, to develop his own ideas, very different from the conventional wisdom of his father the Viceroy. On one occasion he actually expressed them in public, much to his father's distress. But for the most part he seems to have learned his lesson: he was a dutiful son and secretary.

Early in 1880 Disraeli was defeated at a General Election and Gladstone became Prime Minister for the second time. As a result, the Duke had to give up his Viceroyalty, and Jennie and Randolph returned to London. Randolph was delighted to be in opposition: it gave far more scope to his natural combativeness. Furthermore, it gave him a chance to attack his own party leadership as well as the government, and he loved to fight on several fronts at once. The Conservative leader in the Commons was a dull but distinguished statesman called Sir Stafford Northcote, the vigour of whose attacks on the government was severely moderated by his very great personal admiration for Gladstone, whose secretary he had once been. Randolph despised this softness, and nick-named Northcote 'The Goat'. Then, with the help of three friends, he launched a brilliant independent attack on Gladstone's administration. The friends were Arthur Balfour, later to be Prime Minister, Sir Henry Wolff, and John Gorst. Borrowing their tactics from the Irish party, who had outraged the previous Conservative government by obstructing its legislation with endless delaying tactics in Parliament, Randolph and his friends provided a far more entertaining and successful opposition than anything Northcote could bring himself to organize. Quite soon, they were established as 'The Fourth Party'—the other three being the Conservatives, the Liberals and the Irish.

'Our house', wrote Jennie, 'became the rendezvous of all shades of politicians. Many were the plots and plans which were hatched in my presence by the Fourth Party, who, notwithstanding the seriousness of their endeavours, found time to laugh heartily and often at their own frustrated machinations.' Ironically, Northcote lived next door to the Churchills in St James's Place; if he heard the laughter that summer, he must have known that much of it was at his expense. By the end of the session the whole House of Commons was laughing with Randolph—except those, of course, who were gnashing their teeth. Within a few months, from being no one of any political importance, Randolph was a public figure.

For all that, Jennie and Randolph were still excluded from the smartest parties. The Prince of Wales had not yielded an inch. Nor, it would seem from a letter he wrote to Jennie while they were still in Ireland, had Randolph:

My dearest,

I enclose you two letters from my mother from which you will perceive that there is a vy pretty quarrel between myself & the Guests. I reserve all comments on the matter till I am with you again. There is no doubt however that Cornelia behaved vy piggily, as she has done before on more than one occasion. As long as she chooses to go out of her way on every possible occasion to toady those who are not ordinary enemies but most bitter foes, so long I shall have a right to think that not merely does she totally disagree with me on most essential points, but also that she cannot have the least feeling or affection for me. & while I do not dispute her perfect liberty of action, I at the same time uphold my right under these circumstances to forget that she is my sister. . . .

Jennie must have been glad that his pugnacity was at last being usefully channelled into politics. She was now twenty-seven, had been married six years and produced two sons. In the thinking of upperclass society she was now 'fair game' for amorous adventurers—always provided, of course, that no Public Scandal should ensue. But though men doubtless tried, there seems no evidence that Jennie did anything more than flirt in the accepted manner of a beautiful woman, and her marriage was certainly *not* foundering, as has recently been suggested. She seems to have been quite open with Randolph about her admirers, and he with her. For instance, while in Ireland, she was much bothered by the attentions of the young and handsome Lord Rossmore. One day she felt obliged to write to Randolph:

I hope you wont be angry to hear that Rossmore called here today— & that I saw him quite by mistake—I was annoyed because it was luncheon time & I had ordered next to nothing—besides being in the midst of my accounts—He did not stay long as I had ordered the carriage at 3—I told him he must not call here any more as living alone I cld not receive any gentlemen & cld not make an exception for him.

Back in England, Randolph felt obliged to write to her in August 1881 about one of the 'continental cusses' Leonard Jerome so much disliked:

As I was writing to Castellane[1] this morning I opened the enclosed in order to find out his plans. I now send it to you with my reply to it. He is a little blackguard & we must have nothing more to do with him, and indeed I think all those French people are great brutes; But I really do think my darling you ought to be more careful in yr manner to men, who are always too ready to take a liberty. I have such confidence in you that I never bother you, but these kind of things are very annoying & vexatious.

Neither of these trivial but flattering incidents suggests a marriage in trouble—except, perhaps, to a fevered imagination. But in 1881 Jennie did meet the man who was to be the great tragic love of her life. Count Charles Kinsky was an attaché at the Austro-Hungarian embassy, a brilliant rider who was the first foreigner ever to win the Grand National—and that on his own horse, Zoedone, in 1883. He was not strikingly handsome, but he had one of the big moustaches which women found so endearing in those days, and even in photographs there is a great intensity about his dark eyes. He was very musical, which must have been something else which Jennie found attractive. That he was

Jennie dressed for a ball

The Drawing Room at
2 Connaught Place

Jennie with Jack
and Winston

'The Fourth Party' by Spy. Left to right: Randolph, Arthur Balfour, Henry Wolff, John Gorst. From 'Vanity Fair', 1880

'He Completely Carries the House'

Jennie with Lady Curzon at the Woodstock Election in 1885

soon paying regular calls on Jennie is clear from the brief diary she kept at the beginning of 1882. The entries for January 3rd and 4th are particularly interesting for they mention not only Kinsky but Lady Blanche Hozier, who was shortly to give birth to a daughter called Clementine. Twenty-five years later Clementine and Winston were to marry.

Tuesday, January 3
Beautiful day. Went out & tried on my habit—took a little walk—lunched alone wrote a lot of letters—Charlie Fitzwilliam[2] & Kinsky called later Col. B.[3] who had had a good day's hunting with the Baron[4] at Leighton—They wanted me to dine & go to the play—but I couldn't make up the party—went to spend the evening with Blanche Hozier but she had gone to bed—Am longing to get down to Oakham & hunt—

Wednesday, January 4   Oakham
Fine—Randolph arrived from Ireland—had a long talk & then went out & breakfasted with Blanche Hozier—only Emily Yznaga[5]—took a little walk then went home. The Star[6] & Cornelia turned up—Sir H. Wolff & Gorst came to luncheon—took the 5.30 train to Oakham went to bed very early—had a long talk with Custance[7] before going.

Randolph had been spending Christmas, as he always did, with Lord Justice Gerald FitzGibbon, one of the friends he made in Ireland. Now he and Jennie went hunting for ten days, then returned to London to lunch and dine the Fourth Party. After that they went to Blenheim, where the children were staying.

Tuesday, January 17
Cold and raw—Gave Winston his lessons, then painted till luncheon—went to the stables—then walked with R & the Duchess till 5—read to the children . . . played billiards with the Duke & Ld. Alfred Churchill—[8]

Wednesday, January 18
Very cold & foggy—Randolph & Georgie[9] went out hunting—Drove with the Duchess to Stonesfield to give away blankets etc—practised a bit in the afternoon—wrote letters & read to the children—Ld. Lytton[10] & Sir Henry Wolff arrived—

Thursday, January 19

Dull. Went out driving with the Duchess—painted all the afternoon—
Went to a meeting at Woodstock to hear Lord Lytton—very good
speech & delivery—but voice weak. Randolph & Sir H. Wolff, also
made speeches—

The diary gives a revealing glimpse of Jennie's life. She has a small
circle of London friends, otherwise it is politics, hunting, and charity
with the Duchess. That she did *not* neglect her children seems obvious.
Winston was now eight: one wonders what lessons Jennie felt herself fit
to give him. She did not care for Blenheim: 'Dull,' she wrote on 30
January. 'Most uneventful week.' The truth was, as she had written to
her mother a year earlier:

I quite forget what it is like to be with people who love me. I do so
long sometimes to have someone to whom I could go and talk to. Of
course Randolph is awfully good to me and always takes my part in
everything, but how can I always be abusing his mother to him, when
she is devoted to him, and wd do anything for him—The fact is I
loathe living here. It is not on account of its dullness, *that* I don't
mind, but it is gall and wormwood to me to accept anything or to be
living on anyone I hate. It is no use disguising it, the Duchess hates
me simply for what I am—perhaps a little prettier and more attractive
than her daughters. Everything I do or say or wear is found fault
with. We are always studiously polite to each other, but it is rather
like a volcano, ready to burst out at any moment. . . .

She must have been glad to get back to London. But on 26 February
Randolph fell ill. Lots of people came to see him, which cannot have
helped. After dinner he was worse, and Jennie went to fetch Dr Clayton. On Tuesday 28 February she wrote: 'Up half the night with R.' He
was seriously ill, though that did not stop her going to a small dinner
party with friends at the Café Royal the following evening. Nor did it
stop streams of people calling, including the ever faithful 'Star', and
Kinsky. But on 2 March Jennie noted: 'wrote letters & sat with R. who
nearly fainted tonight after hot bath'. She did not write in her diary
again till the 14th, and on the 16th she took Randolph to recuperate near
the Crystal Palace. Doubtless the idea was to remove him from the ex-
citements of London, but 'The Star' still called every day. They paid £80,
Jennie complained, to eat old roosters surrounded by black sausages. In
April Jennie took Randolph to America for a month, but on their return
he was still not right. Though they stopped briefly in London, and saw

Sarah Bernhardt in *La Dame aux Camélias,* Jennie took another house in the suburbs, this time at Wimbledon. It was not until 3 July, more than four months after he first fell ill, that Randolph returned to the House of Commons.

In the next four years Randolph was to become a dominating figure in the Conservative party, and to hold great offices of state. He made speeches all over the country, as well as in the Commons, and he intrigued night and day. It was a very exhausting life, even for a fit man; but Randolph was never quite well. He smoked far too much—Jennie's first note to him at Cowes begged him not to, it will be remembered—and people often commented on how ill he looked. He was not one of those people who pretend to be all right when they're not, and he consulted doctors frequently, though to little avail. All they ever seem to have recommended was holidays. Randolph was glad enough to take them, often by himself, or with Tommy Trafford or some other masculine companion. Once he went abroad with Blandford. Jennie took her own holidays, too—usually going to see her mother and sisters in Paris. In their class, husbands and wives led very independent existences, and it should not be thought, though it has been, that separate holidays meant any more serious form of separation. That Jennie and Randolph still loved each other is clear from their letters when they were apart, most dramatically in a series written in December 1882 and January 1883. Randolph, still not recovered from his illness of the spring, was in Algeria. Jennie was in London, furnishing their new house, 2 Connaught Place, at Marble Arch. Usually she had wonderful health, but now she fell ill herself. On 17 December she scribbled a little note:

Dearest R—

I am sorry to say I am in bed with a slight feverish attack. Laking[11] says I will be all right in a day or 2, if I remain perfectly quiet, so here I am an angel—taking my medicines and not stirring. I like Laking—He says in yr absence, he must be very strict & wont allow any imprudence—By the time this reaches you I shall probably be as well as ever—Mind you enjoy yrself—Mama & Leonie are here & are nursing me. I wrote to yr Mother today—everything is going on well—drawing room a success parquet nearly done. I will write you a letter every day—but until I am up dont expect [a] long epistle—It is no use my trying to write with ink, I always make such a mess—

Yours

J.

Dont you worry I am taking great care of myself—

The note is in pathetic and feeble writing, for Jennie's 'slight feverish attack', though no one told her, was typhoid. She managed another note two days later:

> 2 Connaught Place, W.
> Tuesday 19th

Dearest R I hope it wont distress you to hear that I am still in bed & I am afraid am likely to be for a little while longer—Mama thought she wld like Gull[12] to come & see me just to be sure that Laking was treating me right—& so I saw Sir W. who was very kind—he says I've got a low fever what he called a febrile attack—which wld keep me here a fortnight, & then I shld get up perfectly well—I've got a nurse & am taken the greatest care of—& not allowed to do anything—When you see me you wont know that I've been ill—Now *dont* worry about me please—Write & tell me that you are happy & enjoying yr holiday—otherwise I shall be miserable—If you were here you couldn't do anything for me, so like a darling, dont worry—yr Mother has been to see me today & will tell you all about me—I shall write a line now & then —in fact I think a short line every day wont hurt me—I was so glad of yr letter. Take care of yrself & mind you enjoy yr little trip.

> Yours
> J.

Randolph did not get these letters for several days, in fact not until the 28th. He telegraphed in great alarm for news; but there was a muddle about the address and he did not at once receive the reassuring message Jennie sent him. She wrote again on the 29th:

> 2 Connaught Place, W.
> Dec. 29th

Dearest R Yr telegram distressed me so—particularly when I found from the one to Mama that you had not received the one I had sent you—The fact is I cld not make out the address, it looked like Batna, & of course I thought that you were going on to Biskra and wanted to find a telegram on arrival[13]—I had misgivings but Dr Laking brought me the telegram you had sent him, & that was even more illegible—so after much consideration & looking at map & geography books—we came to the conclusion that it must be meant for Biskra You poor darling I did feel so for you last night & until the hour when I thought you wld get my telegram I was quite miserable. I know how you worry—How naughty of you!—No news is always good news—& if I had been seriously ill, dont you suppose they wld have telegraphed it to you at once? I hope now your mind is *quite* at rest. Today my temperature is quite normal & if it will keep so for 2 days, I shall get up—It has been a mild attack of fever—& I have never once been bad. . . .

Randolph's letters, once he knew Jennie was all right, show not only how much he loved her, but how dependent he was on her. They are, for the most part, on Connaught Place writing paper, but from the South of France. The first was on New Year's Day, 1883.

My darling

I have been in such a state of mind about you ever since last Thursday. I did not receive your letters telling me you were ill till just as I was starting for Batna, & when I first read them it did not appear to me that you were vy bad. I therefore telegraphed to you & Laking to telegraph to me at Batna how you were; this was at two oclock in the afternoon & on arriving at Batna at eight I fully expected to find an answer. There was none however & I waited all the next day till nine oclock in the evening without getting any reply. I got perfectly wild with anxiety & alarm. I made sure the most dreadful things had happened, & that I shld never see you again. I never passed such a day & on reading yr letter over again I saw that you must be vy seriously ill to have had Gull & a nurse and I made sure it was typhoid fever. Well the whole day from morning till night I worried & fretted at getting no answer. I don't know what wld have happened to me if dear Wolff had not telegraphed to Constantine that he had seen you & that you were much better. The telegram arrived at Batna just as the office closed at nine oclock. I cant tell you my relief & joy, for I had quite given you up. I daresay you will think this vy foolish but you must remember that being so far away added to my anxiety & getting no answer to my telegrams was inexplicable. I had had such a fright however that I determined to return to England, & I cld not bear the idea of yr being ill without my being with you to look after you; particularly when I remembered how you used to look after me when I was ill. So I left Batna on Friday & got on board a steamer at Phillippeville[14] which landed me here last night when again I had the delight of receiving good news of you and I have just received a telegram from Sir W Gull saying that you are going on well. I am so thankful darling I cant tell you; and as you & all my people do not wish me to return I will go on to Nice. But you must come out there as soon as you are able to travel. If you will do so, I will throw over the

Birmingham meeting & stay with you here till you are quite set up again. What a bad illness you must have had. I am afraid you are not out of bed yet & you must be awfully weak. I am sure for my sake you will take the greatest care of yrself & not do anything imprudent. Why dearest if anything happened to you my life wld be broken. I cant think of that day I passed at Batna without a shudder. I worked myself up into such a state. I was all alone you see & cld not get back till the next day. The trains telegraphs & posts in Africa are abominable. I cld not have travelled there with any more pleasure & enjoyment & felt I must place myself within reach of you. Up to that Thursday last I had enjoyed myself vy much. The drive from Algiers to Constantine five days was delightful, beautiful scenery fine air & splendid weather. Rather cold than warm however. It did me a lot of good and I shld be vy well now if I had not caught a cold at Batna which I have not got rid of yet. I shall go on to Nice tomorrow & hope to find Trafford there. Gorst too is at Mentone. I have been quite unable to write to you or to anyone else since I heard of your illness. Please thank Wolff for his letters & particularly his telegrams. I dont [know] what I shld have done without his telegrams of last Friday. I wld give anything to see you again. Mind I order you to come to Nice the moment you are well enough to travel. Write to me Poste Restante Nice, to say when Laking thinks you will be strong enough to move. I hope in ten days or so. We had a lovely passage across from Phillipeville here; sea quite smooth & warm weather. Today is vy fine & bright. Please thank dear Leonie for her letters to me. It has been such a comfort to me to know that yr Mother & Leonie were with you. I am sorry poor little Winston has not been well, but I dont make out what is the matter with him. It seems we are a sickly family & cannot get rid of the doctors. I think Laking seems to have been vy clever and attentive. I dont make out yet what has been the exact nature of yr illness but am writing to Laking to know all about it. I am sure you have been getting seedy for some time, & that accursed house in St James Place poisoned you. I hope poor Clara will be none the worse for living there. I hope some time or other we may go together to Biskra. I believe it is a most lovely place, an immense plantation of palms in the middle of the desert & such a climate. A much better place to spend the winter than the Riviera. I am vy glad I went to Algeria it is a charming country. Constantine is one of the finest situated cities I ever saw. Such rocks & precipices & hills all round. I saw an English paper for the first time this morning for a fortnight. There does not seem to be any great news, except about poor Gambetta[15] who seems to be in a bad way.

Goodbye my darling, Do get well quickly & be vy careful write or make Leonie write every day to say how you are.

Yrs ever
Randolph

P.S. I wish you all a vy happy new year.

Jennie was on the mend, but slowly; she had been much more ill than she realized. Her convalescence was not helped by money worries:

2 Connaught Place, W.
Jan 3rd

Dearest R—I have just this moment received yr letters & telegram, & am delighted to think you have gone to Nice—but you poor darling I am *wretched* to know that you have been so worried—how cld you get so alarmed—you wld have been telegraphed to instantly had there been the slightest cause for anxiety—dearest *petit* R—I cant bear to think of yr being unhappy—& on my account—However now it's all over thank heaven—& we have I hope but our meeting to look forward to—

As I telegraphed you I am still in bed, & this makes the 20th day—but my temperature has been very erratic the last few days, & this morning it is 2 degrees below normal so Laking thinks it is the 28th day, as he reckons that I had the fever a week before I sent for him—if so this is the turning point & I shall be up in a couple of days Of course there is always the danger of a relapse but he has no fear of it—as I lie here perfectly quiet & there are no complications of any kind—Gull said I had a splendid constitution & even Laking is surprised at my strength—I dont feel at all weak, tho' of course I cld not walk—I get rather depressed—but feel quite cheery to-day—I dont know if you wld like me to stay at Cannes with Clemmy[16] Of course I wld much rather stay with you at Monte Carlo—but I cant help thinking of the expense—& indeed I am more worried than I can say when I think of our money difficulties—R. Payne[17] has sent a bill for £246 for wine & I shall have to pay over £500 before I leave England—& that does not include *one* bill for the house—I mean furniture—I have not had any from Cooper[18] as yet—I dont allow myself to worry much—for fear of putting myself back I am so anxious to get well—but sometimes these thoughts *will* press on me. . . .

I'm a bag of bones—but both Gull & Laking tell me I shall have to guard against getting too fat, once I get well—You may imagine I am tired of being in bed & being fed every 2 hours on the same slops—soup—milk & brandy—& medicine—the sight of jelly makes me sick—*Mais on se fait à tout dans ce monde*[19]—& I dont find it so irksome now—tho' every day my bones get more tender—I have had heaps of letters from all my friends. . . .

That Jennie really *was* feeling better comes out in a little bit of gossip she passed on. Randolph's sister Georgiana had just got engaged to Richard George Penn Curzon, later fourth Earl Howe, who was only twenty-one:

I was told they call yr mother now—'the Baby snatcher' on account of young Curzon—How ill natured people are—She has been awfully kind to me, & writes & telegraphs continually to know how I am.

Jennie's letter ends: 'Now goodbye *cher petit* R—your letter made me cry—you must never worry about me again—*à bientôt* I hope. Yours J.' Randolph was overjoyed by it:

My dearest   Jan. 5th
    I have just got yr darling letter of the 3rd. Such a joy to me. I had had a horrid thought that yr little pencil scrap which I received at Constantine written when you first got ill was perhaps the last I shld ever get from you. I cant tell you how I felt about it. I cld not bear to read it. However I am rather angry with you for writing to me so long a letter for it must have tired you vy much. I know how it used to tire me to write when I was ill. Pray dont write any more. Get Leonie to write to me. I was overjoyed at Laking's telegram received yesterday saying that your 'progress was most satisfactory'. I had been vy anxious again till I got it. You must certainly in any case come here for a few days as this place will cheer you up; we might stay with Clemmy afterwards if she likes to have us. I am afraid you have been vy ill indeed poor little darling & I think I ought to have been sent for. It wld have done me good to look after you. As it is the worry & anxiety about you has made me rather seedy & the cold I caught pulled me down, but the fine weather here will set me up again. The weather is vy bright & sunny but the air in the shade is cold. Mind you bring yr *fourrure* with you. I hardly dare however expect you in a fortnight after such a long illness. I shall go to Marseilles to meet you. My darling child do take great care of yrself & get well quickly. I am so anx-

ious about you still. I dont know what I shld have done without yr photograph which you know I brought away with me. It has been such a comfort to me. Yesterday I went over to Mentone to see Gorst, & I drove back in a carriage. It is such a beautiful drive. I stopped ½ an hour at Monte Carlo on my way back but did not see anyone I knew. Tommy Trafford has not turned up here yet. Perhaps he has altered his plans. Gorst comes over here today to stop the night on his way to England. I shall tell him to go and see you on his arrival to tell you all about me—so you may look out for him on Monday. I am going to write to Milward[20] to tell him I cannot go to that Birmingham meeting I dont feel at all inclined to begin politics again. I am afraid our money affairs are rather in a mess, but it is not worth while worrying about money. Milward must arrange. You need not pay all Payne's bill. Pay half. My tour has been rather expensive. I have spent about 150£ up to now. What an escape Leonie had from that little beast Gebhart.[21] You know I never liked the appearance of the youth. I feel vy lonely sometimes particularly at breakfast and dinner. It is so horrid eating alone. & the time passes slowly when one is alone. Do make haste & come out to me. But still dont travel till you are really fit. Mind you see Gull before you start & get his leave I keep wishing so I had gone home from Marseilles. We cld have gone to Torquay or Bournemouth together. I am afraid of the long journey here for you. Perhaps Wolff cld make the Rothschilds get the P & M to give you one of their new 'salons'.[22] They are vy comfortable. Tell Clara to write to me. I wonder when you can have caught yr fever. Is it possible that the drains are not right in the new house. You shld inquire abt this from Laking. I am so glad to hear Winnie is right again. Give him a kiss from me. Goodbye my darling I think always of you

Ever yrs
Randolph S.C.

Randolph sent a note to Jennie next day via Gorst. He also sent her a present—though he had forgotten it was her birthday on the 9th. Jennie was delighted with her oyster-knife: 'I think it is lovely, so quaint & so effective—I hope you did not give too much for it—I think it was so sweet of you to think of getting it for me—it [is] just what I wanted I was so tired of my arrow.' She was 29, but 'I shall not acknowledge it to the world 26 is quite enough.' She had walked her first rather shaky steps and was determined to come out and join him. Randolph sent her careful instructions about the journey:

Villa Carmen,
Monte Carlo,
My dearest   January 11th

I was so glad of your letter yesterday & to learn that you liked the little 'oyster knife' which I sent you. I am ashamed to confess I forgot all about yr birthday. What a brute I am, but my memory is so bad. I hope next year you will have a more cheery one than this last. Well now when you start, you had better go by tidal train to Paris; telegraph to the station master at Folkestone the day before for a cabin. The steward on board the boat will get you a coupé at Boulogne. Stop that night & next day in Paris, & leave in the evening by the 7. oclock train if you are coming straight thro to here, or by the 7.15 if you mean to break the journey at Marseilles. You must send to the station in Paris in the morning for a 'SALON' this is one of the new coupés— which will cost you 500 frcs. but will take yr maid. It is the only carriage to travel in, & if you cant get one you must wait in Paris till the next day. The sleeping car places are always taken some days in advance. 50£ will pay yr journey here with yr maid well. I almost wonder whether you cld manage to come when my father comes. I think he starts abt the 16th or so. I dont think the journey will tire you vy much. But perhaps you had better break it at Marseilles. I am sure you are not so much pulled down as people usually are, but still you must not be imprudent. There is a capital little doctor here who will look after you if necessary. I think we wont be in a hurry to go to Clemmy's at Cannes it is much pleasanter here, & vy dull there. . . . I had such a nice letter from Leonie. Please thank her vy much for it, she wont mind my not writing to her as I tell you what little news I have to tell. Fancy Annie being Mistress of the Robes.[23] She will be more uplifted than ever. The weather is a little better today & may take up now. The last 3 days have been unparallelled for 4 yrs. I had a long letter from Gorst telling me all about you & two from Wolff who 'entre nous' does write such dull letters & never tells me any news. However dont you tell him this. Well now darling I have nothing more to say. Telegraph to me when you start, & also when you leave Paris. I will meet you at Marseilles. Such a joy to see you again darling. Take great care of yrself. Bring all yr warm clothes. I dont think you will be too hot. If you are you can get something at Nice where there are vy good shops. Goodbye my darling love to the children

Ever yrs
Randolph SC

I suppose Winston will go back to school in a few days. Give him a little money from me before he goes.

Jennie had overestimated her capacity to recover from such a serious illness, and worry probably held her back. First there was Randolph's own health: 'I cant bear to hear of another new doctor—I do hope you dont mean to try any fresh treatment—the fresh air & sun & above all a quiet mind will do more to put you right than any amount of medicines.' Then there was money: 'I have had my *quart d'heure de Rabelais*[24] over my house books', she wrote on the 11th, and on the 12th: 'I do hope Milward will be able to settle with them for the £15,000. I suppose there is no chance of our laying our hands on the surplus—how handy it would come in!' Randolph wrote admiring some of the ladies he saw. 'Wait till you see how nice *I* look!' she replied. But she could not join him as soon as she had hoped.

Jan. 16
2 Connaught Place, W.

Dearest R, I'm afraid I have been rather remiss about writing the last few days—& you are so good—I get a letter nearly every day—But since I go downstairs somehow it seems quite difficult to write. The last 2 days it has been fine for a couple of hours so I have gone out with Leonie for an hour in a hansom—& it was delightful but my whole morning seems to be taken up in dressing—such a business & such a lot of things I have to put on—& I cant wear any stays or any of my dresses on account of my 'stomachino' being tender & my waist is about 2 yards around—but I daresay it will all get right—I am already fatter—& shall look quite respectable by the time I get to you—but when will that be?—I had hoped to have started today, & had made Perry begin to pack—but Laking wld not hear of it, & was quite cross with me—& said he certainly wld not allow it before Sat. I feel quite in despair—However if I leave Sat I can be with you Monday—but I will telegraph to you—Yr Mother came to see me Monday, & was very kind —she proposes that I shld travel with the Roxburghe's who leave for Paris on Sat—Annie wrote to me this morning & said they wld look after me—but I don't think they can be of much use to me, & I can get on better alone with Perry—However if I go in the same train of course we go together—but I mean to be quite independent If I go Sat —I shall have to go by Dover as the tidal train from Folkstone leaves at the unearthly hour of 6.30 a.m. I see in the *Morning Post* this morning that Sir H Wolff's 2nd son is laid up at Rome with enteric fever & that Lady W. has gone out to him—I shall write to poor Wolfino at once—both he & Gorst came to see me the other day—tho not together —Wolff told me he had had a talk about you with Chenery,[25] who said you were the only man who cld lead the Conservative party—also Cairns[26] praised you up. . . . Laking never told me that it was typhoid till a day or 2 ago—I had no idea one cld have it so lightly— but I am glad he did not tell me it wld only have worried. I think now I have had an escape—Well *cher petit* R. I must get up it is nearly one —This is a dull letter but I feel stupid & no energy to think—Winston is pretty well—Laking advises Herne Bay for a week—before he goes back to school—I'll write tomorrow I do so wish I was with you.

Yours J.

The weather on the Riviera remained bad, but Randolph's doctor told him it was doing him good. If he had been well, it seems likely that he would have gone straight back to England. As it was, he would not

feel really happy till I have got you safe out here. Dont draw any cheques except what you want for the journey. We may want to make a little tour later to Venice or somewhere & shall want money. I have written to Milward to tell him that the money put by for furnishing the house is practically gone & that he must find some more. So please dont reduce the balance you know we dont get any more till the 15 March. . . .

Next day he wrote again, delighted to hear that Jennie would at last be coming soon:

Villa Carmen,
Monte Carlo,
January 17th

My dearest

I have just received your telegram & am delighted to hear that you may be able to start on Saturday. I just got a letter from Gorst saying how much better he had found you & that you were going to start Wednesday but I thought that was too good news to be true. I think I shall go to Toulon on Saturday to meet my father & probably remain there Sunday. But I will telegraph to you before I start. This morning being very fine I went out at 8, and ascended M. Agen on a donkey; it is over 5000 ft high. & the last thousand feet being vy steep I had to walk. The view was lovely & I enjoyed it immensely. I did not get home till two oclock, & then I dressed myself & went to sleep for an hour & dont feel a bit tired. so I am sure I am getting much stronger. I have not seen anything of anybody today. Shall you be able to do all

my commissions for me? I do wish you wld just see Gull before you
finally leave London just to be certain you are all right & fit for the
journey. I must say I think Gladstone is in a bad way & Gorst tells me
he is told that all the news about Northcote's complete restoration to
health is all humbug. I have told Gorst I shall do as he & Wolff wish
about returning for the meeting of Parliament. You had better have a
parting interview with Wolff before leaving to hear what he says.
Goodbye my little darling I do hope & trust you are vy careful of yrself
& shall continue to feel anxious about you until I get you under my
own care

Ever Yours
Randolph S.C.

This touching correspondence reveals how much Randolph and Jennie still loved each other. One can see him, sitting in his Batna hotel
room, miles from anywhere, staring at Jennie's photograph, thinking she
might be dead, that his whole world had collapsed; while she, feverish
with typhoid, the most dreaded illness of the Victorian age, lay on her
sickbed and worried that *he* would be worried. They, and Winston,
might be sickly, but the marriage was strong indeed. Further evidence
comes from the final letter: what Wolff and Gorst couldn't commit to
paper, they could tell Jennie. She was trusted with Randolph's political
secrets. She was trusted altogether.

1. The Castellane family was ancient and noble, with several branches. This blackguard may have been Marie-Eugène-Phillipe-Antoine-Boniface de Castellane, grandson of a Marshal of France, monarchist politician, novelist and playwright. He was the father of the Marquis Boni de Castellane, who married an American heiress, and was a friend of Jennie twenty years later.

2. Son of Earl Fitzwilliam, and passionate admirer of Jennie's sister Leonie. When rejected, he went to India.

3. Probably Colonel Burnaby, a dashing soldier whose interest in politics was such that he stood for Birmingham in 1880 and would have done so again in 1885 with Randolph, only he was killed, sword in hand, at the battle of Abu Klea.

4. Baron Ferdinand de Rothschild.

5. One of three American sisters who, like the Jerome girls, did very well in English society. Emily did not marry, but Consuelo became Duchess of Manchester, and Natica married Sir John Lister-Kaye.

6. Evelyn Edward Thomas Boscawen, later 7th Viscount Falmouth, had been on the Duke of Marlborough's staff in Dublin. He was an admirer of Jennie for many years.

7. Harry Custance, a jockey.

8. The Duke's brother, with whom he had quarrelled over Church Rates.

9. Randolph's fifth sister, Georgiana, as yet unmarried.

10. Lord Lytton had been Viceroy of India from 1876–80. He was the son of the novelist Bulwer-Lytton.

11. Francis Henry Laking practised at 62 Pall Mall and 13 Addison Road, Kensington. Dr Clayton seems to have been given up as useless.

12. Sir William Withey Gull, Bart, was one of the most eminent physicians of his day. He practised in Brook Street, Grosvenor Square.

13. Randolph was on his way from Constantine to Biskra, on the edge of the desert. Batna was about halfway. It was there he got Jennie's two letters.

14. Now called Skikda.

15. Gambetta, the French statesman, died on New Year's Eve.

16. Randolph's aunt Clemmy had married again and was now Lady Clementine Green.

17. Randolph Payne & Sons, Importers of Wines, Spirits and Liqueurs, 61 St James's Street, S.W.

18. Probably Henry & John Cooper, upholsterers, cabinet-makers, art decorators and designers, 8, 9 & 10 Great Pulteney Street, W.

19. But one puts up with everything in this world.

20. Robert Harding Milward, unfortunately, was a solicitor employed by the Churchill family. Though a JP, he went bankrupt for £97,000, was struck off the rolls, and sentenced to six years penal servitude for fraudulently converting to his own use monies entrusted to him. He died almost immediately after entering prison in 1902.

21. Freddie Gebhart was a wealthy American whose party trick was to crow like a cock. Leonard Jerome liked his company, but was glad when Leonie rejected him. Gebhart consoled himself with Lily Langtry.

22. The Paris-Marseilles railway. See next letter.

23. Annie's husband had succeeded to the Dukedom of Roxburghe in 1879. She herself was Mistress of the Robes from 1883–5.

24. Quarter of an hour of bad language.

25. Thomas Chenery (1826–84), editor of *The Times*.

26. The Lord Chancellor under Disraeli, who had found Randolph's apology to H.R.H. so ungracious. This passing remark shows how Randolph had won the attention and admiration of the senior members of the Conservative party.

6

TRIUMPH

I

By December 1884 Randolph's position in the Conservative party was such that Lord Salisbury, the Tory leader, had had to come to terms with him. Part of the deal, not committed to paper, was that Randolph should become Secretary of State for India in any future Conservative administration. Randolph had, again, not been well, and a visit to India, it was hoped, would serve both to prepare him for government office and to give him a chance to get fit again on the long voyages there and back. There was no place for Jennie on such a trip, which involved much meeting of politicians and Indian administrators and dignitaries, so he took with him his secretary, Frank Thomas. The family went to see him off:

Dec. 5th, 1884
Brighton

My dear Papa

I hope you had a good passage and were not sick at all on board?
Was it rough at all?

I should like to be you on that beautiful ship We went and had some Hotel soup after you went, so we did not do amiss. We saw your big ship steaming out of harbour as we were in the train. I cannot think of anything more to say. With love and kisses I remain yours affect

Winston

P.S. I had not any foriegn Paper, so you must excuse me.

By 'foriegn Paper' Winston meant the special thin paper which was used for writing to distant parts, like modern airmail paper. Jennie had some, and she used it the same day:

Dearest R. I have just received yr little letter, & feel so sorry for you—but the gale seems to have abated, & I hope by this time you are all right—You poor thing I am afraid the first few days will be anything

but pleasant—it certainly is rather a wrench to go at the last moment—
We got back all right but the children were half starved—however
they made up for it when we got home—The house looked so melancholy I cld not bear to stay in it—so went off to Clara's for
dinner. . . .

While Randolph was away, Jennie was to see a lot of Clara, who had
married the dashing but unfortunate sportsman Moreton Frewen in
1881. (His speculations in such ventures as gold-crushing machines were
to earn him the nickname 'Mortal Ruin'.) She was to see even more of
Leonie, who had married John Leslie in October 1884, much to the
distress of his parents. Leslie was in the Guards, and while his family
remained huffy, he and Leonie lived with Jennie at 2 Connaught Place.
After retailing family gossip, Jennie went on:

> The children have both gone—I shall have Jack back before Xmas
> as I cld not undertake to manage Winston without Everest—I am
> afraid even she can't do it. . . .

Mrs Everest was Winston's devoted nurse, of whom, in *My Early
Life*, he wrote with the deepest affection. She was, he said, his
confidante, and it seems to have been she who drew Jennie's attention to
the marks of the continual beatings he had received at his first appalling
preparatory school. That autumn he had been removed to the gentler atmosphere of Brighton and the more tender care of the Misses Thomson,
where his health and spirits soon improved. Not so, however, his
behaviour, which remained lamentable. He was just ten.

Years later, when he wrote his biography of his father, Winston
printed many of Randolph's highly entertaining letters from Malta,
Suez, the Red Sea and India. But he omitted all reference to an incident
concerning himself. On 18 December 1884, Jennie received the following letter from Winston's headmistress:

29 Brunswick Road
Dear Lady Randolph Churchill   Dec. 17th

Soon after writing to you this morning, I was called to see Winston
who was in a trouble that might have proved very serious. He was at
work in a drawing examination, and some dispute seems to have
arisen between him, and the boy sitting next to him about a knife the
tutor had lent them for their work. The whole affair passed in a
moment, but Winston received a blow inflicting a slight wound in his
chest.

Dr Roose assures me that he is not much hurt, but that he might have been. As this was not the first time we have had to complain of a very passionate temper in this boy, I decided to send him home at once. He is a candidate for the *Britannia*,[1] and if it is known that he is expelled, he will be disqualified. I have told his parents that if you wish him to be publicly expelled, I shall do it: but I leave that decision to you. If you approve the milder course he will quietly disappear from the school, and we shall think the punishment sufficient. I am quite sure that it is very necessary to impress upon these young boys the necessity of their learning to govern their passionate impulses, and so serious a punishment falling on one of their school fellows, will I hope, help to do so.

Dr Roose tells me that Winston is going to town with him on Friday: so he will be able to give you his medical report.

> Believe me
> very faithfully yours
> Charlotte Thomson

Dr Edward Charles Robson Roose, who practised in both Brighton and London, was to be the Churchills' doctor for the next ten years. His son was at the Misses Thomsons' school, too, and a friend of Winston's. Writing to Randolph the following day, Jennie took a thoroughly realistic view of the incident:

> Jack came back from Bournemouth yesterday looking most fit— Winston arrives with Dr Roose today—I was much startled yesterday by receiving the enclosed from Miss Thomson—I had a telegram from Dr Roose at the same time saying that Winston was all right—but fancy what a serious affair it might have been!—I have no doubt Winston teased the boy dreadfully—& it ought to be lesson to him—I will not close my letter until I have seen him & can tell you how he is—His holidays are not over until the 20th of Jan. I hope I shall be able to manage him—I mean to make him do a little writing etc every morning. . . .

She went on to talk of Leonie and John Leslie, who had offered to pay £20 a month towards the housekeeping. Leonie had hired a second piano, and she and Jennie played all day 'until our fingers ached'. Then she added:

> Dr Roose & Winston have just arrived—the latter is all right—the penknife however went in about a quarter of an inch but of course as

I thought he began by pulling the other boy's ear—I hope it will be a lesson to him. . . .

Randolph was in Bombay when he got this news. He wrote to Jennie on 9 January 1885:

My dearest

I have just telegraphed to you wishing you very many happy returns of the day, & now reiterate the same with every wish that you were out here with me. I got your long letter of the 19th on Tuesday on arrival here from Beejapore; What adventures Winston does have; it is a great mercy he was no worse injured. . . .

It was his only comment, except to add on 24 January, from Lucknow:

Also tell little Winny how glad I was to get his letter which I thought was vy well written. I suppose he is back at Brighton now. I hope there will be no more stabbing. . . .

He seems to have been resigned to Winston's bad behaviour, but not too much bothered about it. It was only later, when he was near the end of his life, that he became so angry with his son. Meanwhile, he was thoroughly enjoying himself, though he had again been unwell. Mr Thomas wrote to the Duchess from Indore, on 15 January:

Dear Duchess,

I fear you will think I have forgotten my promise to write to you. I did, however, commence a letter some time ago, but finding that Lord Randolph was writing by the same mail I thought it useless to proceed with it. I ought to tell you first that Lord Randolph is quite well, though he does not *look* as well as I could wish. This is no doubt owing to the long railway journeys we have undertaken. He has also lost that feeling of giddiness which attacked him at home, & which returned for a few days after landing at Bombay. . . .

Jennie's letters are full of domestic details, mainly about the house which she was thinking of selling. It was 'abominably built', and the nasty smell which she had succeeded in removing from her room had reappeared ten times stronger in the library. In fact 2 Connaught Place remained the Churchills' home till 1892. On 13 February she wrote:

I went to Brighton to see Winston yesterday—& took Jack with me—
They were so happy together & Winny was wildly excited but I
thought he looked very pale & delicate, & Miss Thomson said that she
thought he was far from strong—What a care the boy is!—He told me
that he was very happy, & I think he likes the school but I fancy that
he does not get out enough—We witnessed the performance of a play
in which Winston appears as a woman 'Lady Bertha' & he acted quite
wonderfully & looked so pretty—I shall see Roose in a day or 2 & will
have a talk about him. . . .

Jennie had been to a party and met Lord Hartington, the Liberal Secretary of State for War who 'chaffed me, & said he hoped you were not
coming back too soon—"Quite soon enough to worry you" I said'. Everyone was asking after him. She sent him all the political and social gossip.

She had been to see Lily Langtry in *The School for Scandal*, '& I see
today in *St Stephens Review*—a sketch of me in a box—with Harry
Chaplin[2] & a lady—& underneath is written "Mr Chaplin interviews Ly
Randolph"'. But there was not much to report. 'How quickly the time
passes when one leads a quiet life. The winter is slipping away without
my realising it. Jack Leslie is again at the Tower on guard & Leonie & I
left to our own devices.'

Jennie looked forward to Randolph's return. She was lonely without
him, even with Leonie and Jack Leslie. On 20 March she wrote her last
letter of this series:

London
March 20th
Dearest R—I sent you a telegram yesterday which I hope you got
before starting today—& this epistle I trust you will find at Suez—I can
hardly realize that in 3 weeks you will be nearly home—Living like a
mouse here without stirring—the time has passed very quickly for me
—but I daresay to you it seems ages—when you think of all you have
seen & done—Remember you promised me never to go on another
such a journey without taking me—Life is too short for such long sepa-
rations don't you think so?

The letter ends 'Shall you be glad to see me?' There seems no reason
to suppose that Randolph wasn't.

II

Randolph returned in April 1885. In June Gladstone resigned and Lord Salisbury agreed to form a minority Conservative government. He was most anxious to include Randolph, whose standing was now very high in the country as well as the party. But Randolph had his terms, and was not at all sure they would be met. His talk, according to Rosebery, was both striking and despondent. 'I am very nearly at the end of my tether', he said. 'In the last five years I have lived twenty. I have fought Society. I have fought Mr Gladstone at the head of a great majority. I have fought the Opposition Front bench. Now I am fighting Lord Salisbury. I have said I will not join the Government unless Northcote leaves the House of Commons. Salisbury will never give way. I'm done.' It was a strange mood to be in, for as Rosebery told him, Salisbury could not form a government without him, but it indicates how exhausting Randolph felt his career had been already. Now it was to become far more so, for Salisbury did yield, Northcote did go to the House of Lords, and Randolph became Secretary of State for India.

In those days it was necessary to seek re-election on appointment to government office, so there had to be a bye-election at Woodstock. Randolph had recently quarrelled with Blandford over the sale of treasures from Blenheim, a process begun by their father who had died in 1883. Randolph decided it might be wisest to keep away. His new office gave him an enormous amount of work, and the result of the election was not in doubt, so he sent Jennie to conduct his campaign for him. Though she stayed at Blenheim, she made her headquarters the Bear Hotel at Woodstock. Helping her was Randolph's sister Georgiana. They felt most important, as though the eyes of the world were upon them. Jennie, revelling in the hustle and bustle of the committee rooms, felt like a general conducting a battle. But her greatest effectiveness lay, literally, in the field rather than the committee room. Georgiana had brought down her tandem with her, and she and Jennie drove about the countryside canvassing the electors, their horses gaily decorated with ribbons of pink and brown, which were Randolph's racing colours.

Sometimes we would drive into the fields, and, getting down, climb the hayricks, falling upon our unwary prey at his work. There was no escaping us. Many of the voters of those days went no farther than their colours. 'I votes red' or 'blue', as the case might be, and no talking, however forcible or subtle, could move them. Party feeling ran high, and in outlying districts we would frequently be pursued by our opponents, jeering and shouting at us; but this we rather enjoyed. We were treated to jingling rhymes, the following being a specimen:

> 'But just as I was talking
> With Neighbour Brown and walking
> To take a mug of beer at the Unicorn and Lion
> (For there's somehow a connection
> Between free beer and election),
> Who should come but Lady Churchill, with a turnout that was fine.

> 'And before me stopped her horses,
> As she marshalled all her forces,
> And before I knew what happened I had promised her my vote;
> And before I quite recovered
> From the vision that had hovered,
> 'Twas much too late to rally, and I had changed my coat.

> 'And over Woodstock darted
> On their mission brave, whole-hearted,
> The tandem and their driver and the ribbons pink and brown.
> And a smile that twinkled over,
> And that made a man most love her,
> Took the hearts and votes of all Liberals in the town.

> 'Bless my soul! that Yankee lady,
> Whether day was bright or shady,
> Dashed about the district like an oriflamme of war
> When the voters saw her bonnet,
> With the bright pink roses on it,
> They followed as the soldiers did the Helmet of Navarre.'

It was an exhausting business, but years later Jennie remembered this election, of all the many she fought for Randolph and Winston, as the one she enjoyed most. Thanks to her efforts, Randolph was returned with an increased majority, and when the result was announced she appeared at a window of the Bear Hotel and made a speech to the crowd, thanking them from the bottom of her heart. She was so delighted at her success that she felt as though she had been elected herself, and when she got back to London she was quite disappointed that she wasn't acclaimed in the streets like a national hero. Doubtless she was much teased for this, but she received many gratifying congratulations, too. Among them was a letter from Randolph's close friend, though political opponent, Sir Henry James. He had been Attorney-General in the Liberal government, and introduced the Corrupt Practices Act of 1883.

My dear Lady Randolph,

You must let me very sincerely and heartily congratulate you on the result of the election, especially as that result proceeded so very much from your personal exertions. Everybody is praising you very much.

But my gratification is slightly impaired by feeling I must introduce a new Corrupt Practices Act. Tandems must be put down, and certainly some alteration—a correspondent informs me—must be made in the means of ascent and descent therefrom; then arch looks have to be scheduled, and nothing must be said 'from my heart'. The graceful wave of a pocket handkerchief will have to be dealt with in committee.

Still, I am very glad.

Yours most truly,

Henry James.

Jennie was particularly pleased with this letter, which came from a man who had proved a very good friend indeed. The previous year he had given a dinner party at which Randolph and the Prince of Wales were formally reconciled. Randolph's manner, according to Francis Knollys, 'was *just* what it ought to have been'. Thus in five years, from almost nothing, Randolph and Jennie were not merely restored to favour, they were one of the leading political and social couples in England.

The Duchess, naturally, was delighted with the way events had turned out. Since the Duke's death, Randolph's career had become the overwhelming interest of her life. Another who followed it closely was Dr Robson Roose:

Private   9 Regency Square,
                                                          Brighton
                                                          20 June 1885

Dear Lord Randolph Churchill

Permit me to congratulate you on your Victory, and to wish you health and happiness for your great office! I feel *now* you will have an additional strain upon your strength and I shall feel so deeply grateful if you will permit me to come and see you if you are ailing or overworked not only in London but any part of England in fact *anywhere*, and let me render my services as a complimentary labor of *deep respect*, as well as of *grateful* appreciation of your many acts of kindness —Please do not be offended at this request; or think me pushing, I am only *so* desirous of helping you and yours, and, apart from my respect-ful regard, I am desirous for your country's sake of helping with my small abilities to maintain in health your invaluable life—Forgive me if I have annoyed you, I mean so kindly by this letter. With compls.

Yrs Faithfy

Robson Roose

P.S. I venture to send a copy of my book which you were good enough to say you would accept.[3] It is dedicated to Gull as I belonged to his Hospl. and etiquette demanded it.

I have been quite seriously ill and have been ordered to go to America and back in a White Star Liner and I propose leaving July 16th. for 1 month only. but if the pressure of the end of the session is trying you I will gladly put off my voyage.

Randolph's health remained very doubtful. In September the Queen wrote to Jennie through a lady in waiting to enquire how he was. Every-one was anxious. But he set to at the India Office, and was soon making a generally good impression.

III

The political events of 1885 and 1886 are extremely complicated, and in spite of an immensely detailed recent work on the subject, still not en-tirely clear.[4] There was not only a struggle between the two main par-ties, but within each of them a ceaseless manoeuvring for position among the leaders. Furthermore, politicians of both sides intrigued with each other quite as much as with their colleagues, in an effort to es-tablish a new centre party which would command wide general support and give a new generation of men the chance to seize power from the old leadership of Gladstone and Salisbury. Ireland was the main issue on which manoeuvre and compromise could take place, as both parties were uneasily split.

Randolph took a leading part in these intrigues, trying one policy, then another, in an effort to gain a dominant position for himself, but it would be unrealistically glib to see his behaviour as simply opportunist. He believed that the old order of government by a small and wealthy class must give way to a new and more democratic one: hence his inven-tion of 'Tory Democracy'. Nonetheless, like any politician, he had to start from the situation as it was, and throughout this period he was scheming and plotting night and day with an energy and single-mindedness which left him very little time for ordinary life. For a significant part of the period he held high office, with all the burdens that entailed. Furthermore, he was making many speeches, both in and out of Parliament, and speeches as calculated as his take a long time to write. It cannot be emphasized too strongly that he was driving himself exceedingly hard. Not only his health, but the enormous amount of work he got through must constantly be borne in mind throughout the events which follow.

His first spell of office was not lengthy, for Salisbury's government fell in January 1886, though not before Randolph had presided over the British annexation of Burma. In opposition again, he turned his attention to the burning issue of Ireland. Although he had earlier made overtures to Parnell and the Irish Nationalists, he now completely switched positions, and in February made his famous, or infamous, speech in Belfast in which he declared that 'Ulster will fight, and Ulster will be right.' Political passions were running extremely high. But in the midst of all the excitement, Randolph and Jennie were suddenly summoned to Brighton, where Winston had fallen dangerously ill with pneumonia. It was touch and go. Dr Roose gave up his London work to stay by Winston's bedside. When the danger was over, Mrs Jerome wrote to Jennie: 'Yr whole life has been one of good fortune & this the crowning blessing that little Winston has been spared to you.' Randolph and Jennie must have been enormously relieved: Randolph sent Roose a substantial cheque. Roose gushed his thanks:

45, Hill Street,
Berkeley Square, W.

Dear Lord Randolph Churchill   31/3/86

In acknowledging the receipt of your too kind and thoughtful letter with its munificent enclosure what am I to say? When I realize, as I do daily, that through *you* I have opportunities introductions, and a kindly sympathy which is making for me a leading London career, I feel I *cannot* do too much for you and yours, and with this feeling of deep gratitude, I accept your cheque almost with pain! I cannot refuse what you wish to send, but I do feel that *without fee* no attention I can shew to you or yours can fulfil in any way the debt I owe to you— Please do not be offended with me for saying again and again that I have no desire no anticipation of fees from you, and that no amount of work I can do for you will redeem the immense service you have and do render to me by your mention of my name to so many

Ever yours gratefully
Robson Roose

P.S. I could write *so* much more but I think you understand what I feel.

The private crisis was soon over; the public one continued. On 8 April Gladstone introduced his Home Rule Bill: the fight over it was to last almost two months. Just before Easter, Randolph and Jennie both took brief breaks. Jennie went to stay with friends in Ireland, while Randolph went over to Paris for a few days. Most interestingly, his companions there included Charles Kinsky:

Hotel Vendome,
1 Place Vendôme,
Paris
April 20 1886

My dearest

I write a few lines to tell you I am all right and find the change vy pleasant. I hope this will find you tomorrow safe back from Dublin. There were no apparetments at the Bristol sufficiently spacious for me & Harry Chaplin and Kinski who arrive tomorrow, so we have moved here where we are all together. I have been to the races today with Henry Hoare.[5] Very few people there. Last night I dined with Trafford & his wife & daughter & we went to the new Cirque. Tomorrow Ferdinand Rothschild gives us dinner and we go to see the Fiacre 117.[6] I have been to see Lady de Grey[7] who is looking vy well indeed. She is stopping with the Jancourts.[8] I met Minnie Paget[9] at breakfast at the Rothschilds yesterday also looking most flourishing.

That horrid young Cairns[10] is here. He tried to speak to me but I snubbed him. I shall return Sunday so you might get some one to dine. If possible Henry James as I shall want to hear the news. I hope you had a good time in Ireland.

Ever yours
Randolph S.C.

Then it was back to the Home Rule debate, which went on throughout May. Randolph played a leading part in the defeat of the Bill, which came on 7 June. A General Election was called immediately. In those days, a General Election took place over several weeks. There was no single day on which everyone voted, or on which all the votes were counted. Results came in in dribs and drabs, and it took some time before it was clear who was going to win.

Randolph was exhausted. He decided to make only two speeches in his new constituency, Paddington. (Woodstock had been abolished.) In them he violently denounced Gladstone, and said the Home Rule Bill was simply 'to gratify the ambition of an old man in a hurry'. He was much cheered. When he and Jennie and the Duchess attended a meeting together, the crowd rose and sang *Rule Britannia*. It was all very heady stuff, and Randolph was sure the Conservatives were going to win, and there would follow a long term of Conservative government in which he would be a dominating figure. He determined to take another holiday while he could. Early in July he left to go fishing in Norway with his old friend Tommy Trafford. It was a remote place, with only two posts a week, and they reckoned it was 1500 miles from Connaught Place. He wrote to Jennie on 10 July:

> I have heard no election news since Tuesday, when things seemed to be going well. I am expecting the post with telegrams every moment. This is doing me a lot of good. I felt vy seedy leaving London & it took me some days to get right. We had one rough night in the North Sea which decidedly upset me. This is a most lovely spot & very solitary; no tourists no natives. The House which is rough to look at is comfortable enough inside. & Tommy is as amiable & charming as ever. He sends you many messages. . . .
>
> . . . Are you having some good fun with dinners or balls? Post just come in; with telegrams from Moore[11] and Rothschild. Certainly most satisfactory news which confirms all my expectations. . . .

Three days later he was still delighted with the news, but worried over his and Jennie's financial situation:

> I expect the Tories will now come in & remain in some time. It seems to me you want the 5000£ a year badly. But really we must retrench. I cannot understand how we get thro so much money. . . .

The answer was simple enough: by never stinting themselves of anything. Clearly their debts at this time were beginning to worry both of them. The political situation, however, could not have been better. The Conservatives won the election handsomely, and on 21 July Gladstone resigned. Three days later Randolph was back and bombarding Salisbury with suggestions for the new administration. There had been a good deal of speculation in his absence about what post he himself would be offered. Gossip had even reached Dr Roose, who wrote Randolph a significant warning letter:

> 45 Hill Street,
> Berkeley Square, W.
>
> Dear Lord Randolph Churchill   23 July, '86
>
> I hear rumours that you may be induced to take the post of 'Irish Secy.' or 'Foreign affairs' and I venture to send you this note, as your

responsible medical adviser, of warning not to do so! Apart from the great anxiety of Ireland you would have *frequent railway journeys* most trying to one of your constitution, of course there is not this objection to the post of Foreign Minister but *that* entails, I am told, an increasing work and unceasing anxiety which you ought to avoid!

I would respectfully suggest that you should go back to your old post 'India' as *that*, altho' arduous, is liable to be less trying to your constitution than the others I have mentioned—I hope you have returned better for your change? I go for 3 weeks rest from August 14th—

> yrs gratefully
> Robson Roose

Please forgive this letter written in the interest of your health.

The previous September Randolph had been advised to take a rest. Overwork had made him irritable and the doctor prescribed digitalis as a sedative, which he proceeded to take in large doses. The effect of this drug is to depress the heart's activity; but it can be dangerous, as the action can be accumulative, and giddiness, acute depression and other nervous symptoms follow. We do not know for how long Randolph continued with this treatment. However, instead of avoiding work and anxiety, he now accepted a double load of both. Within a week of Roose's clear warning, Randolph was Chancellor of the Exchequer and Leader of the House of Commons. Furthermore, it was generally recognized that he was next in line to be Conservative Prime Minister. It was an astonishing triumph for a man who six years earlier had been a backbencher.

Lord Salisbury had wanted Sir Michael Hicks-Beach, the previous Conservative Leader of the House, to take the post again, but Beach refused, saying that since Randolph would in fact *be* the leader, he should have the official position, too. But, he wrote, 'I had very great difficulty in persuading Lord Randolph to agree. I spent more than half an hour with him in the Committee Room of the Carlton before I could persuade him, and I was much struck by the hesitation he showed on account of what he said was his youth and inexperience in taking the position.' Here was the crux of the matter: Randolph's inexperience meant that he had to make excessive demands on his energy. Lord Rosebery said it used to take Randolph up to forty-eight hours to compose a speech and during that time he was unapproachable. He drove his staff as hard as himself. His very able secretary, A. W. Moore, collapsed from the strain at the end of the year and was sent away for a rest, but he never recovered from his exhaustion and died two months later at the age of forty-six. Randolph was living on his nerves, and smoking cigarettes incessantly. He was capable of sustained exertion, concentrated on the problems in hand, but was left with no energy for anything else. He knew he was taking on far too much. 'How long will your leadership last?' Rosebery asked him. 'Six months', Randolph answered gaily. 'And after that?' 'Westminster Abbey!'

Jennie's family were delighted at Randolph's success, though Jennie herself had again not been well. Her mother wrote to her on 5 August from Buxton, in Derbyshire, where she had been visiting Chatsworth and Haddon Hall and taking the baths.

Dear Jennie,

I was so pleased this morning to get yr letter I do hope now the excitement of both society and politics, are in a measure finished, that rest, and quiet will make you feel all right again. Do try to take care of yourself my dear Jennie—I cant tell you how pleased I am that Randolph got the Office he wished. I have done nothing but read the newspapers the past three weeks. I think I have seen everything that has been written about Randolph, both in praise & against him. I am so delighted that he has triumphed over his enemies. I know he will do great credit to himself & party in spite of the predictions to the contrary. Let us pray for health & strength for him, his duties will be so trying—I do so hope to live to see Randolph Prime Minister. . . .

She ended: 'I do hope that you will get well & strong, and be able to enjoy all yr autumn pleasures.' But for Jennie that autumn was to offer no pleasures at all.

NOTES

1. H.M.S. *Britannia* was the training-ship for cadets in the Royal Navy: now the Britannia Royal Naval College, Dartmouth.

2. Conservative MP and political friend of Randolph's, later Viscount Chaplin.

3. *Gout and Its Relations to Diseases of the Liver and Kidneys.* One doubts whether Randolph read it very carefully, but others did. It went into seven editions.

4. *The Governing Passion,* by A. B. Cooke and John Vincent.

5. Sir Henry Hoare, 5th Bart, b. 1824, had been a Liberal MP, but was now better known as a social and racing figure.

6. A play.

7. Gladys, daughter of Lord Herbert of Lea. Lord de Grey was the heir to the Marquess of Ripon.

8. Friends of long-standing. Jack went to stay with them at their home in Presles in 1898.

9. Minnie Stevens, an American, married to Arthur Paget, the son of a general who became a general himself.

10. Lord Chancellor Cairns had died in 1885. This is his son, the second Earl.

11. Mr A. W. Moore was Randolph's secretary.

7

TRAGEDY

In August something went very wrong indeed with Jennie's marriage. She was convinced there was another woman. Her mother, Clara and Leonie were all away from London. The only people she could turn to were her in-laws. She went first to Randolph's sister, Lady Cornelia Guest, whose intervention only made things worse. Then, swallowing her pride, she went to the Duchess, the woman who had made her early married life so trying, and who still openly disapproved of Jennie's smart social life. Jennie's letters to the Duchess do not seem to have survived, but the Duchess's to Jennie have. The first is dated 8 September, from Huntercombe, the Duchess's house in Buckinghamshire, near Burnham.

Confidential

Dearest Jennie

Huntercombe
Sept. 8

I thought so much about you that I was very glad to get your Letter I will begin with the end of it. Rely on one thing which is—I may not be able to do any good but I will do no harm & not like poor Cornelia put the fat in the Fire in my desire to help you. Meantime I PRAY you do not breathe thoughts of Revenge agst *any one*. It will bring you no blessing. Accept your present worry & anxiety patiently & strive to dispel it by the exercise of DOMESTIC VIRTUES!! looking after the Children & the new cook etc.—avoiding excitement & the Society of those Friends who while ready enough to pander to you would gladly see you vexed or humbled as they no doubt are jealous of your success in society. How dull & tiresome you will think me & how little comfort —I think Ly Mandeville[1] would be true—but oh she is indiscreet & things do come round so. I wish so much you had your sisters for they are to be trusted & I really would trust no one else. Try dear to keep your troubles to yourself—this is hard for you have a tell tale Face— though you do tell little Fibs at times—It is a horrid time of year for you to be in town. If you do not go to Scotland with him dear Jennie do come and vegetate quietly here. Bring Jack & we will try to make

you as happy as possible. I am sure it will show R—you care for him &
he has a good Heart & will give you credit for it—If I were you I
would not if it killed me let the heartless lot you live with generally
see there was 'a shadow of a shade of a shred' wrong only *He* should
know it & feel that it makes you miserable—And meantime though it
is a hundrum task try to make yourself so essential to him that he
must recognize it. He hates trouble—& yet he likes things to be nice &
well managed. Oh dear Jennie you are going through a great *crise* of
your Life & on yourself will depend whether your hold & influence
becomes greater than ever or not—But the question is—Is it not worth
it & you who are clever & young & attractive can do it if you choose.
You must now sacrifice yourself & your pleasures & give yourself stead-
ily up to the task—perhaps for many a day. I have no doubt of your
success for I *know* in his Heart he is truly fond of you—& I think I
ought to know—But I have told you all this & will not preach any
more. Sunny[2] came ysy & looks well and gives a good Acct of your
Boys.[3] Perhaps it will be as well for you to go there for next Sunday.
But pray be very careful with Blandford. He is so indiscreet to say the
least of it and does set people by the ears. I dare say there is some
ground for Ly M's story. I can believe any thing of those sorts of
women. They seem to like to spoil a menage. But that *species* of pro-
ceeding will defeat its own end. God bless you I pray for you & my
dear R. every Day that God may give you patience strength & gentle-
ness & that He may watch over dear R. & keep him straight

Believe me
Yrs most aff
F.M.

I had such a nice note from dear Col Boscawen[4]—Perhaps you
might look out for a very tiny token for *me*—in some old shop—There
are 2 in Davies St—something he could use to *suit* my poverty stricken
Pouch.

It seems that Jennie did take the Duchess's advice to go to Blenheim,
but not the rest. She wrote the Duchess three letters in the next forty-
eight hours. She was desperate. Whom she suspected is not clear—but
she obviously thought there was someone. The Duchess was less convinced; she thought the indiscretion might have been Jennie's.

Huntercombe
Sept. 10

Dearest Jennie

I have your 3 Letters & they make my Heart ache. I know not what
to advise except patience—I cannot make it out. Have you told me ev-

Randolph in 1893

Jennie in
San Francisco in 1894

Count Kinsky

Jennie with Winston and Jack

George Cornwallis-West

erything? Can anything have got to his ears, or some Diabolical Mischief been made—I must see him—I shall go up on Monday Morng but I think its better you should not be there & He cannot think it a Cabal. His Letter does not allude to you—He only says he shall be glad to see me Monday—Perhaps it would be well for you to stay for the Show—or until your Mother comes to you—for I dread your being left alone in London & she is sure to give you good advice. I could tell you more after I have seen him—You will have the Children at Blenheim & could you not write to him from there. Even if he does not answer he must read your Letter & you could tell him how miserable you are & appeal to him not to break your Heart. Do not be afraid of my saying a word to make matters worse. I may indeed do no good but He will listen to me so Pray try & be calm dearest Jennie, its a heavy trial for you—worse for an impetuous disposition like yours—take it dear as quietly as you can & pray for strength to bear it—I never preach but in heavy sorrow only God can comfort one & He will help you dearest Jennie I do feel so sorry for you. All words seem so cold. If you wish to see me in London Monday please let me have a telegram at 46 Grov. Sq. otherwise I shall return here to lunch. I can say no more. You will have your Children to cheer you—After seeing Randolph will write you a long letter. I cannot understand his being so hard if he realizes all you suffer. Perhaps he is full of other things. I *cannot* believe there is any other woman . . .

The state of relations between Jennie and Randolph at this moment is clear from a curt note Randolph sent from the Treasury to greet Jennie on her return from Blenheim. The Duchess had been to see him, and Lady Mandeville seems to have tried to put things right, with no success.

Treasury Chambers,
Dear Jennie   Whitehall. S.W.

I have ordered lunch for you. My mother has been up this morning & has gone back. She is coming up Wednesday for Primrose League meeting.[5] Read enclosed which is vy droll & return it to Consuelo who sent it to me. I shall not be in till late tonight

Yours ever
R.S.C.

Randolph was wrong: the Duchess had not gone back. She had stayed in London and had lunch with Jennie. No doubt they had thrashed the whole thing out in detail. She scribbled a note from Paddington station on her way home:

> Missed the train dear & saw it just go out of the station. Am waiting till the 5.10—thought it no use to go back & bore you. I cannot say more & can only hope you will take my advice. I know how hard it is. But do try dear—& once more be *very* close & discreet & have patience & God bless & guide you
>
> Yrs most aff
F. M.
>
> You can tell R. I found so much to do I went to you for lunch.

So the Duchess was not above telling little fibs herself at times. It is clear that she was genuinely sorry for Jennie, but also that she was very anxious that nothing should get out, particularly now, when Randolph was doing so well. And he was doing well, though as Leader of the House of Commons he was having a very awkward time with the Irish, who were obstructing government business in almost as masterly a manner as Randolph himself had employed in 1880. But he won high praise, even from the Queen, who never trusted him, for his geniality and patience. He was also extremely busy at the Treasury. But if in public he was all self-control, in private he sometimes gave vent to temperamental outbursts which deeply shocked his colleagues, and made them think him unfit for his high office. After an incident in which he berated Hicks-Beach in front of Lord George Hamilton, for which he apologized next day, inviting both men to dinner, Hamilton wrote:

> It is said, 'All is well that ends well', but after this experience of Churchill's waywardness I looked with great anxiety upon his future leadership. On thinking the matter over, I could only come to the conclusion that his nervous system was overstrained and that we might soon again have an outburst which would be irremediable.

What outbursts there were at 2 Connaught Place we can only guess, but that the atmosphere was tense and unhappy is certain. Even if, as seems probable, Lady Mandeville had now denied the rumour she originally spread, Jennie still suspected someone—though it is hard to see how Randolph could have found the time to carry on an affair. But what other explanation could there be? He was still keeping his distance. Jennie, meanwhile, was trying to keep up a front by continuing her social round. Randolph wrote her another cool note from the Carlton Club on September 25th:

Dear Jennie

I think the Allsopps'[6] will be vy pleasant but Wilton[7] dull & cold, so advise you to refuse the latter. I go to Huntercombe this afternoon & to Newmarket on Monday by 2.30 train. We finished Parliament finally this morning. A great relief. I think you are quite right not to come up to London but to go straight from Duncombe Park[8] to Newmarket. Everybody has bolted from town. I had a long interview with the D of Cambridge[9] yesterday, and also a vy satisfactory one with Hatzfeldt. I fear Russia means business which will be awkward. Accounts from Ireland are fairly good. Au revoir at Newmarket.

Yours ever
Randolph S.C.

I had a vy gracious letter from The Queen yesterday.

The Queen had written to congratulate him on the skill and judgement he had shown in leading the Commons through a difficult session, but his behaviour outside the chamber caused much irritation to his colleagues. His frequent conversations on foreign affairs with Count Hatzfeldt, the German Ambassador, may have been satisfactory to him, but they annoyed Lord Salisbury very much indeed. It seemed that Randolph wanted to meddle in everyone else's business as well as his own. There were mutterings about him in the Cabinet. Meanwhile domestic matters continued to go badly. As always when a marriage is under strain, money troubles came to the fore. While Randolph was visiting his mother at Huntercombe, she received another letter from Jennie. Her reply was sharp:

Huntercombe
Sept. 26

Dearest Jennie

Thanks for your Letter. I am glad you have enjoyed yourself. Randolph came yesy & seems in good Health & spirits—He has been very affect. & cheerful though Sarah[10] & I were quite alone. I leave him very much to himself & I really think he likes it best. I am much concerned & grieved to find that there has been a new settlement of his Affairs required & more money borrowed of Mr Montagu.[11] It has come about accidentally my knowing abt. it as my signature was necessary & it made me rather sorry that you have never been able to confide entirely in me though I do not see how I can shew you more affection and sympathy than I do—I reproached R. for his extravagance gently enough for God knows I cannot bear to add to his anxieties & he said he had relied on *you* doing for him as I used to do for his Father keeping things straight. Now dearest Jennie I would not for the world pain or judge you harshly—But indeed if you wish to regain your influence over him & make him fonder of you, you *must* sacrifice yourself & lead a different life. You must feel now that life cannot be all pleasure & oh dearest Jennie before it is too late I do pray you to lay my advice to heart & give up that fast lot you live with racing flirting & gossiping. Indeed it is real affection that dictates my words. You will be happier I know if *once* you break off with the past & live for a better and more useful existence. I believe you are as I told you at a great crisis of your life. I should be so glad if I could be of use to you & persuade you—But I have told you all this before & I do not want to lecture & bore you. If I could be of any use to you in Household matters you know I would. He tells me he is now going to give you an allowance for Housekeeping etc—But I do not like to seem inquisitive & you have never confided to me your money difficulties—As to other matters I feel sure you have no cause for jealousy in that quarter. But I feel there is a great deal of talk & I fear dear you have not been able to conceal things as you should have done. Mrs Stirling[12] Ly Mandeville Ly Londonderry[13] & others have talked & it has come round to me from Mary & my Children I do pray you to be *very* discreet this week I hope & trust for both your sakes that nothing will be observed at Newmarket. But you must be very careful Dear—And now God bless you—I shall think constantly of you & only wish it was in my power to do you any good.

We expect the Curzons this Evg which will be nice—

Randolph seems quite satisfied abt. things in general & he has cause to be—Ever

Yr most afft
F.M.

Did he, though, have good enough cause? He was behaving in the most extraordinary way for a Cabinet Minister, enraging his colleagues, interfering, causing ceaseless trouble. On 2 October he went to Dartford and delivered what was virtually his personal programme for the government of which he was a member. It seemed deliberately designed to upset everyone with whom he was supposed to be working. And then he did something even more astonishing: as though to challenge his colleagues to see how they could manage without him, Randolph set off for a European holiday, under the instantly penetrated disguise of 'Mr Spencer'. He was now a famous politician on the continent as well as in England, and many people quite wrongly believed the pseudonym was to enable him to conduct secret negotiations with European statesmen.

Cabinet Ministers were not amused. When the Duchess came up to London to say goodbye, Jennie was not there. She had not answered the Duchess's letter about their financial problems, it seems:

Huntercombe
Oct. 3
8 o/c

Dearest Jennie

I was sorry not to find you in town. . . . I saw Randolph but only for a very short Time as he appeared full of business & thought—He said he should go today or Monday for a fortnight. I said would you take Jennie & he said No only T. Trafford was going with him but that you were going to Bradford[14]—I said no more dear Jennie feeling it was wiser to trust to Time to put things straight. I still believe you have no cause for jealousy of that Lady—& that you have the future in your own Hands—only there must be sacrifice & self denial & great patience & can you *will* you exercise it? Meantime dear you say nothing abt. the *Money* question which I wrote to you & which worries me very much. However perhaps when we meet we can talk it over. I have little to tell you. If you feel inclined to come here you know we shall all be glad to see you. But I fear its very quiet. The Lawn Tennis is at an end & so we shall not have many visitors. . . . I do so like being here so quiet & so cheery. The Days fly by. Blandford is coming today for a night. I am longing to read Randolph's speech & hope it will be a great success. The Londonderrys seem doing very well in Dublin I get an Irish Paper daily & it reminds me of the old Times—I went to a very successful Primrose League Meeting the other Day with Georgie where they recd. me like Royalty!!—Georgie & I were so amused. She is very popular & we both *orated*—God bless you Dear— I hope your Mother is better—I wish I could put a wise cold Head on your shoulders! Its easy to preach to others I know though as you say very hard to do right oneself.

Yrs aff.
F.M.

I have just finished reading Dear R's magnificent speech & never have I read one more statesmanlike tactful & forcible. It must go down in the Country as it has done on my mind—so straightforward & yet discreet—so eminently *common sense*. It has been a great treat to me to read it—the story abt. the Dutch Generals—the Return of political Economy from the Starry regions to which Mr Gladstone consigned them & above all his words abt. the Unionists *must* forcibly strike everybody. I have no words to express my admiration & approval. If he is not gone will you give him this little bit of my Letter as I will not bother him I trust & pray he is well & will now get rest.

Tell me his address abroad.

Rest does not seem to have been Randolph's object, for he travelled rapidly round the capitals of Europe. His first note to Jennie came from Berlin:

> Der Kaiserhof,
> Berlin
>
> Dear Jennie   October 6, 1886
>
> You will like a line to let you know we got here safely after a vy long journey. From 6.30 am leaving Flushing to 11 oclock PM here. It was a vy hot day travelling. This is not much of an hotel rather dirty & bad waiters, but we discovered a restaurant this morning where we got a vy civilized breakfast. It is certainly not a vy lively town but worth seeing. Tommy & I spent an afternoon in the Zoological Gardens which are even better than ours. Tonight we go to a theatre where the attraction is a big ballet & tomorrow we leave at noon arriving at Dresden at five in the evening. It is certainly vy pleasant getting away from England and if the weather only keeps as fine as it is now travelling will be vy pleasant. My cold has not troubled me and is practically gone.
>
> Yours ever
> Randolph S.C.

The next letter is slightly warmer in tone, and reveals that he and Kinsky were still friends:

> Hotel Bellevue
> Dresden
>
> Dear Jennie   October 8, 1866
>
> We arrived here yesterday afternoon glad to get away from Berlin which is certainly most dull and unattractive. I was much amused to get this morning a message through Iddesleigh[15] from H. Bismark[16] hoping I would go and see him if I went to Berlin. I wired to Iddesleigh that I did not intend to go to Berlin but that from here I was going to travel in Bohemia. I found here a vy interesting letter from Kinski. Please thank him for it & tell him I will write & tell him how his house at Prague is looking. Yesterday we went to a kind of Music Hall vy stupid & bad, but crowded with Saxons who seemed immensely amused. Of course we have done the Raphael, which cer-

tainly exceeds all one's expectations. The gallery is immense and would require a month to go over it properly so we did it in 45 mts. We go on tomorrow to Prague & the following day to Vienna. Tonight we are going to the opera which is said to be well done here. How spiteful the Radical papers are. That *Pall Mall* most mischievous. I hope Lady Salisbury does not read it or she might take alarm for the position of 'Robert'.[17] Tommy is vy flourishing & most amiable. We have found a vy good hotel here. Unfortunately the day has been pouring wet so have been a good deal in our rooms.

Yours ever
Randolph S.C.

From Dresden the travellers went on to Vienna.

Frohner's Hôtel Imperial,
Wien

Dear Jennie   October 12, 1886

We got here last night & I found yr letter of Saturday; I return Winnie's which you enclosed. I am hopelessly discovered; at the station yesterday I found a whole army of reporters at whom I scowled in my most effective manner. Really it is almost intolerable that one cannot travel about without this publicity. How absurd the English papers are. Anything to equal the lies of the *Daily News* & *Pall Mall* I never read. W. H. Smith[18] is here & we had a long talk last night. I have got him to go and see Paget[19] who wanted me to go and dine with him & tell him that as I saw no one at Berlin I did not wish to see anyone here. The reporters have been besieging the hotel this morning but I have sent them all away without a word. The weather is fine & bright tho there is an autumn chill in the air. We have got 'Gugel' Kinsky's cabdriver, and are going tonight to the theatre an der Wien & afterwards to the Orpheum. where I hear the programmes are vy good. Prague is a most interesting place. I got you some Bohemian glass things for flowers & also a toilette for myself. They will reach Connaught Place in about a fortnight. I expect we shall leave this for Paris on Friday or Saturday. This pottering about Europe *de ville en ville* suits me down to the ground if it were not for the beastly newspapers. Tell Mama all about me. Old Kodolitsch[20] called this morning but I said I was out. I thought he would be such a bore. I am going to try & find a Sandringham present for 'Tum' here.[21]

The tone of this, though not exactly warm, is certainly not hostile. Randolph is buying Jennie presents; later, in Paris, he saw to a commission of hers at a jeweller's. It is exasperating that he, who kept almost every letter Jennie ever wrote him, did not keep the ones he received on his European tour. In any case, he was playing the part of a correct husband, writing regular but non-committal accounts of his doings.

Among the reporters clamouring at the station was one from *The Times*. 'Mr Spencer', he said, looked fatigued. He refused in emphatic terms to receive anyone whatever, but walked about Vienna both morning and afternoon, and visited a leather goods shop, before going to see Millöcker's operetta *The Vice-Admiral* in the evening.

Meanwhile there had been a small fire at 2 Connaught Place. Randolph was unperturbed. He wrote from Paris telling Jennie to do what the carpenter recommended. He was rather bored, as Tommy Trafford had gone to see his wife and children, but there were several old friends about to keep him company. He had received a letter from Winston which pleased him: he replied enclosing stamps and some of the autographs for which Winston was always beseeching him. (Winston seems to have sold them to his school-friends to supplement his pocket-money.)

If Jennie was hoping for kinder treatment on Randolph's return, she was disappointed. Once again she appealed to the Duchess, who replied:

Huntercombe
Dearest Jennie   Oct. 24

Do not fear for anything you have said to *me*—for it will go no further. But I do intreat you to put such thoughts away from you & I quite agree that perhaps it is best not to talk abt. them for it intensifies them & I am sure it works you up to exaggerate things. I know well how impulsive & excitable you are & it will be very hard for you to keep a watch over your words & *thoughts* even—But do my dearest Jennie make a firm resolve to *seal* your lips & govern your thoughts & do not let any friend *male* or *female* beguile you henceforth into confidence & be calm & gentle with him—Keep your place as a Matter of course & do not rush about for destruction I know so well how hard it is for you & pray believe it's no want of sympathy makes me say this but simply that it is the only possible way of getting his Love & respect & of preserving your own Dignity—It will bring you a blessing if you accept patiently this trial & look on it as a sort of retribution for indiscretions or errors—Also I fear there is already a lot of talk abt. it & women who have long been jealous of you & your success are ready to *carp* & rejoice at what makes you unhappy. The Curzons are come home. Rosamond leaves tomorrow. We have had a quiet Sunday &

Blandford who is here appears in a peaceful Amiable frame of Mind.
God bless you. Please send me local Papers & a Telegram after his
speech.

Yrs most aff
F.M.

I am sure Leonie is a good guide & confidante. You require NO other &
must have *none* in future, I feel sure of her Discretion & believe in her
calm judgement.

Jennie accompanied Randolph to Bradford, but they seem to have
parted again soon afterwards:

Eridge Castle,[22]
Sussex

Dear Jennie   November 1, 1886

HRH tells me he expects us to stay over the Sunday at Sandringham so you had better write to Mrs Allsopp to tell her we cannot go down till the Monday following. Please send brougham to
Charing Cross on Wednesday morning at 10.20

Yours ever
Randolph S.C.

The weekend at Sandringham was not happy. Jennie was unable to
conceal her distress:

Huntercombe Manor,
Maidenhead

Dearest Jennie   Nov. 19

My heart aches for you but I feel you intensify Matters and worry
yourself in vain. If you could only be quiet and calm—I feel sure everybody at Sandringham saw your jealousy—& I know there is just as
much talk abt. it as abt. the Brooke[23] affair. And people will not pity
you the idea is that you who have led so independent a life are foolish
now to be so jealous & you have been too successful & prosperous not
to have made Enemies.

I saw R. on Tuesday for a short Time & said a few words for you
which he took in a way that made me hope for you. I only said I
thought you were not well—that you seemed to me very unhappy &
that I thought you fretted abt him—He muttered you had no cause—
you were so excitable—to this I agreed but I said you were very warm
hearted & affect. & quite devoted to him & I hoped he would be good
to you—Something of that kind & he kissed me & seemed to acquiesce

& he said no more except occasionally referred to you, said you had a
pretty Ball Dress. I cannot exactly say why but I left him with the impression he really could not get away from London. Dear Jennie I can
say no more—Rosamond writes some friends of theirs went to the Ball
& that he was the great attraction & you were very much admired.
Will you come here dear any Day after Sunday—We stay till the 3rd
or 4th. . . .

Goodbye—I can only pray for you & hope for the best.

> Ever yrs affct.
> F.M.

Still Jennie's misery went on; and still she tried to keep up appear-
ances, though with little success. She and Randolph went to dine at
Windsor with the Queen, who thought her very handsome and dark.
Randolph, Victoria thought, looked very ill. Then they went to stay
with the Salisburys at Hatfield House. On 29 November the Duchess
wrote that she'd been told it was Jennie who looked ill there, with Randolph 'out of sorts'. The whole social world was buzzing with rumours.

So was the political world. Randolph's quarrels with his colleagues in
the Cabinet were now an open secret. He enraged them, for instance, by
passing pieces of information to *The Times*. Salisbury described him as
having 'a wayward and headstrong disposition': nowadays he would be
called manic. The crisis finally came over his budget. He insisted on cuts
in defence spending, and threatened to resign if his demands were not
met. People did not take these threats seriously.

Relations between Randolph and Jennie can be gauged from her account of what happened next. Randolph was again invited to dine at
Windsor. Jennie did not accompany him this time. She was busy drawing up the guest-list for a reception they were to give at the Foreign
Office. The cards had been printed, but she wasn't sure about one or two
people, so she sought Randolph's advice on his return. They were just
going to the theatre with Sir Henry Wolff. She was puzzled when Randolph answered by saying 'Oh, I shouldn't worry about it if I were you;
probably it will never take place.' He wouldn't explain himself, and no
doubt she did not dare to press him, things being as they were. So off
they went to see *The School for Scandal*. Shortly after the first act, Randolph slipped away, saying he was going to his club. In fact he went to
The Times and showed the editor the letter of resignation he had written to Salisbury from Windsor. The first Jennie knew of it was when she
read it in the paper next morning. She went down to breakfast, the
paper in her hand. Randolph was calm and smiling. 'Quite a surprise for
you,' he said. Nothing more. Jennie felt too utterly crushed and misera-

ble to ask for any explanation, or even to remonstrate. Moore came rushing in, pale and anxious. 'He has thrown himself from the top of the ladder,' he said in a faltering voice. 'He will never reach it again.' He was right.

Later, in Rome, Randolph confirmed Rosebery's opinion that the Windsor letter was not a resignation letter; he only meant it as the beginning of a correspondence. The real fact was, Rosebery stated, that nervous, impulsive, overstrained and impatient of opposition as Randolph was, he discharged this menace of resignation at Lord Salisbury as he had flung a similar threat in the previous year, without calculation, and as a warning rather than a positive act. Salisbury, however, this time took him at his word. The resignation was accepted, with relief, and the government found itself perfectly able to carry on without him.

The resignation caused an immense sensation, and at once all that had been whispered about Jennie's marriage became openly discussed. Gossip suggested a Public Scandal might lie behind Randolph's seemingly inexplicable behaviour. An American journalist heard the rumours and wrote to Jennie:

> Hotel Metropole
> Charing Cross
> Jany 14th, '87
>
> My Lady,
> An article furnished me this week for enclosure in my Saturday cable to the *New York Sun*, deals with the details of a separation which the writer alleges to be pending between yourself and Lord Randolph.
>
> Unwilling to publish so grave a statement without having first made every effort to verify its exactness, I called twice, hoping to see either Lord Randolph or yourself in order to be guided in correcting, or entirely withholding the article in question, by what you might wish to say. If you will make an appointment for me before noon tomorrow, when my despatch is sent, I shall be pleased to wait upon yourself or Lord Randolph.
>
> I endeavoured to see your Father, Mr Jerome, whom I have met but could not learn whether he had gone from the Langham. I may add that a cable received today from New York informs me that rumours are current there of the story of which the article sent to me purports to be a confirmation.
>
> Believe me My Lady
> Very truly yours
> Arthur Brisbane
> Cable Correspondent, *The Sun*, New York
>
> Lady Randolph Churchill

Jennie took the letter straight to Randolph. The draft of his reply survives:

2 Connaught Place, W.
Jan 14, 1887

Sir,

Lady Randolph Churchill has handed to me the vy singular letter which you have today addressed to her.

If as I assume you have regard to the credit of the newspaper in New York to which you act as correspondent I would advise you not to be a party to furnishing them with information and causing them to circulate statements which are utterly false libellous & unfounded.

It passes my comprehension how such rumours could have been started, how anyone of position or respectability could pay the smallest attention to such scandalous gossip, & how an American gentleman could write such enquiries as you have written to a lady & to one moreover who is a compatriot of his

I am
Yours obediently
Randolph S. Churchill

Arthur Brisbane Esq.

Brisbane did his best to defend himself:

The Hotel Metropole
London, S.W.
Jan 14, 1887

Sir—As London correspondent of *The Sun*, it is my duty to forward by cable such statements as are of public interest, and which reach me through the ordinary news channels. The assertion in regard to which I wrote to Lady Randolph Churchill was sent to me for publication in the usual way. Instead of publishing it forthwith, I called three times at your residence intending to place the communication before you, but was unable to see you.

I was informed this evening that you were not in London, and it was for that reason that my letter was addressed to Lady Randolph Churchill instead of to yourself—

I learn this evening that a duplicate of the communication addressed to me had been sent to a second American newspaper and would have been published in America as current rumor, had I not chanced to speak with the representative of that paper.

I thank you for your trouble in replying to my note, while regretting the interpretation which you put upon my efforts to save a lady and a compatriot from the uncontradicted publication of scandalous gossip—

Very truly yours
Arthur Brisbane

Lord Randolph Churchill

Randolph at first felt genuine surprise at the way events had turned out over his threat of resignation. The strain of the last few months had been too great and probably impaired his judgement. Having made the threat, and finding himself obliged to make it good, he did the honourable thing and resigned. Once the decision was made, and he was shorn of his responsibilities, he began to feel relieved. As he said later to Rosebery, 'I would not live the last four years again for a million a year' —and that was something coming from a man who was very short of money.

The immediate result for Jennie was a reconciliation with Randolph. For when, early in February, he once more went on an extended foreign holiday, it is clear from both their letters that all is well again. For Jennie the crisis was over, and when Randolph reached Biskra, from which he had turned back on hearing of Jennie's illness in 1882, he found long, effervescent, gossipy 'epistles', full of affection, and perhaps relief.

On 6 February, for instance, she wrote about a dinner party she had gone to at the Mandevilles, where she met Lord Dunraven, Under-Secretary of State for the Colonies, who was about to follow Randolph's example and resign from the government. Then she had had a visit from the Prince of Wales. 'He came at 5. & remained over an hour, & was most cordial—insisted on kissing my hand when he went away & declared himself our "best friend"!' (A cynic might suggest that perhaps he was hoping to take advantage of the troubled marital situation.) Randolph had written to the Queen apologizing for the fact that his resignation had been reported in the papers before she had been informed. The Queen's private secretary had replied briefly and coldly. The Prince thought the letter curt, but he explained that it would not be proper for the Queen to enter into a discussion on the subject, even if she approved. 'Of course Tum indulged in a few arrows—but they have not stuck into me,' Jennie wrote.

She had been to dinner the night before with Sir William Harcourt, who had been Home Secretary and then Chancellor of the Exchequer under Gladstone. The dinner was dull and nasty, the talk all political. George Goschen, a Liberal Unionist, had taken Randolph's place in the Conservative administration. (He is the man Randolph is supposed to have 'forgotten' when he resigned.) 'Harcourt was very pompous—he said he rejoiced when he heard that Goschen had joined for 2 reasons— that it kept *you* out—& wld break up the govt.' There was much chaff about the Chancellor's official robes. The tradition of passing them on from one Chancellor to another had been broken by Disraeli in 1853, when he refused to hand them over to Gladstone. Harcourt asked Jennie if Randolph was passing his on to Goschen. 'No,' she replied, 'they are put away in a tin box for a few months until they are wanted.'

After dinner Jennie went to a party being given by the Prince of Wales at the New Club in Covent Garden. Lord Hartington, leader of the Liberal Unionists and heir to the Duke of Devonshire, was there with 'a large party of lovely ladies'. He was most amiable, and talked to Jennie the whole time. 'Randolph is so right to go away,' he said. 'I envy him—he has had his day, and off he goes.' They talked of a speech that W. H. Smith had just given. Hartington thought Smith had spoken very well. 'No fireworks!' said the Prince, with a giggle at Jennie. 'I believe you,' she answered, 'but when you are in pitch darkness people are very glad of fireworks to show them the way.' Hartington told her she had scored, and indeed she defended Randolph splendidly.

At lunch that very day she had sat next to Joseph Chamberlain, who had broken with Gladstone over Home Rule, and was now a leading Liberal Unionist. He and Randolph had been intriguing together a good deal over the last two years. He was nice to Jennie 'for the first time', she wrote. 'I wish I cld remember all he said—However he is not in the least vexed with you—& thinks you are perfectly right to go away—that it is yr best game—you have but to wait—He quite agreed with me that you & he were the only 2 possible leaders in the future—but that you must agree in private, as to the amount of public abuse you were to shower on each other.' Chamberlain was very bitter about Goschen, and said he would *never* again be in a Liberal Cabinet or get in for a Liberal seat. Mrs Jeune, the political hostess who was giving the lunch, told Jennie that Goschen was nervous and unhappy, and would be a failure. Dicey, the editor of *The Observer*, was there, and Jennie made a point of being civil to him. But the letter was not entirely political. In a PS Jennie wrote: 'The children are all right. It is Jack's birthday on Wed. 9th 7 years old! How time flies—'

When Jack was born, Randolph had been nobody: now the great moments of his career were over, though naturally neither he nor Jennie knew it. She wrote on the 15th about a dinner-party at the Dunravens. She had sat next to Hartington:

I asked him how he thought '*his*' Govt: were getting on—'Very badly the last week,' he said—'Randolph wld never have allowed the waste of time—5 days before a minister spoke'—He chaffed about yr robes & asked if he shld try & sell them for me to Goschen—I said I thought the bargain wld be too hard a one—'Do you mean Goschen wld go in for the "old clo" line?' everyone laughed—However, said Hartington, Randolph won't want them in the future, as he will be P.M. next time. . . .

The letter had a P.S., revealing the twelve-year-old Winston's passionate partisanship of his father:

Winston was taken to a pantomime at Brighton where they hissed a sketch of you—he burst into tears—& then turned furiously on a man—who was hissing behind him—& said 'Stop that row you snub nosed Radical'!!

Randolph was delighted with this news, and asked that Winston be sent a sovereign for his loyalty. A few days later Jennie was invited to dinner by the Salisburys. She was not sure whether she should go or not, and whether Randolph would approve, but she took her courage in her hands and went:

2 Connaught Place
Feb 21st

Dearest R. I was very glad of yr telegram today from Constantine or rather last night, as I had no idea where to write to. I hope you found Biskra warm. It is rather hard to go so far & find snow—I feel I have heaps to tell you, but don't know where to begin—First of all about my dinner at the Salisbury's—There were a lot of small tables & Lady S. made me sit at hers next to Abercorn[24]—She wanted to be very amiable & said she hoped you were well & enjoying yrself—After dinner Ld S. came and talked to me for nearly an hour about every imaginable thing except you—He was very nervous & jerky & after a time the conversation turned on you, a propos of the cold weather abroad. I told him that you wrote you did not give 2 thoughts to politics & were quite happy—'I am sure the rest will do him good,' he said—'Randolph's brain works so quickly that it must wear out his nervous system.' 'I don't think so,' I said, 'but it is true that his brain works with rapidity so rapid—that he generally arrives at a conclusion 6 mths before most people.' I can't repeat all he said but my impression was that he wanted to be friendly—but not in a political line—He evidently did not want to discuss you—so of course I did not force it. He abused Henry James & said that he was very jealous of Goschen— Meanwhile I hear on every side that the Liberal Unionists are very low, even Hartington, as they know they will never be re-elected & things are going *very* badly in Ireland—I do so hope dearest that you will not disapprove of my having gone to the Salisbury's if it does no good it can do no harm—& I am sure it will stop some of the carping— There were lots of the enemy about & they looked so astonished at see- ing me in confab with Ld S. . . .

Jennie had been to dine with Mrs Jeune. Henry James had been there, and Harcourt, Chamberlain, and Ritchie, President of the Local Government Board. Mrs Jeune thought there had been a great change in Randolph's favour in the last few days. Even Ashmead-Bartlett, a long-standing enemy of Randolph's in the party, now believed that the Conservatives could not get on without him. Ritchie had only one refrain—Randolph must come back. Goschen was not a success: 'He looks like a man who has got on a kilt for the first time', Ritchie declared. But Randolph's supporter, Dunraven, had made a hash of his resignation: 'it was a fiasco'. Chamberlain sent his love.

Jennie gave a slightly different version of her dinner with the Salis- bury's to Leonie, and incidentally revealed her mixed feelings about Randolph's resignation:

I had a long talk with Ld. S. after dinner but I did not get much out of him. He was very shy and nervous and I had the greatest difficulty to get him to speak of Randolph. It is too long to repeat but I rather had the impression that they could never come together again. Don't repeat this, of course it is impossible to say what may happen in the House. As Arthur Balfour said—their difficulties haven't com- menced yet and when they do—they may have to go to Randolph. But Sniffy I feel very sick at heart sometimes. It was such a splendid posi- tion he threw away. In the bottom of my heart I sometimes think his head was quite turned at the moment and that he thought he cd do *anything*. However 'it is an ill wind that blows *no* good' and R. has been so much easier and nicer since that I ought not to regret the crisis. He writes most affectionately and very often and I hope all will be righted when he returns. . . .

Jennie felt she could speak her heart to Randolph again now. A letter of 5 March says all that need be said about the end of this unhappy epi- sode:

I was very glad to get yr letter from Tunis & to hear such a good account of you. It is a blessing to think that you are well & happy. It reconciles me to much that is disagreeable here—where people are as venomous & ill natured about us as possible—But you are good to me & I trust you utterly, & don't care twopence what they say—Enjoy yrself as much as you can & come back well, ready to fight the whole lot—And if you are only glad to see me, & understand how much I think of you & all that you are to me—I shall be quite happy—

NOTES

1. Consuelo Yznaga. Lord Mandeville became Duke of Manchester in 1890.
2. Blandford's eldest son.
3. Who were staying at Blenheim.
4. Jennie's old flame 'The Star' was marrying the Hon. Kathleen Douglas-Pennant.
5. Jennie and the Duchess were both founder-members of the Primrose League, a Conservative Party organization founded in memory of Disraeli at Blenheim in 1883.
6. Samuel Charles and Georgiana Millicent Allsopp. He became the second Baron Hindlip the following year.
7. Wilton House, Salisbury, home of the Earl of Pembroke.
8. In Yorkshire, home of the Earl of Feversham.
9. Cousin of Queen Victoria, and Commander-in-Chief of the British Army 1856–95.
10. Lady Sarah Churchill, Randolph's youngest sister, who later married Lieutenant-Colonel G. C. Wilson.
11. Probably Samuel, head of Samuel Montagu & Co., foreign bankers. He was the Liberal MP for Tower Hamlets, Whitechapel Division: later Lord Swaythling.
12. The Hon. Mrs Norah Stirling, daughter of Lord Rossmore. Her husband was in the Royal Horse Guards.
13. Lady Theresa Susey Helen, daughter of the Earl of Shrewsbury. Her husband was Lord-Lieutenant of Ireland from 1886–9. She was a famous hostess.
14. Where the conference of Conservative Associations was being held at the end of October.
15. Sir Stafford Northcote had taken the title of Iddesleigh on his far from noble elevation to the House of Lords. He was now Foreign Secretary, and still a victim of Randolph's dislike and contempt.
16. Herbert Bismarck, son of the German statesman.
17. Lord Salisbury.
18. Secretary of State for War.
19. Sir Augustus Berkeley Paget, British Ambassador to Austria since 1884.
20. Colonel Kodolitsch once invited Jennie to inspect his Hungarian regiment on a charger. Like Kinsky, he spent much of his time in London.
21. Shortly after his return, Randolph and Jennie went to stay with 'Tum', the Prince of Wales, at Sandringham.
22. Now demolished, then home of the 5th Earl and 1st Marquess of Abergavenny.
23. Daisy Brooke, the beautiful Countess of Warwick, was having an affair with Lord Charles Beresford. Much scandal was to follow, before she became the mistress of the Prince of Wales.
24. Son of the Duke whom Randolph's father had succeeded as Viceroy of Ireland.

8

LOVING AND LOSING

'The moment a man is out of the Cabinet', wrote Randolph in 1894, 'he is lost, he is not a bit worth more than any other Member of Parliament.' It was something he had learned slowly and painfully. He remained in the Commons till his death, and for some years his reputation remained high. But as it declined, so did his health. He turned with some success from politics to racing, winning the Oaks with L'Abbesse de Jouare, popularly known as Abcess on the Jaw. But typically he was abroad at the time, and missed his biggest racing triumph. Jennie wasn't there, either—she was boating on the Thames and got the news from a lock-keeper. In April 1891 Randolph decided to go to South Africa and try to make some money. 'I was a very poor creature after your departure,' wrote Jennie, but she perked up when he bought some shares in the Rand Mine, and sent her some diamonds. She was delighted:

I suppose by now you are comfortably established at Fort Salisbury and are 'prospecting' to any amount—I was agreeably surprised & delighted by receiving another diamond from you—it is a beauty, & for the present I have had it made into a pin, with a screw at the bottom for safety—How *dear of you* to send it to me. . . . Last July in London Clara had the fortune teller Mrs Soundy at her house—& after telling me my character etc. she looked into a glass ball & asked me to wish something—Of course in my mind I wished that you might make a lot of money & succeed out there. After a pause she said 'Yes you will get yr wish but not easily—& it won't be realized for a year & a half' May she prove right!

After bringing him up to date with all the racing and social news, she ended: 'Well goodbye I have got on both yr diamonds they are much admired—I dont in the least mind being like an ape—& can accommodate any more you choose to send! Best love.'

In spite of diamonds and Rand shares, however, the financial situation went from bad to worse. In the autumn of 1892 Jennie and Randolph had to sell 2 Connaught Place, and move in with the Duchess at 50 Grosvenor Square. For Jennie it was very bitter, as she admitted in a letter to Randolph that December:

> *Quite between ourselves* I don't think yr Mother cares about my staying here if she goes away & she has postponed her departure indefinitely. I am not going to bother you with it all & I shall try & do the best I can for myself & the boys—but I feel rather 'mis' over it all— I know 'beggars cannot be choosers' but I feel *very* old for this sort of thing. I have been to Hudson's[1] & settled what is to be sold—a certain amount will come here—but not all—as some things I do not want— and there is only room for very little—Yr mother does not want to part with any of her things & rather discourages us moving upstairs—But it really does not matter if you have what you want & I have my rooms all right—the boys can very soon manage with yr mother's furniture things will all settle themselves. . . .

During Randolph's South African trip, Jennie was living at Banstead Manor, near Newmarket, a house Randolph had first rented the previous year to be near his race-horses. A frequent visitor was Charles Kinsky. With Winston and Jack he played the part of a genial uncle, and they liked him very much. In 1890, Winston had given him chicken pox, but he doesn't seem to have minded, indeed he wrote Winston a friendly note. Sometimes he sent the boys stamps for their collections. That summer he took Winston to the Crystal Palace to see the German Emperor, some wild beasts and some splendid fireworks. Winston, aged sixteen, was tremendously impressed by the way Kinsky handled the head-waiter and crushed the fingers of an insolent Kaffir in his powerful grasp. They drank champagne, and on the way home, with Kinsky driving his phaeton with a fast pair of horses, they passed everyone on the road. Later, at Banstead, Kinsky set up a target for Winston and Jack to shoot at, and wrote from Vienna promising a gun. Jack, when he went to Harrow, had a picture of Kinsky in his room—probably the one of him on his Grand National winner Zoedone which Winston later offered a sovereign for. He wanted to put it in his room at Aldershot Barracks.

Jennie kept no letter from Kinsky of this period. Perhaps, when the affair was over, she sent them back; perhaps, in rage, or out of caution, she destroyed them. That she was discreet is plain. Writing to Randolph in October 1891, about a house party she'd been giving, and what a success it had been, she noted that 'Kinsky slept at the Farm opposite as there was no room for him & he did not mind—Everest has been ill with pleurisy—poor old thing, & of course I would not turn her out.' It's almost as though she wanted Randolph to know just how careful she was being.

Kinsky was not by any means in permanent attendance. He had his diplomatic duties (though they were hardly arduous), and was moved from embassy to embassy, though he always kept a flat in London and hunters in the Shires. He was discreet, too, and perhaps he kept his distance when Randolph was at home. But he and Jennie were often to be found at the same week-end house-parties. Those in the know, in Edwardian England, kept it to themselves, but acted on their knowledge.

Though Randolph seems to have been unaware of the progressively more obvious effects of his illness, the last years of his life were agonizing for all who knew and loved him. The time came when his speeches in the Commons made so little sense that friends went to Jennie and begged her to stop him coming. It was partly to keep him away, and partly in a last vain effort to help him recapture his health by travelling, that she set off with him in June 1894, against doctors' recommendations, on his final voyage. They were to go round the world. With them, as well as menservants and a doctor, they took a lead-lined coffin. It was necessary to be prepared. Jennie must have set out to do her duty in particularly low spirits, for her relationship with Kinsky had become unsettled. There was very little, anywhere, that she could any longer feel sure of.

They went first to New York, then to Maine, then across Canada to Banff Springs. From there Jennie wrote to Leonie about Randolph's urge to keep moving:

> As soon as he gets a little better from having a rest and being quiet he will be put back by this travelling—and *nothing* will deter him from doing what he likes. He is very kind and considerate when he feels well—but absolutely *impossible* when he gets excited—and as he gets like that 20 times a day—you may imagine my life is not an easy one. . . . I can't look ahead very far—Keith[2] thinks that R. will eventually get quite well, & I think so too—if only he would give himself a chance. Meanwhile I try to make the best of it.

From Banff Springs they went to Vancouver, and from Vancouver to San Francisco, and from San Francisco they took a boat to Japan. Randolph got no better, he got visibly worse. There were angry scenes, with the doctor 'énervé', and a manservant sent home. Randolph insisted on going to Burma, which in happier days he had annexed. It was there, on top of all the horrors of the voyage, that Jennie received a telegram from

Charles Kinsky announcing his engagement to Countess Elizabeth Wolff Metternich zur Gracht.

She was shattered. Even to Clara, to whom she never let herself go, she wrote: 'I HATE IT. I shall return without a friend in the world & too old to make any more now.' Leonie, who knew much more of what Jennie really felt, went with Winston to take Jack out for the day from Harrow. He wrote to his father, in a letter which Randolph probably never read:

> Aunt Leonie and Winston came down to see me last saturday they [didn't] stop very long however. She told me Count Kinsky is going to be married and that he says he is the happiest man in the world. To think I have not been really happy for nearly 6 months since you left. O how I wish I could express my thoughts and soul towards you and Dear Mama, but I can't and if I try I only write bad English.

Kinsky can hardly have expected Leonie to believe him, but what she really thought she was too sensible to say to a fourteen-year-old. It was to her that Jennie could express all her 'thoughts and soul'. In a remarkable, but partly lost letter, written early in December, as she was steaming from India to Egypt, Jennie revealed everything:

> . . . it is not likely—but of course in R's state anything is possible— Our mail comes in Tuesday & I hope to get letters from you—I suppose Charles has written to you about his engagement he wired it to me—& from his last letter I was not expecting it. Oh Leonie darling do you think it is *too late* to stop it? Nothing is impossible you know. Can't you help me—for Heaven sake write to him. Don't be astonished at my writing this—after my last letter—But I am frightened of the future all alone—& Charles is the only person on earth that I cd start life afresh with—& if I have lost him—I am indeed paid out for my treatment of him—The only thing I reproach F.W. for, is for telling me give Charles up—knowing that he himself did not intend to stick to me—Leonie darling use all yr cleverness & all yr strength & urge him to put off his marriage. Anyhow until I have seen him—He cared for me until quite recently—& if I am only given the chance—I will redeem all the past. The world wld forgive him knowing his devotion to me—& if he still cares for me—the girl I am sure wld be willing to give him up—particularly as there is someone else—she cld go back to—Leonie dearest rightly or wrongly work for this tell him that I am so suited to him that my troubles have sobered me & that I cld be all he desired—besides I cld help him in his career—The future

looks too black & lonely—without him—Oh! why have things gone so
wrong—Perhaps you can put it right—don't let him marry until he has
seen me—It is only a month to wait—*P. & O. 'Carthage' Red Sea—Dec
10th*—Dearest Snippy—As I found we were going as fast as the Mails,
I have kept my letter back until Today—we part from this ship tonight
at Ismailia—but it will take on my letter which will reach you the 18th
if you are in London—We go to Cairo for 8 days, as we have to wait
for our Messageries boat which we join at Alexandria for Marseilles
where we arrive the 20th. We have had a very good passage & R. is
very quiet. I think he will be easily managed henceforth. His will is
very feeble—I had to give in about Monte Carlo as he set his heart on
going there instead of Cannes—We shall go to the Metropole at first,
& make plans later—Perhaps if we remain at M.C. we can take a small
villa at Beaulieu. Write to me c/o Smith Bank on M.C. I don't know
if the Duchess will come out or not it may be too long a journey for
her—in which case we wld return to England after a bit—If she comes
perhaps Winston will bring her out—He can go to Germany a little
later—As for Jack if he does not stay at Deepdene³ you might look
after him if necessary—but I dare say the Duchess will have made arrangements for him—You will let me know all yr plans—Give my love
to Mama & Clara—of course I will write—*Don't breathe* what I have
written about Charles to anyone— Yr loving
Jennie

So that was it. Pressure had certainly been brought to bear on Kinsky
by his family, who felt it was more than time he married, and preferably
a catholic with the requisite number of quarterings. But he had resisted
that for years. Now that he believed that Jennie no longer loved him,
and knew she had betrayed him, he resisted no longer. And Jennie was
distraught. Who was F.W.? We do not know. But it might have been
Frederic, Lord Wolverton: Jennie certainly knew him, he has the right
initials, he was one of the Prince of Wales's circle: furthermore, he
married in January 1895, which is suggestive. But there is no evidence,
and it may just as well have been someone else. Whoever it was, his attraction had proved fatal.

Jennie and Randolph were back in London for what must have been
a grim Christmas. On 3 January Jennie wrote to Leonie:

. . . Don't dream of coming over at present & until it suits you. There
is little to do here & I am really much in a better frame of mind than

you can possibly imagine as regards this wedding. The bitterness if there was any, has absolutely left me. He and I have parted the best of friends and in a truly *fin de siècle* manner. So darling don't worry about me on that score. I am not *quite* the meek creature I may seem to you. Pity or mere sympathy from even *you* is wasted on me. No one can do me *any* good. He has not behaved particularly well & I cant find much to admire in him but I care for him as some people like opium or drink although they wd like not to. *N'en parlons plus.*[4] Randolph's condition and my precarious future worries me much more. Physically he is better but mentally he is 1000 times worse. Even his mother wishes now that he had died the other day. What is going to happen I cant think or what we are to do if he gets better. Up to now the General Public and even Society does not know the real truth & after *all* my sacrifices and the misery of these 6 months, it would be hard if it got out. It would do incalculable harm to his political reputation & memory & is a dreadful thing for all of us. We cant make any plans for the next few days. My life is dreadful here, so disorganised & uncomfortable, no place to sit, everything in confusion. I've got a cold which makes me feel 'like mud'. . . .

On 9 January, Kinsky was married. On the 14th Jennie wrote to Jack, who was staying at Deepdene with Duchess Lily:

My darling Jack

When am I going to see you again? Don't you think you might put pen to paper—I feel very lonely never hearing from you—You will have seen in the papers of poor Papa's sudden attack the other night. It was very serious but he has rallied altho' on the whole he is not so well—I am writing in bed which will account for this scrawl—Winston writes from Hindlip that it is pleasant there. I believe Sunny & his sisters go there today—I think he will probably come back Wed: give my best love to Aunt Lily—I wish I cld see her—but I do not feel I can leave the house for an hour at present—You might come up & see me one day if Aunt Lily approves

Yr loving Mother
J.S.C.

Write to me about yr clothes—how are they?

Even at a moment like that Jennie could worry about her son's school clothes.

Ten days later Randolph died, of General Paralysis of the Insane, leaving substantial debts: his Rand shares, which would have made his children millionaires, were sold to pay them off. Within a few days Jennie had lost the two men she had loved most.

NOTES

1. William Hudson, household furniture remover and fireproof furniture depositors, Hudson's buildings, Wilton Road, S.W.
2. The doctor who accompanied them.
3. Home of Blandford's second wife, known as Duchess Lily. Blandford had died in 1892.
4. Let's talk no more about it.

9

GEORGE

Jennie was resilient. She'd surprised her doctors by her powers of recovery in 1883, and she must have surprised her friends now. Instead of moping and mourning, she went to Paris with Leonie. She deserved a little fun after all she'd been through, and even the Duchess was only mildly disapproving. 'She carped a little at your *"apartement"* in "the gayest part of the Champs Elysées" but was otherwise very amiable—or rather not particularly malevolent,' wrote Winston in February 1895. A frequent visitor to the Avenue Kléber flat was Bourke Cockran, the celebrated American orator whose rhetorical style was to be such an influence on Winston's. But in April Jennie and Leonie had to return. Their mother, who had retired to a bleak life in Tunbridge Wells after Leonard Jerome's death in 1891, fell ill and also died. Jennie found herself even more alone. But she had her boys.

The story of how she took her parental duties more seriously after Randolph's death can be followed in the biography of Winston. But though he has naturally received far more attention from historians than his younger brother, Jack too benefited from Jennie's greater interest. In some ways he was closer to her than Winston, able, as he grew up, to tease her about her admirers and adventures in a way Winston never did. Also, at times, he and Jennie formed an alliance of amused exasperation against Winston's ceaseless demands and of mock despair against his perilous reputation-seeking as a young army officer. For all Jennie's endless social round and constant struggle against financial disaster, they were a remarkably united and loving threesome.

The social round hardly ever paused long enough for Jennie to catch her breath and collect her thoughts, but sometimes she felt dispirited. Her old friends George and Mary Curzon were going to India as Viceroy and Vicereine, and many parties were given to speed them on their way. One night, at Welbeck Abbey, home of the Duke of Portland, Jennie found herself next to Curzon:

> In a despondent mood I bemoaned the empty life I was leading at that moment. Lord Curzon tried to console me by saying that a

woman alone was a godsend in society, and that I might look forward
to a long vista of country-house parties, dinners, and balls. Thinking
over our conversation later, I found myself wondering if this indeed
was all that the remainder of my life held for me. . . .

This must have been in 1898. In June of that year Jennie was invited
to stay at Warwick Castle by Daisy Warwick, who had had a long reign
as the Prince of Wales's favourite mistress. The Prince enjoyed Jennie's
company very much: he was getting difficult to amuse as he grew older,
but she knew how to do it, and so was frequently invited where he was
going to stay. Among the other guests was a handsome young officer in
the Scots Guards, George Cornwallis-West. George was twenty-four,
just sixteen days older than Winston. His father owned 10,000 acres in
Wales, round Ruthin Castle in Denbighshire, and was Honorary Colonel of the 4th Battalion of the Royal Welch Fusiliers, but for all his
rank, he was really something of an aesthete, and had spent his youth in
Italy, copying old masters and begetting three illegitimate daughters. In
1872, having inherited and decided to become respectable, he married
Patsy, the beautiful grand-daughter of the Marquess of Headfort. Patsy
quickly produced two girls and George, to whom she seems to have
taken an early dislike. She was, however, ambitious for her children, and
had married her elder daughter, Daisy, to the immensely rich Prince of
Pless: Shelagh, younger than George, was to marry the Duke of Westminster, no pauper himself. It was, in shooting terms, a left and a right
for a family who had nothing like the cash to match their acres. But
Patsy wanted only the best: for George's godfather, she had acquired the
Prince of Wales himself.

In his amiable memoirs *Edwardian Hey-Days,* subtitled *A Little about
a Lot of Things,* George described that weekend at Warwick Castle. He
was at Hythe doing a course of musketry when he received his invitation. Leave from a course was almost unheard of, but an invitation to
meet the Prince was virtually an order, so George quickly got permission, and off he went. Warwick Castle is one of the most splendid places
in England, standing on its bluff above the river Avon, and Daisy Warwick at this time was, as George put it, 'at the zenith of her beauty'. But
it was Jennie, not Daisy, that took his eye. She was forty-four, but
looked not a day over thirty, and her charm and zest for life were un-
diminished. She always, even when she was old, treated people of all
ages as equals: George was enormously flattered by her attention. Before
anyone knew what was happening, they were out on the river together.
According to George, Jennie talked about Winston, about the great faith
she had in him, and her ambitions for his career. He would rise to great

things, she was sure. But they cannot have confined their conversation to Winston's prospects, for they had fallen instantly in love.

In his memoirs George leaves it there, and goes on to write of how he introduced the Mauser automatic pistol to the School of Musketry, the rise of French restaurants in London, and one or two polo-players he knew. He was discretion itself, in fact. But to Jennie he was quite uninhibited. He wrote from Newlands Manor, his family's other large country house, at Lymington, in Hampshire, on 3 July 1898:

Jennie Dearest, It is perfectly heavenly down here and I do so miss you, & long for you to be with me here. I wonder now what you are doing & who you are on the river with, I am sure Sweetie you are behaving yourself well. I have to go back to that dreary spot Pirbright[1] tomorrow, or rather have to be there, very early, so consequently leave this tonight. Dont forget tomorrow afternoon, if you possibly can, come & have tea with me at Burton's Court, & listen to the band. Good night you dear angel, *à bientôt*, yours always.

G.

Burton's Court is a large green place in front of the Royal Hospital, Chelsea, where the Guards have their cricket-field. To this day the Guards band plays on summer afternoons beneath the trees, and it must be one of the last Edwardian pleasures left in England to go and hear them while Guardsmen bat and bowl, their concentration apparently quite undisturbed by the musical accompaniment. For George, though, in 1898, the excitement of taking Jennie out to tea proved too much. He took to his bed almost at once: he often did in an emotional crisis. The rapidity of the affair was proving too much for his parents, too, who thoroughly disapproved:

In bed at
Dearest Jennie,   50 Park Street[2]
Excuse this scrawl but am still in bed, with every prospect of remaining there at present. Still darling I am better much. My temperature has gone down, it was 104 on Sat night. Much as I hate the idea of not seeing you, I dare not advise you to come here, as one never knows when my mother or father, who arrives today, may turn up. The former found out from my servant where the roses came from, though he had the sense to say they were sent with a note. We had a scene, she required a lot of pacifying & then only by assuring her that you were anxious for me to marry M.G.;[3] & had asked me to

lunch to meet her. It appears two *nice kind-hearted men* (D them) have informed her I am devoted to you. God bless you dearest, I longed to be with you at Eastwell,[4] but Fates are against us. What time do you go to Newmarket tomorrow. Your ever l.

G.

He was soon up again:

My dearest Jennie   July 13th, 1898
    I am much better today, & am down for the first time. The Doctor has ordered me home where I go tomorrow for a bit, how I do wish you were coming too. How is Newmarket, I see your host won a race yesterday. My address after tomorrow will be Newlands Manor.
    Lymington
      Hants.
Will you write me a line there like the angel that you are. I have missed you so the last few days, I have a picture of you before me now one in this weeks *Sketch* sitting at a piano. I have got such blues today. I want you to cheer me up badly. My battalion came up from Pirbright today, so at any rate when I do come up again I shant have to rush off to Pirbright every other hour. I hope you are behaving nicely with your old friend H.W. are you sweetie dear? It is such a glorious day out my thoughts carry me back to Hampton Court & the punt & the river, how I enjoyed that day, you make me forget I felt at all C.D.[5] Au revoir Dearest.

yours always
G.

H.W. was Hugh Warrender, one of Jennie's most staunch admirers, who pursued her and pursued her, and never married anyone else. His brother George, later an admiral, was also an admirer. Their sister Eleanor, another great friend of Jennie's, was a nurse. George had no need to worry. It was high summer, and Jennie thought of no one else. The lovers were only thwarted by George's tiresome duties, such as having to guard the Bank of England. On 19 July, Jennie must have watched him marching off:

    Oh my Jennie darling I did so love seeing you today, how I do crave for you, and longed to rush out of the ranks & tell you so, when I saw you this evening, you are so much, so *very much* to me sweetie. . . .

The *very much* was underlined four times, but George's passion still increased daily:

My Darling   July 25th, '98
   I have just this second got your second note, I am so mis, I had not the *least* idea that you were waiting in the carriage, when the 1st note arrived, or of *course* I would have rushed down four steps at a time to see my beloved Jennie, what a fool the waiter was not to tell me, I cant tell you how fearfully disappointed I am, I would have given worlds to see you. And the note I sent was such a cold formal note, as there were some others writing at the same table, but now they are all playing bridge, so that I can let my heart overflow to my sweetie. Oh darling I do love you, you are all the world to me, I cannot tell you how I appreciate all your confidence in me. How are you, *'Est ce que vos yeux sont un peu culottés'*⁶ but if they are its only because I love you, & my love is reciprocated. Bless you my sweetie, from your own
                                                                        G.

Four days later it was:

   I thought about you all yesterday & built castles in the air about you & I living together, it was such a nice castle, & somehow didn't fall to pieces as soon as most castles in the air do.

Then he was off to play cricket. He was besotted; there being no London mountains, he climbed balconies for her instead:

                                                          50 Park Street,
                                                          Grosvenor Square, W.
My Darling   8.15 a.m.
   Just off to parade feel so fit after a cold shower-bath.
An awful thing happened. I found directly I left I had left my latchkey, on a chain with a cigarette holder case, in your dressing room on the right hand side as you go in. Keep it a little then will you either send it or leave it here in a parcel. I had to climb up the balustrade to the balcony
                                                          Bless you.
                                                          G.

The lovers plotted to spend another week-end at Warwick Castle:

50 Park Street,
Grosvenor Square, W.

My Sweetie   August 1st, '98

Just a line before I start for Latimer, to tell you I am thinking of you & that I love you darling. I hated leaving you last night, I hope you are refreshed by your long sleep I am, & feel fit to make a hundred runs. What a happy peaceful day we spent yesterday, wasn't it delicious. I hope you will enjoy yourself at Cowes. I have just heard my people are going shares in a house there who with I dont know. Got a wire this morning from Lady W. Of course come Warwick any time you like Thursday. *A bientôt* my own sweetie, I long to be coming with you.

from your loving
G.

Jennie, however, was not invited to Warwick, much to George's chagrin, and no doubt her own. Daisy Warwick was piqued, perhaps—not because she had designs on George herself, but because she thought they were being too obvious. Besides, no one in the Prince's circle would have looked with favour on a woman of Jennie's age carrying on so boldly with a man a mere fortnight older than her own son. When she arrived at Warwick, Daisy announced that she had put off the ladies of the party. 'It is too horrid', wrote George. Equally horrid was the interview he had with his father about money:

Perham Down Camp
(Really in the train on my way there!)

Darling little Missus,   August 23rd, '98

As you see by above I am writing this in the train so that my writing will be even worse than it generally is. I left camp yesterday at 6.0 and after an extraordinary round about journey, including travelling by special and luggage trains I arrived home at 11.0 pm five hours to go 40 miles, wonderful speed! I had an unpleasant morning going through accounts with the agent & my father, & found that a most unsatisfactory state of things existed. However I managed after some persuasion to get my father to agree to several things, which I hope will put matters straight for a time at any rate. There is nothing so unpleasant as my position of having to regulate my fathers expenditure, it is in most cases the other way round. How I long to be with you now, you who are so sensible, would I know give me such good advice, and all my petty worries would vanish at once if I were with you dearest. We march to Wilton on Sat next, and will be there about

four days. I do wish you were going to stay with the Pembrokes, or somewhere near Salisbury, wouldn't it be nice. I hope you have had all my letters, the post at Perham is somewhat vague as regards delivery & collection. Goodbye my sweetie, I love you so. I forgot to say I fear I couldn't manage to go to the Mintos[7] as well as the Guthries[8] so soon together. Excuse writing. Love from your loving
George

Jennie was about to set out on her autumn travels, starting at Blenheim. George wished he could have gone, as there was a Fire Brigade competition which would have interested him very much. Jennie wasn't too happy about leaving him alone for several days. George assured her she could trust him:

I love you, & if you think for one instant you cant trust me by myself in London, you are quite mistaken, but there I know you were only chaffing me. . . .

Perhaps she wasn't 'only chaffing', though. George was easily impressed by feminine beauty, and was already leading a full sexual life, it would seem, at eighteen. He and some fellow Old Etonians took three tarts out on the river at Maidenhead one day. When they reached Windsor, the 'Perfect Ladies' ('at the very top of their profession and all young and pretty') asked to be shown round Eton College, including the Chapel. There, one by one, the young men abandoned them out of shame: 'Somehow it seemed rather beastly—those three tarts in Upper Chapel.' Off religious premises, though, George seems to have had few qualms. His susceptibility to women and theirs to him made life very easy in some ways; but not for those who hoped for some steadiness of affection.

Jennie cannot have imagined the affair would last long at this time, for she tried to get George a post with Curzon in India. Curzon was not interested:

You recommended young Cornwallis-West. He seemed a nice boy at Warwick but I don't suppose there is a chance of my having room for him, as I fancy I can only take one English officer from here & I have 50 applications.

George seemed quite keen to go, too. He asked Jennie if she'd heard anything. Jennie and Patsy seem to have been on friendly terms, because he thought Jennie might have told Patsy first.

The Executive Committee of the Hospital Ship 'Maine'.
From left to right: Lady Essex, Mrs Griffiths, Mrs Van Duzer,
Mrs Von André, Mrs Ronalds, Mrs Leslie, Jennie, Mrs Arthur Paget,
Mrs Blow, Mrs Moreton Frewen, Mrs Haldeman, Mrs Field

The Hospital Ship 'Maine' at Durban

A Ward below Decks on
the 'Maine' (above left)

Jennie's Cabin (left)

Jennie with the staff of
the 'Maine' (above)

'Sisters of Mercy'.
The Princess of Wales
thanking Columbia.
From 'Punch', November 22,
1899 (right)

Jennie with her injured son Jack, aboard the 'Maine'

They met again at Duart Castle, the Guthries' house on the Isle of Mull. Jennie wrote to Jack with bad news on 20 September:

> Fancy what a bore for me—I have sprained my ankle & can hardly put my foot to the ground—I was 4 miles from home when I did it—& managed to hobble back—but today it is so swelled I have to send for a doctor—

Her sisters said it served her right for pursuing George over the moors: a man should never be interfered with while he was at his sport.

There are many letters from George to Jennie over the next two years, mostly full of accounts of army manoeuvres, hunting and shooting. As letters, they do not begin to compare with Randolph's, any more than George compared with Randolph as a man. But they have a likeable boyish frankness, and moments of real tenderness, and George's absolute devotion to Jennie is beyond question:

> You are such an angel, I know you understand, & even if you did feel hurt you would never show it. And I love you for it very dearly. There is no one like you, you never get what I call 'Heroics', and never want me to do anything you think I'd rather not, in fact you spoil me, you angel I should love to give you a big hug before [I] start. I will go direct from the station & dress & come to you, put on your dear Jappy dress if you are alone. My cold is much better, thanks to ammoniated quinine. . . .

> I have just awoke from the 40 winks, you prophesied I would take; & feel all the better for them. You sweetie I hated leaving you last night; it seems unnatural that I should have ever to go away. I am none the worse, and got a cab almost immediately. Your telephonic conversation was nice but very inadequate, I wanted to be shot along the wires myself. . . .

> I dreamt about you last night, only too vividly, some-one tried to take you away from me, I can never allow that, the mental pain was awful even in my dream, Heaven knows what it would be if it actually happened. . . .

The only bar to Jennie and George's happiness was the strong disapproval of their affair being shown by all their friends, and particularly by those who took their social responsibilities gravely, such as the Prince of Wales. He wrote to Jennie and told her she was being foolish and compromising her social position. George was miffed:

I really do think its exceedingly cool of H.R.H. to write the kind of letter you mention in your letter. I wonder why our friendship should annoy him. I gain everything by your love for me, I fear you lose by it. I wish it were otherwise. . . .

Jennie thought she was being unwise herself at times. At any rate she would not even contemplate marriage, and George accepted it:

Ford Manor,
Lingfield,
Surrey

My darling little Missus,   November 9th, '98
    I was so glad to find your dear letter awaiting me, when I arrived in from shooting this evening. You must not be afraid Missus mine, I do really love you, & appreciate your cleverness & good qualities; really I would give up everything for you, I feel this more when I am not with you, as when I am, you are always trying to make me realize the folly of it all. I should say though only part of it, as there is no folly in being devoted to you my sweet, even if we cant get married. And I feel every day more & more like a creeper clinging to & growing on you. I may add that it is my prayer that this creeper may be 'evergreen'. We had a good day today about 600 pheasants, some high mostly otherwise. Tomorrow is to be the best day they expect to get 600 pheasants before lunch & 800 rabbits afterwards. If you want to bet, put a very little on Turkish-Bath & Chevy-Chase on Saturday at Liverpool, I heard from the trainer today, he thinks they will win. This is private as I never give away stable secrets, but there is no such thing as a secret between your loving George & my sweet little Missus.

No secrets, and no marriage. Marriage would be ridiculous and unbecoming. It was out of the question.

NOTES

1. Where his battalion was stationed.
2. The Cornwallis-Wests' London house.
3. Mary (May) Goelet, American heiress, who married Randolph's nephew, the Duke of Roxburghe, in 1903.
4. At Newmarket, where Jennie was staying with Lord William de la Poer Beresford, V.C., who had married Blandford's widow (Duchess Lily) in 1895.
5. Seedy.
6. Guards' Officer French for 'Have you got bags under your eyes.'
7. The 4th Earl of Minto, who was Governor-General of Canada 1898–1904, and later Viceroy of India, had a house at St Boswell's, Roxburghshire, where Jennie often stayed.
8. Walter Murray Guthrie was married to Olive Leslie, Leonie's sister-in-law.

IO

LOVE AND LETTERS

I

1899 was the busiest year of Jennie's life. She was forty-five, looked thirty, and must have felt eighteen. She was bursting with energy, so that not even an affair with a man the same age as her eldest son, or that son's endless demands for her assistance in every aspect of his career, could use it all up. She continued to think about her conversation with Lord Curzon. What should she do *really* to fill her life?

Among her many accomplishments, Jennie was an excellent musician, and the picture George had admired in *The Sketch* showed her sitting at a piano with Mademoiselle Maria Janotha, a popular performer in royal circles, and Pearl Craigie, an American of thirty-one who wrote novels and played under the name of 'John Oliver Hobbes'. The three women had played Bach's Concerto in D Minor for three pianos at a concert at the Queen's Hall. It was the only time, Jennie said, she ever enjoyed playing in public, though she did so often for charity. Perhaps this was because of Pearl Craigie, whom she had met through the Curzons. Jennie made few friends with women outside the immediate family circle, but for Pearl she felt real affection:

> A woman of great sympathies, her unselfishness has been realized by all who ever came in contact with her, and her valuable time was always at the disposal of anyone she could help. . . . A brilliant and clever conversationalist, she could hold her own with all manner of men, and yet in the more frivolous company, which she often frequented and thoroughly enjoyed, she never talked over people's heads. She had the art of drawing everyone out and making them appear at their best. So different to some clever women writers I have met. . . .

That was in 1907. Some years later Jennie wrote of her again:

It was impossible to know her and not love her. She was so human, so sympathetic and her brilliant and delicious mind so deep a well to draw from.

I remember a day we spent together in the country. We went for a walk. It was one of those days the English climate never wearies of giving—grey, raw, damp, odious. But we became so interested in our talk that it was some time before we noticed that we had wandered into a ploughed field. To me, it seemed, listening to her, that the field was enamelled with flowers, and that a warm sun beamed on us. She had the rare quality of making you feel at peace with yourself, and inspiring you with unfailing hope.

No other woman ever made Jennie feel like that; it was men who led her into ploughed fields. But the reasons why she found Pearl Craigie so attractive are obvious. Jennie was no intellectual, but she was intelligent, and though George provided everything she required in a physical way, mentally he gave her nothing. A talented, accomplished woman like Pearl Craigie was precisely the sort of person Jennie felt could help her with the problem of what to do with her life.

She had many literary friends. Among them had been Oscar Wilde, now disgraced. Jennie was once accused of misquoting from *The Importance of Being Earnest*. She made a bet that she was right, and wrote offering Wilde a beautiful pen-holder if he would vouch for her accuracy. He replied:

>   The Cottage,
> Dear Lady Randolph,   Goring-on-Thames
>   'The only difference between the saint and the sinner is that every saint has a past and that every sinner has a future!' That, of course, is the quotation. How dull men are! They should listen to brilliant women, and look at beautiful ones—and when, as in the present case, a woman is both beautiful and brilliant, they might have the ordinary common sense to admit that she is verbally inspired.
>   I trust your bet will be promptly paid, as I want to begin writing my new comedy, and have no pen!
>   Believe me,
>   Yours sincerely,
>   Oscar Wilde

Now Jennie decided to start a new literary magazine, and Pearl Craigie helped in many ways.

She introduced Jennie to the people she needed: Sidney Low, who was to be Jennie's assistant editor, John Lane, the publisher, Cyril Davenport, who chose the covers—which were copies of fine bindings. Doubtless Pearl Craigie suggested contributors, too. 'On looking back at the early period of the *Review*', Jennie wrote, 'I often wonder how I should have succeeded without Pearl Craigie's intelligent help and advice.'

The advice she got from other people was confused and contradictory, but Winston took a close interest and thought it an excellent idea. He wrote on 1 January 1899:

> I have no doubt that the business will go on. If it does you will have an occupation and an interest in life which will make up for all the silly social amusements you will cease to shine in as time goes on and which will give you in the latter part of your life as fine a position in the world of taste & thought as formerly & now in that of elegance and beauty. It is wise & philosophic. It may also be profitable. If you could make a £1,000 a year out of it, I think that would be a little lift in the dark clouds.

The patronizing tone of that is breath-taking, from son to mother, and as a New Year message it cannot have gone down too well with Jennie. But Winston was genuinely enthusiastic, and asked her to keep an editorial chair available for him, should he choose to take it. He shivered, though, at Jennie's choice of name, *The Anglo-Saxon Review*. The idea of an Anglo-American alliance was a wild impossibility, he said, and would find no room among the literary ventures of the day. Jennie and Pearl Craigie, both Americans, obviously thought otherwise. Indeed, Anglo-American co-operation was to dominate Jennie's thinking that whole year.

It is sad to have to say that, though *The Anglo-Saxon Review* was successful in giving Jennie something to do, as a magazine it was a failure. It was extremely expensive, for one thing: a guinea was a lot to ask, even with the fine binding, and there were never enough people willing to pay it. Instead of making money, it lost from the beginning. More important, there was no real editorial principle behind the selection of material. Jennie knew everyone, and those she didn't Pearl Craigie and Sidney Low knew, and they bullied and cajoled and got people to write as editors should. But the magazine existed to fill a gap in Jennie's life rather than one in the literary world. There were plenty of reviews at the time, and most of them not only cheaper, but frankly better. Not that *The Anglo-Saxon* did not have some excellent material: the first issue had a long story by Henry James, for instance. (Henry James the author of *The Turn of the Screw* and *The Golden Bowl*, that is; not Randolph's friend.) Other contributors included Swinburne, with a poem on the Battle of the Nile, and 'John Oliver Hobbes' herself with a long poetic drama unpromisingly called *Osbern and Ursyne*. There were pieces about Lady Mary Wortley Montagu and Wireless Telegraphy and the Treaty of Paris. There was an article by Lord Rosebery on Sir Robert Peel. But somehow it didn't add up to a magazine with any definite personality. Such as it was, the tone was vaguely aristocratic, and the review was mocked for having so many contributors from high society. In later issues such men of distinction in their different ways as Lord Crewe, Edmund Gosse, George Bernard Shaw, John Gorst, Stephen Crane, H. de Vere Stacpoole, George Gissing, Maurice Baring and William Archer were liable to find themselves between the same covers as *Angling Reminiscences in England and the Tropics* by Susan, Countess of Malmesbury. Daisy Warwick's contribution must have caused a few smiles. It was called *Some Minor Miseries of a Book Lover*: no one had imagined her problems lay in the field of bibliophilism. But it is easy to mock, and *The Anglo-Saxon* did run for twelve issues and fulfil its main purpose. It gave Jennie a sense of a full and purposeful life. She wrote to Jack on 24 February:

I am getting on very well with the review—but it is anxious work—I have got the people I want for the staff—which is important—& am getting money for the syndicate—I am so tired of writing about it that I don't think I will go all over it again—You will have more than enough of it when you return.

Jack was in Egypt, acting as secretary to Sir Ernest Cassel, the financier. He had been made to go into the City. *Someone* in the family had to make some money, and as Jennie only knew how to spend it, and Winston was too busy, it had to be Jack. He hated, but accepted it. He does not seem to have taken much interest in the magazine. George took an interest, but thought he knew his limitations:

I often wonder if you would object if I were to send you endearing telegrams, I often want to when I pass a telegraph office. You angel I didn't like leaving you one bit yesterday. I wish I could be of more help to you in your enterprise, I fear my talents (if I have any) are certainly not literary.

As a matter of fact George was later to extend his range from the amorous telegram to several full length books.

II

At the end of April 1899 Jennie was invited to stay with the Cornwallis-Wests at Ruthin Castle for Chester races: the Prince of Wales was going to be there. 'H.R.H. appears to be very anxious to meet you. Odd isn't it?' wrote George. Perhaps he meant to lecture her between the races. Obligatory guests included Lord Marcus Beresford, who managed the Prince's horses, and Mr Reuben Sassoon, who placed his bets. Among those chosen for other reasons was Miss Muriel Wilson, daughter of Arthur Wilson, in whose house, Tranby Croft, the famous Baccarat Scandal had taken place in 1890. Muriel was an heiress on whom many mothers had their eye for their sons—including Jennie, who thought she might do very well for Winston. Patsy obviously wanted her for George, which must have caused some tensions in the party, though none between Jennie and George, whose devotion continued unabated throughout the summer. By this time Jennie was beginning to waver on the subject of marriage. On 16 February she had written to Jack, noting Lord Crewe's engagement to Lady Peggy Primrose: 'only 22 years between them!' But she had a conscience about the gap between herself and George. It gave her bad dreams. George would have none of it:

> Dreams always go by contraries, and *yours* was no exception to the rule, and darling I feel it will always be the case as regards us two. No one shall come between us. . . .

Not even Winston, who was now back in England and had retired from the army to fight a by-election at Oldham. Jennie put on the dress she wore for her concerts and appeared with him at meetings. 'There are thousands of true hearts in this constituency which have a warm corner for Lady Randolph Churchill,' said the *Oldham Daily Standard* on 27 June, and on the 28th it recorded that 'Lady Randolph Churchill had a most enthusiastic reception as she accompanied Alderman Whittaker[1] to the platform. Her charming and graceful presence gave an added interest to the proceedings. She listened intently to the speeches, and seemed especially pleased and amused with Mr Bottomley's[2] vigorous and humorous address.' She did not, it seems, speak herself, but her very presence was thought to contribute to the Conservative cause. This time, however, it was to no avail, and Winston was not elected.

Soon after Jennie's visit to Oldham, she and George must have agreed that they would marry, in spite of everything:

Pirbright Camp,
Woking
My darling little Missus,   July 11th, '99

I am sending my servant up for some things, so take the opportunity of writing you a line before you start for Newmarket. You are such a darling. I loved your bringing me to the station last night.

I was awfully chaffed this morning as someone saw me, and remarked I kept my head in the carriage some time. I passed it off by saying 'Well if a man cant be driven to the station by his own sister he cant be by anyone.' They believed me. Some day soon I hope to be able to say wife instead of sister. Dont forget you have a pony to play with for me. We had a parade this morning it *was* hot. Bless you my own Precious one, till Thursday. Your own

G.

Four days later he wrote saying:

I went to see Mrs Greaves[3] after I left you, I told her in the strictest confidence, that I was going to marry you, she was very pleased, and declared she had never known an instance of two people marrying when the man was the younger, that was not a success.

Their engagement was, of course, to remain an absolute secret, and, equally of course, it didn't. Things came to a head in August: George was invited on board the Prince's yacht *Britannia* at Cowes:

The Prince of Wales took the opportunity of taking me aside and pointing out to me the inadvisability of my marrying a woman so much my senior. He admitted that this was the only argument against our engagement, told me that no one could possibly say what might happen within the next three months, and begged me to do nothing in a hurry.

The Prince meant that the situation in South Africa was serious, and it looked like war. '"If there *is* war", he added, "you're sure to go out. There'll be time enough to consider it when you come back."' Unfortunately the Prince was too late; the engagement leaked into the papers, where much was made of George's closeness in age to Winston. The wedding was forecast for October. Though these reports were denied, some public comment was unavoidable, for Cowes had a strange effect on Jennie. It was there, of course, that she had met and become engaged to Randolph, and *their* romance had got into the papers, somehow, too.

The Marquis Boni de Castellane explained how it happened this time. One evening Jennie told him about it, making him promise to keep it a secret. A few hours later he discovered she'd told his whole party. .

After all this excitement, Jennie and George went to Paris for still more. They took a trip to Versailles, though that was not what excited George most:

> I did so enjoy my two days, & nights!! in Paris my love, they were the happiest I have ever spent in my life, & trust they were only a foretaste of what is to come. . . .

Jennie went from Paris to Aix, to take a cure and think. George went back to London, where he saw Jack. Jack did not always care for Jennie's admirers, but he seems to have got on all right with George:

> Jack came to dine, and we talked of you. You would have been amused at the menu, we had grouse for dinner, but as it was the 11th only, they were put down as *'Dindonneaux d'Ecosse'.*[4] I went to see my doctor today, as I was not quite well again after Paris, I suppose it never *had* got *quite* well, and overdoing it brought it on again, its so difficult to write what I mean without being crude. However he said it was nothing and would be well in a few days. Darling precious Missie I am counting the days before we meet again. . . .

In Aix, Jennie was regretting her indiscretion at Cowes and having serious doubts again:

> Arthur's
> St James' Street. S.W.
> August 14th, '99
>
> Little Missie mine, your letter today made me rather sad. You said in any case no matter what happens we will stick to each other, but precious you dont mean by that, we should not marry, do you? When I am away from you I feel all the more determined, but be as you wish, (whatever that may be) I'll always stick to you, and can no more bear the thought of our being separated than you can. The adjutant took me aside today & wanted to know if it was true I was engaged, and Col Paget[5] had written to him to find out. I told him it was true in this way, that I would marry you tomorrow if you would me, but that you were not willing, still at the same time it didn't follow that I did not intend to persevere in the idea. The opinion here is that *I*

acted too prematurely & had it put in the papers, & that you evidently had it contradicted, it is unpleasant for me, and several sarcastic things have been said to me, but I dont mind one *little* bit dearest one, and am only telling you this, to make your mind at rest, & show you that you are in *no way* held up to ridicule. . . .

Jennie continued to have doubts, and to worry George with her letters. On his way from Scotland to stay with the Wilsons at Tranby Croft, he assured her that *his* mind was quite made up. When he got there he found trouble—though not from Muriel:

> Tranby Croft,
> Hull
> August 20th, '99

My own precious little Missie, I cant tell you how delighted I was to find a letter from you, on my arrival here after having been travelling all day, and another one this morning, I do love getting your dear letters so. 'Missie mine', I have written to you every single day since you left, so that as you got no letter one day, you will probably get two on another. I had a letter from the adjutant today, saying that Col Paget wishes to see me on the 25th I know what this means he is going to have a go at me about you, but dont be afraid my darling love I shall be strong, as if possible I love you more than ever; still it is a bore if he uses threats I shall say I shall leave the regiment, you wont desert me Missie, will you? I couldnt bear it, it would break my heart. Perhaps he will try & persuade me to go abroad, but I wont go, I cant leave you Missie, for I love you better than my life, and any prospects I might have would become empty & hollow without you to share them with. I've got such blues, & how I long to be with you, so that you could drive them all away. But enough of this strain. I am sorry to hear about your bother with American subscribers, it is such a bore being so far away, we must go over there in October together. Have you started your article yet? . . .

Coming back to London, he went out to dinner:

> I compared all the women there with you or rather tried to, but it was impossible for me to do so; you are my idol my precious, and are set up far above anyone else in this world. When I went to bed, I cried out 'Missie! Missie! I love you, are you thinking of me?' were you? I wonder? . . .

Next day, though, he got another letter from Jennie that he didn't like. She reported that she'd heard from the Prince. 'You might have added that you didn't propose to carry out the Prince's suggestion,' George complained. But Jennie was wondering. The Prince, at another spa, was writing to her in a firm but kindly manner. A woman could do pretty much what she liked, he considered, so long as she wasn't mischievous, but a marriage to George would be not only mischievous but foolish, for it would never bring the happiness she fondly imagined. She was old enough to know better. Such advice was doubtless coming to Jennie from all quarters and by every post. When the story reached India, for instance, Mary Curzon wrote to ask whether to send a wedding-present or not: 'And shall you yield to prayer and persuasion then? Jennie solo is so delightful that I am still not reconciled to Jennie duet. . . .' It wasn't only prayer and persuasion, though, that Jennie had to consider. The Prince's advice contained a warning: if she went ahead and married George, she would cease to be his friend. History must have seemed to be repeating itself. The social life of the Prince's set meant even more to Jennie now than it had done in 1876: she certainly did not wish to give it up again.

Jack, meanwhile, was more concerned about Winston's romance with Pamela Plowden, a girl he had been pursuing for some time. He told George his doubts:

> Jack dined with me last night, and opened his heart to me about Miss Pamela, he doesn't often talk so I was pleased with his confidence. He doesn't think much of her, in fact he dislikes her, he says she is such an awful humbug, and is the same to three other men as she is to Winston. He tells me they went about at Blenheim as if they were engaged, in fact several people asked if it was so. I am sorry for Winston, as I dont think he would be happy with her, I cant make her out, she is certainly very clever, in a doubtful sense of the word. . . .

When Jennie returned from Aix, she and George went again to stay at Duart Castle on the Isle of Mull. There she seems to have told George quite definitely that marriage was off. He was desolate:

Duart Castle, Craignure,
Isle of Mull
Sept 12th, '99

My darling little Missie,

I feel so low & miserable this morning, and I miss you terribly. I wonder what you feel. I hope you were not tossed last night, I heard the wind blowing as I lay awake. The little dog Jennie came to sleep in my room last night; can you guess why? They are all going to Oban for the games, but I am going stalking instead, more amusing I think. You are lucky in having a fine day to go through the canal, I have always heard it is quite lovely. The London papers have had a miscarriage today so I dont know how matters are going in London. Bless you my darling Missie, I love you very dearly & will stick to you even if we dont get married. I cant write more now I'm too mis.

Your loving
Georgie

He went on being 'mis'. Two days later he wrote:

. . . . Oh my little Missie I have been so depressed since we parted; to think that all our arrangements and little plans for the future, as man & wife, have burst like a soap bubble, and nothing will ever remain but a pleasant recollection in some ways, and very bitter in others, of what has proved to be nothing but a 'Castle in the air'. Little Missie I would have made you very happy despite all drawbacks, but if you think I would have injured you socially, and made you a subject of ridicule, had I married you, then you are right to let matters remain as they are. I love you dearly and shall never love another woman as much. Please God the day will never come when you will regret the decision you have come to.

She seems to have regretted it at once, for she sent him a telegram, to which he replied:

WISH IT COULD BE SO TOO LATE BOATS ARE BURNT HAVE WRITTEN MY RELATIONS YOUR OWN FAULT GEORGE.

NOTES

1. Chairman of the local Conservative association.
2. Horatio William Bottomley, 1860–1933, journalist, company promoter, fraud, bankrupt, eventually imprisoned: MP for South Hackney 1906–12 as a Liberal, and 1918–22 as an Independent.
3. Mrs Rosamund Angharad Greaves, only child of Edward Lloyd of Flintshire. She married secondly Lord Henry Grosvenor. She lived in Scotland.
4. Young Scotch turkeys.
5. Colonel Arthur Paget, married to Jennie's old American friend, Minnie Stevens. He became a general in 1900.

I I

WAR

While this private drama was being enacted, a public one, of rather greater moment, was just beginning in South Africa. The Prince of Wales had been right: war was coming with the Boers. In October, George's Battalion of the Scots Guards was sent out under the command of Lord Methuen. At his interview with Colonel Paget George had given a verbal undertaking not to marry or become officially engaged before setting out. For this he was well rewarded. He wrote to Jennie on 6 October:

> I had a pleasant surprise when I went to the Orderly room this morning, but dont say anything about it, as it is not definitely settled. Col Paget has recommended me to a general as his aide-de-camp, he wouldn't tell me who he was, but only that he was certain to get a command, and he had asked him (Arthur P) to recommend someone. Of course I accepted at once. It would be far better to [see] the fun from a horse than from the flat of one's feet. Ah Missie I am glad to go out as a soldier, but I do hate leaving you my precious one. I saw Winston today in St James Str, dont tell him I said so, but he looked just a young dissenting parson, hat brushed the wrong way, and at the back of his head, awful old black coat and tie, he is a good fellow but very untidy. . . .

George was busy buying his kit, and looking spick and span. He didn't realize that pressure had been brought from a royal quarter to get him his job as A.D.C. He soon found out:

> My dear George West,   October 15th, '99
>   I had the opportunity of speaking to Lord Methuen at the station yesterday when I took leave of Sir Redvers Buller, and strongly urged him to take you on his staff, so I hope it may be all satisfactorily settled.

I envy you going out on active service with so fine a battalion, and wish you good luck and a safe return home.

Yours very sincerely,
Albert Edward

Jennie had written rather crossly to the Prince, calling him a fair-weather friend, and pointing out the great sacrifice she was making in not marrying George. Perhaps the Prince wished to prove how deep his friendship really was. He was not only helping George in his military career, he was making sure he would mix with senior officers with the right ideas. When George came back, with any luck he'd have forgotten all about his romance with Jennie, and all risk of danger and ridicule would vanish.

George's regiment set off to South Africa from Chelsea Barracks at five o'clock on a dark autumn morning. There was a slight fog, and the streets were, in any case, poorly lit. Wives and sweethearts joined in the march, linking arms with the soldiers, and when they reached Westminster Bridge, on their way to Waterloo, there was a large crowd waiting to see them off. Bottles of whisky were pressed on the delighted troops, and in the semi-darkness it was difficult to prevent the march becoming a disorganized rabble. But at Waterloo itself the police prevented civilians going in with the soldiers, and there were many heart-rending farewells.

Though George went off, as a young soldier should, with excitement and expectation, his own parting with Jennie had been pretty heart-rending, too:

S.S. *Nubia*
4.45 p.m.
My own darling little Missie,   21st Oct. '99
   I did so love getting your two dear little notes before I started, I shall treasure them, and they will be always in the pocket next to my heart till we meet again. My precious one it was agony simply agony leaving you, but Thank God as you say, I know you love me dearly and it is returned as you, in your turn, must realize.

   The ship was just starting when Mother came on board, she got out at Southampton and came to the docks on chance of seeing me, I wish in a way she had not as it upset me very much, she looked so ill & worn. Oh my precious little Missie how I do love you, you never have been more loved in all your life; your sweet face was such a comfort to me today, I am glad you came. I must not be low but its very hard having to be parted from THE one thing that is most joyful and beloved in ones life. I am sending this by the Pilot, who gets off when we pass the Needles. We touch at St Vincent, a port in the Cape Verde Islands. Au revoir my own darling precious little Missie, I *do* worship you so, and loathe parting from you, but it is fate, and I will return soon to your dear arms. Bless you again my true love, I love you I love you

your own loving
George

George took his own pony with him, called Toby, but the voyage was long and tedious. It took twenty-eight days to Cape Town, but the monotony was relieved, to some extent, by the fact that Alfred Rothschild had generously presented the Officers' Mess with twenty cases of 1887 Perrier Jouet.

Those were the days. Winston was also on his way to South Africa, and also equipped with adequate supplies of liquor—including eighteen bottles of ten-year-old Scotch whisky, six of Very Old Eau de Vie, and twelve of Rose's Cordial Lime Juice, perhaps for hangovers. He had refused to intervene in Jennie's situation, though Colonel Cornwallis-West had obviously urged him to do so. 'After all I don't believe you will marry', he told Jennie. 'My idea is that the family pressure will crush George.' Meanwhile he had become War Correspondent for the *Morning Post*. Jack, too, though Jennie didn't know it, was planning to escape from the life he so disliked in the City and go to the war.

Deprived of her menfolk, Jennie found *The Anglo-Saxon Review* not nearly sufficient occupation, and getting restless again, she wondered how she could contribute something to the war. Mrs A. A. Blow, an American lady who had lived in South Africa, had the perfect answer: Americans in Britain could not do anything to participate in the war directly, as America was neutral. But why not send a hospital-ship? Furthermore, there was an American millionaire ready to provide one. Jennie responded enthusiastically, as the official report made clear:

It was on the 25th of October, 1899, that at her invitation the following ladies met at her house: Lady Essex,[1] Mrs Blow, Mrs Joseph Chamberlain,[2] Mrs Arthur Paget, and Mrs Ronalds, to formulate this generous idea, and to further cement with their active sympathy for the wounded that bond of brotherhood which exists between the Anglo-Saxon Nations, by establishing a fund destined to equip and maintain the Hospital Ship *Maine*, which vessel was generously lent to the British Government by The Atlantic Transport Company through Mr Bernard Baker, the Chairman, who has from the first contributed very largely towards the expenses, showing in this practical manner his public spirit and international sympathy in the cause of humanity. Thus, entirely at the cost of Americans not only in the United States, but those residing in England and other countries, has this vessel been sent on her errand of mercy in charge of American Doctors, Nurses and Orderlies selected for the Committee by Mrs Whitelaw Reid.[3]

Jennie was made Chairman of the General Committee, with Mrs Blow as Hon. Sec., and Mrs Ronalds as Hon. Treasurer. The last was a very old acquaintance of Jennie's indeed, from the days when Leonard Jerome had got her to sing for him in his private theatre in New York. Fanny Ronalds was a social figure of some eminence, as well as a singer, and in spite of her affair with Leonard, she had manged to remain a friend of Jennie's mother. She had lived in Paris when the Jeromes lived there, and then in London, where she fell in love with Sir Arthur Sullivan, the musical half of the team of Gilbert and Sullivan. Jennie had known her all her life.

With splendid American energy, the ladies set about raising £30,000 ($150,000). Subscriptions were implored, and firms badgered to provide free supplies. Lily Langtry gave a concert in New York, Mrs Ronalds raffled a diamond and moonstone pendant, 'entertainments' were put on at Claridges and the Hotels Cecil and Carlton, and Barnum and Bailey donated a performance at Olympia. The Queen took a great interest, and sent a Union Jack, presented to the ship by the Duke of Connaught, her third son, and the close friend of Leonie. The Committee had hoped for a Stars and Stripes from President McKinley, too, but there was strong anti-British feeling in America about the war, and the *Maine* had to go without. When the American nurses and doctors came, Jennie took them to Windsor, and the Queen talked to her for half an hour, asking about everything, and who had helped most on the Committee. Jennie wanted to say that Clara and Leonie had been a great help, but to Clara's great annoyance, she hesitated, and the chance was lost. Two days later she was bidden to dine and sleep at Windsor, and was again closely questioned by the Queen.

That there were great ructions on a committee of rich and self-willed women was only to be expected, but in spite of jealousies and back-biting the target was exceeded by more than a fifth. In the middle of all the work, Jennie suddenly heard that Winston had been captured. She received a deluge of sympathetic letters and telegrams; among them was one from Charles Kinsky, now in St Petersburg, and another from Patsy Cornwallis-West. Patsy remained friendly. Perhaps, like others, she believed the affair was over. Rosebery wrote, for instance: 'May I say without impertinence that I am sure you are wise after the crisis of which you spoke to me at Guisachan, to throw yourself into work and such good work as the *Maine*?' But Jennie had not forgotten George, nor he her. He wrote on 3 December with alarming news:

> Orange River,
> South Africa
>
> My own darling little Missie,   December 3rd, '99
>
> Stirring events have happened since I wrote to you a week ago, but, as is usually the case people in England have a better knowledge of facts than we have who are actually taking part in the campaign. I wrote to you last from Enseling siding, and two days afterwards we had the hardest fight that has taken place in any part of the colony since the war began. 13 hours hard fighting was the time the battle of Modder River lasted, and I can tell you it was a near shave, at one time I thought we should be driven back, but thanks to our Artillery we just managed to win the day. I went out with my General & his staff at 4-0 a.m. and we reconnoitred their position, at least as far as we could. It is impossible to see these Boers they hide themselves so successfully, and they are so cute that they will not open fire on our reconnoitring patrols, as by so doing they would give away their numbers and position. The other day, we could only see a few on our right flank partially concealed in an old reservoir and in some trenches, as we could find no others, the General naturally concluded that the village of Modder River, on our left, was unoccupied, and therefore ordered the whole of his infantry to advance across an absolutely open plain, they got within 800 yards of their goal when suddenly a terrific fire was opened on them, this started at 6.0 a.m. and did not cease till 7 p.m. The men started without breakfast and went the whole day without food, and water, having finished their water long before noon. It was a terribly hard day, and the heat was terrific. I was knocked over by sunstroke at 3-p.m. and dont remember anything till the evening, when I found myself in hospital. I was sent down to De Aar where I remained for four days. I am all right now my darling Missie so dont be anxious, and am off to the front again first thing tomorrow. Oh my own little Sweet Missie I am so sick of this war, three big battles in six days is enough for any man, and I think most of us think the same. I want to be back to you my sweetheart, my love for you grows stronger every day. So far Thank God I am safe, but one can never tell what may happen to one. Well Missie

mine if anything does, you will always know that you are the only woman I have ever given my whole heart & soul to, and that I love you better than anything in the whole world. How busy you must be Missie mine, what with your ship, which appears to be a great success, and your Maggie. I do hope this number will turn out well, I expect to hear from you as to the returns of the last number. I wonder if you will be able to come out here I wouldn't risk the *Review* not being a success if I was you, but my darling I would love to see you, and to have you to nurse me if I was wounded. This will reach you about Christmas time, I wonder if you will be at Blenheim again. How I do long to be with you, and hold you tight in my arms once more. I am yours precious one absolutely, and I know you are mine. I heard a cynic the other day say 'I like women and admire them they are so much more sensible than we are, They may like one man best, but they are quite happy with some one else when the other is away, and dont fret like men do over one woman.' I rose like a trout, and of course got awfully chaffed. Still in my case I was right wasn't I my precious one. Well my little Missie I must stop now as it is bed-time. God bless you my own darling. I kiss your sweet lips many many times,

> your own loving
> George

I have re-read this and it seems such a stupid letter, but I have so little time. Bless you darling.

George's sunstroke was entirely due to his own carelessness. He had been galloping about with messages on Toby, and got roundly cursed by a senior officer for riding too close to the General, thereby attracting enemy fire and risking the General's life. George had therefore handed the pony to his orderly and lain down and kept quiet. When the General and his staff moved off, neither Toby nor the orderly could be found, and George started to wander about in search of them. He had forgotten to fill his water-bottle. In the intense heat this was fatal, and he rapidly became delirious. Luckily someone found him and brought him back to camp. But it was a serious case of sunstroke.

George's letter makes it clear that Jennie had been planning to come out with the *Maine* for some time. In her *Reminiscences* she said that she felt the Committee ought to be represented on board by 'a person of authority without a salary', but it seems clear that personal considerations played their part, too. She had nothing to keep her in England,

and every reason to go, gossip or no gossip. The ship sailed on 23 December. That day, though, Jennie received a telegram:

INVALIDED PROBABLY RETURNING ALMOST IMMEDIATELY REPEAT MOTHER GEORGE.

It was a staggering blow. What had happened was that George had underestimated the seriousness of his illness and discharged himself from hospital too soon. He had gone back to the front. But after a few days he fell ill again, and was sent to Cape Town, and from there ordered home. The same day as his telegram he wrote:

> Sanatorium,
> Claremont
> My darling little Missie,   December 23rd, 1899
> I am too miserable for words. I have had no communication from you letter, or otherwise for three weeks, the last I got was a cable dated Nov 30th and nothing has come for me from you by the last three mails, although they have sent our letters here straight, & not up to the front; as is proved by my having received my other letters. Oh Missie darling what does it mean? I have been so C.D. and wanted your letters to cheer me up so much. I have sent you three cables in the last ten days, and have had no answer, the last one was selfish I confess. I wanted you to postpone your departure until I arrived, it was horrid of me to want it, when you are coming out to nurse the sick & wounded. Now I dont know when you leave, or whether there is a chance of my seeing you before you start. Oh please my little Missie dont stay too long here, come back to me do!! You dont realize how much I love you, and what it means to me to be going home feeling I shall not be greeted by your dear lips. I hope to be fit by April perhaps, & then I may come out here again if the war is still raging, so we may miss each other again, which would be awful. The doctors had a board on me the other day, and gave me six months sick-leave, they frightened me rather too. But they are only army doctors, & I shall get the best advice when I get home. Sun-stroke is a horrid thing, especially in my case, as I feel it more owing to the results of the concussion I had two years ago.
> I would give 10 years of my life & more to find you in London when I return. Missie I am so miserable, & want you with me so so much. You do love me as much as you used to, dont you darling? I am so glad to see in todays paper that Winston has escaped, and has left Delagoa Bay for Durban. I expect when you come out here you wont (or at

least the *Maine*) wont be kept here permanently, but will be used to convey wounded from Natal to the Base Hospital here, in the same way as the Hospital Ship *Trojan* is used.

Well Good bye my darling little Missie I love you better than anything in the whole world, Please precious dont stay out here too long, I want you *so so* much, ever your loving
George

write to me to Newlands Manor.

Jennie had learned of Winston's escape from the prisoner-of-war camp on 14 December, but it was only the day before she sailed that she heard of his safe arrival in Delagoa Bay. Though she must have felt mightily relieved, she set off in a glum mood about George. She wrote to Leonie on the 24th:

Hospital Ship *Maine*
Dec 24th, '99
Sunday

Dearest Snippy—Here we are off Dover—the Pilot will take this— There was such a fog we could not get out of the basin until this morning—It is awfully cold & wet on board—but I dare say we shall get all right—That fellow from Warings[4] altho' he was here days—left everything undone—no table (I am using my bridge table) no chair no glass—no hooks up—We are however settling everything before we get into rough water—You may imagine that I did not feel over lively last night—I had a cable from George saying that he was invalided home & was probably leaving immediately—You must promise to see him, & write to me all he says—I am so devoted to him that it would be a terrible thing for me if I knew he blamed me for going—Heaven knows this is no pleasure—I *had to go*. Write to me fully—& look after George. The fog is so thick we have once more come to a standstill— We are all rather glad, as it will give us a chance of unpacking. I will do my duty by the ship—but shall be back as soon as I can—Bless you darling & a Happy Xmas.

Jennie and George must have passed each other somewhere off Africa.

NOTES

1. Adela Grant, wife of the 7th Earl of Essex.

2. Mary Endicott, daughter of a former US Secretary of War. Chamberlain's third wife.

3. Elizabeth Mills Reid, wife of Whitelaw Reid, editor of the *New York Tribune,* and Ambassador to Britain 1905–12. Mrs Reid was on the board of the Nurses Training School at Bellevue, New York City, which provided the *Maine's* nurses.

4. S. J. Waring & Sons Ltd, and Gillow & Co., two leading house-furnishers, had just amalgamated to form the firm of Waring & Gillow, Ltd.

12

THE *MAINE*

Jennie wrote about her expedition with the *Maine* no less than three times. First there was her official report to the *Maine* Committee in London. In it she described in detail the operation of the wards, the hours of duty, the method of issue of medicines and linen, the treatment of patients, and even the 'substantial' lunch with which they were provided on discharge—sandwiches, cheese, jam and lime-juice or Rosbach water. She also gave her report on the staff and crew: everyone was splendid, but she thought nursing sisters were probably a mistake on a hospital ship, in spite of the great comfort a woman could give a man in pain. The four on the *Maine* and their Superintending Sister had worked well under trying circumstances. She went on to list all the distinguished visitors they'd had, and to describe the concerts on the poop deck. Eleanor Warrender, sister of Hugh, had gone out with Jennie: she earned praise for her management of the ship's library. (Her unmentioned activities as Jennie's right hand woman must have been rather more arduous.) Religious observances had been kept up: Jennie herself had played the organ at Sunday services.

Jennie felt she had to explain why she had decided to bring the ship home when she did. On arrival in South Africa she discovered to her horror that the authorities wanted the *Maine* to fill up with wounded and take them straight back to England. This was not at all what the Committee had had in mind: the *Maine* was not a floating ambulance, it was a proper hospital, with an operating theatre and surgeons. Jennie had to fight hard against official pressure, but she knew everyone, of course, in South Africa as in England, and with the help of Sir Walter Hely-Hutchinson, the Governor of Natal, and Sir Redvers Buller, she was able three times to frustrate efforts to send the *Maine* home. It stayed in Durban, in fact, for two months, fulfilling its original purpose. But after the relief of Ladysmith on 28 February 1900, there were a great number of sick and wounded to be taken back to England, and Jennie agreed to go. She was partly influenced by the desire to gain the *éclat* of being the first hospital ship to return with the heroes of Lady-

smith, which had been besieged for four months; also, the climate was
beginning to tell. Altogether 28 Officers and 326 Other Ranks had been
treated, and 12 Officers and 151 NCOs and men were brought home.
There had been only three deaths.

Jennie's report is efficient and business-like. Her second version of the
story, written at the same time, but at much greater length, is more 'literary'. It is in the form of a series of letters, which she published in *The
Anglo-Saxon Review* in June. Here she describes in graphic detail the
storms the *Maine* passed through on its way to South Africa, the
difficulty of trying to play the piano on the high seas, and the charm of
Las Palmas, where the *Maine* put in. Jennie thought it was like Mon-
terey, in California, which she had visited on a much less happy voyage
with Randolph. Soon they were at Cape Town, given a berth inside
next to a collier. On shore, Jennie went to the telegraph office:

> Three little women came up, their anxious faces in marked contrast
> to their befeathered, bedraggled attire, and asked me to write a tele-
> gram for them. 'Come at once, hopeless', was the pathetic message.

Not too encouraging a start for someone on a mission of mercy, but un-
daunted, and after an inspection by Lord Roberts, the Field Marshal,
the ship went on to Durban, passing through an astonishing storm with
hailstones the size of small plums. At Cape Town Jennie had been
joined by Jack: she makes no comment on her feelings on finding him
there, though she had left him apparently safe behind in England.[1] He
needed a passage to Durban, so he went on the *Maine*. Winston was
waiting to greet them at Durban, and all three, with Miss Warrender,
went to stay with Sir Walter Hely-Hutchinson at Pietermaritzburg.
There Jack and Winston left for the war, while Jennie inspected hospitals and spoke to the wounded, before hurrying back to greet the first patients to arrive on board. Jennie was not, of course, a nurse, but she
could write letters for the injured and illiterate:

> I was much amused by the letters which those unable to write dic-
> tated to me, generally beginning 'Dear Father and Mother, I hope this
> finds you as well as it leaves me'—then came a great scratching of
> heads and biting of fingers until I would suggest that a description of
> how they were wounded would start them off again—'Won't you send
> your love to anyone?' I asked. 'Not out of the family', with a reproving
> look, was my answer. One very gallant Tommy, who lay with a patch
> over his eye, an inflamed cheek, and a broken arm, asked me to add to

his letter—'the sister which is a writing of this is very nice.' The compliment was fully appreciated.

There were so many visitors to the ship, that Jennie had to limit them to specific hours, with great regret. She was against red-tape in all its forms, and that in military medicine was redder and tougher than most. She became very angry about wounded men's clothing:

> On the subject of clothing it is astonishing how little the authorities have been able to cope with it; at the front many of the men were nearly naked, their khaki hanging on them in shreds, and what else could be expected, the uniform being made of such abominable stuff to wear and having to be worn for perhaps five or six months. But when one thinks of the thousands and thousands that have been spent on clothing for the hospitals, not only by the Government but by private individuals, it seems incredible that the sick and wounded should be allowed to leave a hospital to be drafted to another, or to a hospital ship, in the tattered garments they came with, brought in straight from the battlefield. I saw with my own eyes, among a party of wounded who were being transferred from a tug to the *Maine* and the *Nubia,* a man whose khaki trousers were conspicuous by their absence, both legs having been cut off, a pocket handkerchief being tied round one of his poor wounded legs. This man probably had been through several hospitals, and each time sent off again in his rags. Surely a reserve of uniforms or ordinary clothing might be kept for extreme cases such as this, and the principal medical officers allowed a little discretion in the matter. But when I discussed this point with one of the authorities, he said it would be an impossibility. 'You might as well have an office for recording the wishes and messages of the dying'. What a happy hunting-ground the red-tape fiend has in time of war! He sits and gloats on all occasions.

Jennie hoped that young people, unencumbered with ideas drawn from past and irrelevant wars, would improve things. She was an idealist.

Once the ship was operating properly, Jennie felt free to visit the front line. The necessary passes and permissions were granted, and Hely-Hutchinson lent his private railway carriage. Jennie was thrilled by every aspect of the expedition: on the way up, for instance, the train was searched for spies. She was flattered to find her reputation had gone before her. A gun had been named after her already, and at 5 a.m. she was woken by an officer in the Seaforth Highlanders who gave her a cup of coffee in the dawn, and poured out all his troubles. When the train passed the site of the ambush in which Winston had been captured, the guard rushed to point out the wreck of the armoured train. Jennie looked at the graves of those killed in the action, and thanked God Winston was not among them. Then they were at Chieveley, and the front:

> General Barton and an A.D.C. met us at the station. We were taken all over the Camp—a wonderful sight. The weather-beaten and in many cases haggard-looking men, their soiled worn uniforms hanging on their spare figures; the horses, picketed in lines or singly, covered with canvas torn in strips to keep the flies off; the khaki-painted guns, the ambulance waggons with their train of mules, and above all the dull booming of 'Long Tom' made us realise that here was war! We sat down on the outskirts of the camp near a sham gun guarded over by a middy of the *Terrible*.² Here, too, was the gun which the bluejackets had named after me. Six miles off, through our glasses, we could see Colenso and the enemy's camp, the white tents being the ones they had taken from us. The whole panorama spread out, a grand sight. It was thrilling. I longed to be a man and take some part in the fighting, but then I remembered my red cross.

Breakfast was provided by the 7th Fusiliers—eggs, bacon, kidneys and strawberry jam. It might be South Africa, it might be the front, but by God, a Fusilier likes his British breakfast. The flies were terrible, though. Afterwards, Jennie was installed in the General's tent, to write notes to Jack and Winston:

> I looked round with curiosity and interest at the general's quarters—a camp bed, a washing basin, a box, nothing more. Sitting on a camp stool with my feet on a tin box I was scribbling away, when a rider galloped up, calling out with a cheery voice, 'General, are you there?' His look of blank astonishment when he caught sight of me was most amusing. A woman in the camp and in the general's tent! It was a novelty! I explained. After a few laughing remarks he rode off.

His day must have been made; but alas, he was to be killed the next week.

On her return journey, Jennie visited the remount depot, and saw 2000 horses, most of which had just arrived from South America:

> What a fate! to be penned up for days on a rolling ship, then crammed into an open truck in a blazing sun, to be taken out, stiff,

sore and dazed, given two days' rest, and then sent up to the front only to be food for Boer bullets! Poor things. So understanding. Such good friends. The hardships they have to undergo, and the lingering death many have and will meet, is one of the most hideous features of the war.

Back on board the *Maine* Jennie put such thoughts from her. She pinned up a large map and stuck flags in it to show the patients how the war was going. Then she was entertained by Captain Percy Scott on board HMS *Terrible*, though not without a soaking first. 'I preferred getting wet up to my waist—being caught in a huge wave—to being hauled on board in a wicker basket like a bale of cotton,' Jennie said. It was there that she heard of the relief of Ladysmith.

As soon as they were told of it such a grand cheer went up from the men, and another equally hearty when their captain informed them that they were to have grog all round. Lights were flashed—messages heliographed from Captain Percy Scott's electric shutter—to all the ships in the harbour; the band played itself tired, and the men sang themselves hoarse; and at last, after a bouquet of fireworks, we went to bed.

Jennie was able to visit Ladysmith after the siege had been lifted. She went up there with Winston and Miss Warrender:

One must see it all to realise the stupendous difficulties, the harsh impossible ground to get over, how it had to be gained inch by inch, the smallest mistake costing hundreds of men. The masses of shell and bullets on either side of the line, the dead horses, and the newly made graves, testified to the fierceness of the struggle. At one point we crossed a small bridge built up with sandbags, over which our men had to run singly under a terrible fire from three kopjes; we lost sixty-six men here. After two hours we came to an open plain glistening with the discarded tins of the advancing army, and further on we went through Intombi Camp, broiling in the blazing sun, a place of desolation and misery, and so on into Ladysmith. Blinding dust up to your ankles, scorching sun, shut up empty houses, an expression of resigned martyrdom on everyone's face—such was my first impression of Ladysmith.

Things soon cheered up, though. After making 'a hasty and apologetic toilette', Jennie dined with Sir Redvers Buller in a tent overlooking the town. Jennie brought back a souvenir—a shellcase from the gun named after her, with an inscription telling her of the damage she'd done.

Then it was time to go home. The *Maine* filled up with wounded and set off, stopping at St Helena to water. Jennie was much impressed with the grimness of Napoleon's place of exile. She thought he must have found it torture. The ship put in again at Madeira, and arrived at Southampton on 23 April. It had been away exactly four months.

Jennie's final version of the story was written seven years later, for her *Reminiscences,* and is mainly a précis of the letters in *The Anglo-Saxon,* with one or two additions too forthright, perhaps, for 1900. The behaviour of some army reserve nurses whom the *Maine* had carried from Cape Town to Durban disgusted her, for instance. Some of them had actually brought *maids* with them. Jennie, who can never have gone anywhere before in her life without a maid, was superbly scornful. But it is what she did not put in any of her versions which is most interesting. She never mentioned, for instance, that Jack had been one of her wounded. From her brief diary we find that she heard about it on 12 February, and went on the 14th to Pietermaritzburg to meet him. He carried a letter from Winston:

Chieveley Camp,
Natal

My dearest Mamma,   13 February, 1900

    It is a coincidence that one of the first patients on board the *Maine* should be your own son. Jack, who brings you this letter, will tell you all about the skirmish and the other action he took part in. He behaved very well and pluckily and the Adjutant, the Colonel and his squadron leader speak highly of his conduct. There was for ten minutes quite a hot fire. And we had about ten men hit. Jack's wound is slight though not officially classed as such. The doctors tell me that he will take a month to recover and I advise you not to allow him to go back before he is quite well. He is unhappy at being taken off the board so early in the game and of course it is a great nuisance, but you may be glad with me that he is out of harm's way for a month. There will be a great battle in a few days and his presence—though I would not lift a finger to prevent him—adds much to my anxiety when there is fighting. . . .

Poor Jack! It is hard being the younger brother of a genius. Winston had seen action all round the world, and been under fire more times than he could remember. Now Jack, who had wanted to go into the army, but had a bad eye, and anyway Jennie couldn't find the money—

who had been made to go into the City, which he hated—who had jumped at the chance to come to war—Jack was wounded in his first skirmish, and Winston was glad he was out of the way, he was such a worry to him. He was something of a worry to Jennie, too, it seems. While Jennie was enjoying herself on the *Terrible* she sent a head-matronly signal: TELL MY SON HE IS UNDER MARTIAL LAW AND HAS GOT TO REMAIN IN BED. He stayed with the *Maine,* convalescing, till she sailed from Durban on her way home, when he returned to his regiment.

Another person who is not mentioned anywhere by Jennie is, of course, George. He felt rather jealous when he heard that Jack was one of Jennie's patients:

I was so fearfully sorry to get your cable yesterday morning an-nouncing the fact that poor old Jack had been wounded. Thank Heavens it is not serious, still I hope he has been sent down to the base so that you can nurse him. I envy him darling being nursed by you. I wish it had been my lot. . . .

George was feeling extremely sorry for himself. The sun-stroke had turned out to have very serious side-effects, and the situation at home was far from easy. He wrote Jennie a series of long plaintive letters, ask-ing her to hurry home:

> Newlands Manor,
> Lymington, Hants
> January 18th, 1900

Oh my precious little Missie, I am so miserable at your not being in England, but I know I am selfish, & I suppose you had to go, as you had been more or less the leading spirit in the organisation of the whole ship. I shall never forget my feelings when I got your wire at St Vincent and I am ashamed to say, I thought hard things about you. That if you really cared for me, you would have realized how being ill, I naturally leant all the more to you, and wanted your tender love & companionship; also that if you had wanted to see me you could have gone by the mail steamer, and caught up the *Maine* as I suggested to you in my last cable, inasmuch as your services on the journey out, could not have been required. But now that I have received all your letters I realize that you couldn't very well help your-self; and I am ashamed of ever having had unkind thoughts about my little Missie. Of course darling you know I will wait patiently till you return, and then fly to your dear arms, I shall count the days till the time arrives that I can press you to my heart, and lift up your dear face to kiss your sweet lips. Oh little Missie mine dont stay long out at the Cape I implore you. When I get you again I shall stick fast to you like a limpet. You can count on me to be absolutely true & faithful to you in every act & thought till you return.

I am better considerably than I was; but still not up to much. I am sorry to say that the sun-stroke I had has affected my heart, I had two attacks of 'Angina Pectoris' on the ship coming home; my word doesn't it hurt, I thought I was going to die once. I am going up to London next week to see a good doctor. I haven't told mother or any of my female relations, as they get so easily alarmed, so dont say anything about it to anyone, as it is certain to get back. There is no cause for alarm Missie mine, as every day I get better so *you* need not be frightened. I heard from Leonie on my arrival, I shall go & see her when I am in London. You poor darling what an awful tossing you must have got; I never heard of such an experience, 'hove to for 48 hours' in 'the Bay' sounds too dreadful.

Poor little Patsy looks very C.D. her nerves seem to have suffered in my absence. Naturally they are all thankful to get me back, even in a somewhat debilitated condition. The Former (Patsy) goes off to Daisy tomorrow.

We are anxiously expecting news of Bullers advance in Natal, he ought to have fought a big engagement by now, pray God it is a Victory.

Come back soon to me my precious Missie, I love you so so dearly, and miss you more than you can imagine, its hateful being in England without you.

Your ever loving
George

The tone did not alter:

50 Park Street,
Grosvenor Square, W.
February 2nd, 1900

Oh Missie darling if ever there was a man who wanted the one creature on earth he loved to be with him I am he.

I have just received your wire redirected from Milford-on-sea, saying you are going to remain at Durban a month, your last wire said you were returning as soon as possible, so I thought & hoped, that when once you had arrived at Durban and got things started on board the *Maine* you would think of returning, I felt so much happier than I did before I thought I should [see] my own darling little Missie by the end of February at least, and had thought out all sorts of plans. My doctor has ordered me to go abroad in about 6 weeks time, and I thought how heavenly it would have been to have gone with you somewhere if you would have come. And now all my pleasant ideas & plans are frustrated by your wire, if you leave Durban say the beginning of March you wont be home before the beginning of April, and may miss me altogether as by that time I may be well enough to rejoin my battalion. If you had been ill, and I had been obliged to leave you I should not have wasted a moment in flying back to you at the very first opportunity, but it seems you are different or have altered.

I love you Missie darling as I never have loved, or shall ever love another woman, I have given you all I had to give, and all that was best in me, and shall never regret it until the day of my death. I cant tell you what a trying time I am having at home, when my mother was there it was alright, but now she has gone to be with Daisy. I am alone with my Father who never loses an opportunity of dropping hints about financial difficulties and how easily they could be overcome if I married an heiress, he also takes a pleasure in abusing all your friends, though he knows he dare not mention your name thus to me. Then again I am so fearfully depressed at having to leave all my pals in the regiment up at the front, I feel so useless to them & the regt., not being able to stand a months hard work. And lastly and worst of all your not being here makes it fifty thousand times worse. I meant to write you an amusing letter this mail, but your wire has made [me] feel so wretched. Forgive me *darling,* PRECIOUS Missie mine, if you felt as ill and as depressed as I do you would understand. I only came up for the day to see the doctor, whose account of me was not very satisfactory, and to see H.R.H. who asked me searching questions which I refused to answer. Ah Missie come back to your George who loves you more than you were ever before loved, and who wants you so.

I feel so *selfish* but must write as I do,

George

The Prince of Wales was trying to find out whether absence had made either Jennie's or George's heart less fond. He not only saw and cross-questioned George, he wrote several times to Jennie in South Africa about what he woundingly referred to as her flirtation. On receiv-

ing telegrams from George like this, Jennie must have seriously thought
of giving him up:

SEE NEWSPAPERS MAINE LEAVING IMMEDIATELY YET YOU REMAINING
DURBAN THIS IS YOUR EFFORT TO RETURN

GEORGE

He quickly apologized. Life wasn't easy, he was ill and irritable, and his
only fun was making a golf-links in the park to while away the time till
her return.

On her way home to this importunate lover, Jennie busied herself
writing her report and her article for *The Anglo-Saxon,* which had been
carrying on perfectly well without her. At Madeira she learned of the
Committee's plans for the *Maine.* She wrote to Winston, who was supposed to pass the letter on to Jack:

> The ship is coming out again within a week of arriving as we have
> plenty of money—I am much worried as Leonie is going to have an in-
> fant the 1st week of June & as she has not had one for 11 years & is
> always rather bad—I hate being away—She is counting on me—Yet I
> hate leaving the Ship—tho' HRH. & everyone seems to take it for
> granted that I am not going again & that I shall have done enough—
> Bless you my darlings. . . .

She had asked Leonie to look after George while she was away, and
Leonie had done so to the extent of enraging George's father:

> I am aware that you have assisted Lady Randolph Churchill in her
> insane infatuation for my son—because a telegram signed 'Melanie',[3]
> which I understand is your name, fell into my hands in which you
> invited him to meet the hospital ship *Maine* on its arrival at South-
> ampton.
>
> I wish seriously to ask you if you consider a marriage which I am
> told is again talked of between Lady Randolph and my son can possi-
> bly lead to the happiness of either? To begin with she is older than his
> own mother. She will lose the name in which she is best known to the
> world and its rank and position and she will find herself married to a
> young man of such an impressionable nature that only a few weeks
> ago he proposed marriage to a young and pretty girl who refused his
> attentions—notwithstanding his protestations of love and his repudia-
> tion of your sister. The life of a couple so ill-assorted is doomed, is
> painful to think of—and the marvel to me is that a woman as talented

Jennie as the Empress Theodora at a ball at Devonshire House.
She later signed the photograph for her son Jack

Mrs Patrick Campbell

Jennie electioneering
with Winston at Oldham

Jennie, in the same dress
and seated at the piano,
with Mlle Janotha,
a German pianist, and
'John Oliver Hobbes'
(Pearl Craigie)

Jennie with Winston in 1912

and experienced as your sister could coolly contemplate it as nothing out of the common.

I can only add that if this marriage takes place, it will estrange the whole of my family from my son and so I have told him.

Had George really proposed to someone else? It seems hard to believe. And telegrams do not usually 'fall into' people's hands—people pick them up deliberately. George was right to be wary of his family's snooping. At any rate, the row between him and his father may have been responsible for his failure to come, as promised, to meet Jennie at Southampton:

> Ruthin Castle,
> N. Wales.

My precious little Missie,   April 21st, 1900

I have written to you care of the harbour-master Southampton, to be given to you on your arrival. But in case you dont get it, I am sending this by Leonie to give you on seeing you. I could not allow you to set foot on English soil without receiving a message from me, as I shall not be there myself.

Oh my sweet little Missie the joy of seeing you again and clasping you to me, I *love you* darling I LOVE you. Do send me a wire care of Station Master Rugby, telling me of your arrival, & then I will come straight to you. My train arrives at 5.45. Please Missie Mine lets be quite alone the 1st evening can we do you think? I am counting every hour every minute till we meet.

I am by way of beginning to do duty with the new 3rd battn. on May 1st. I put it off a week, as I want you if possible to come away with me somewhere for that week Do! surely you deserve a holiday. If you cannot, I shall recommence duty at once, as it would not do to stop in London & not do so. Bless you my own, I kiss you a 1000 times.

> Your own devoted
> George

So Jennie was back, and nothing whatever had changed. The long separation—they had not seen each other for six months—had done none of the things devoutly wished by almost everyone except themselves. It seemed they really *must* get married now.

But Jennie still wavered and havered. She decided not to go back to South Africa with the *Maine*, however. Instead she resumed her old social round, dinners and operas and weekends in the country. She could not decide what to do. On 24 May she wrote to Winston:

[I] am more busy than I have ever been—preparing for the 3rd voyage of the *Maine*—finishing my 'Hospital Letters' which Longman is going to publish[4] & trying to cope with bills & bores!—The *Maine* ought to arrive today at Capetown—The Port Medical Officer has been asked to fill her up as quickly as possible—she is to return at once —& go out again—If this trip has not done well without me—I shall probably go out the 3rd voyage—But all my plans are vague—Sometimes I think I may marry G.W. I need not to you go over the old ground—but added to the reasons in favour of it is his extraordinary devotion to me through all these trying times & my absence—Also the fact that it is possible for him to help me in a money way in the future if not at present—There is no doubt that you will never settle down until you have a home of your own, & in the 4 years that I have had this house you have spent about 3 mths in all in it—I mention this to show you why I do not feel that I would be breaking up our home if I *do* marry—But there are so many things against my doing it that I doubt its ever coming off—At the same time do not be astonished if I did—You know what you are to me & how you can *now* & *always* count on me—I am intensely fond of you, & apart from this—my heart goes out to you & I understand you as no other woman ever will—Pamela is devoted to you & if yr love has grown as hers—I have no doubt it is only a question of time for you 2 to marry—What a comfort it will be to you to settle down in comparative comfort—I am sure you are sick of the war & its horrors—You will be able to make a decent living out of your writings, & your political career will lead you to big things—Probably if you married an heiress you would not work half so well—But you may have a chance in America—tho I do not urge you to try—you know I am not mercenary either for myself or you boys— More's the pity! I long to see you & have a good talk—My return home owing to the stupidity of the Committee: was a fiasco—but people are gradually understanding the work I have done, & in any case I have my own consciousness of something accomplished.

That makes it clear that she was not thinking only of herself, or only of her own marriage. Other people were beginning to find the whole subject a bore. At Whitsun, Jennie was supposed to go with George to stay with Daisy Warwick, but she was summoned to Sandringham instead, where she was reported to be 'just back from her hospital ship which had been a boon in South Africa, but fractiously insisting she is going to marry George Cornwallis-West'. George, at Warwick Castle, got more sympathy from a lady he took out in a launch, who said they should simply consider themselves. He asked Daisy if Jennie couldn't have got out of going to Sandringham, and she thought she probably could have done, but it was too late, of course.

If they were beginning to bore their friends, then enough was enough. For Ascot, Jennie went to stay with her old friend Consuelo Yznaga, now Duchess of Manchester: George came too. He hacked over to Pirbright each morning to attend parade, then returned for the racing in the afternoon. On the Thursday of that week, their engagement was announced in the *Daily Telegraph*. At once George received a peremptory order from his commanding officer to go to see him. If he married Jennie, he was told, he would have to leave the regiment. George saw red. Jennie was a friend of Colonel Hamilton's, everybody liked her, there was no rule against subalterns marrying: the ultimatum was an outrage. So he jumped into a hansom and went to see the Adjutant-General of the Army, Sir Evelyn Wood, whom he knew slightly. Wood was on his way to lunch, but let George explain the situation in the cab, and promised to help him. George, however, had gone to the wrong man, for the regimental commander regarded Wood as 'the enemy of the Brigade of Guards', and his intervention was bitterly resented. George was told his presence in the regiment was no longer desired.

He consulted with Jennie, who promptly wrote to Lord Lansdowne, the Secretary of State for War. Lansdowne said George should ignore his Colonel's threats, and as an old friend, wished her all possible happiness. The Commander-in-Chief of the Army, he told her, was entirely on her side. Civil as well as military authority was on Jennie's side by now, too. The Prince of Wales accepted that she was going to marry George, and helped in the crisis. Jennie managed to have a word with him:

Sunday, 8.20

My Precious Beloved, Your dear letter has just arrived, I love it, it was the next best thing to seeing you yourself, and went some way towards making my evening more cheery, although nothing will ever be able to make up for the actual person (your sweet self) not being wherever I am. I am glad H.R.H. is civil, I hope you will be able to have a talk with him this evening. If you do you might suggest I am very anxious to have an interview with him on the subject. But do not like to bother him. I see the Princess of Wales H.S. arrived at Southampton yesterday. I expect your *Maine* going to China will create any amount of envy amongst 'Yeomanry Hospital' *chairmen* & such like!![5] Miss

Warrender came and had a chat with me, she seems nice, but does gabble so, I cant understand half she says. Shelagh & my uncle came but only stopped about 10 minutes. I was not very sorry *entre nous* they are so frivolous.

The doctor does not think I shall be able to go out tomorrow, my cough is very troublesome still. He told me I might come down to the drawing-room so I thought I might as well come down to the library where it is warmer. Oh Missie darling I have been thinking of you all day, & wanting you so, I long to be married, & lay myself out to make the remainder of your life as happy as it lies in my power to do. Bless you my own Beloved Missie, I kiss you 1000 times everywhere.

> Your own devoted
> George

I have been improving my mind by reading a history of France.

Jennie saw to it that George got his interview. The Prince went straight to the point. Did George intend to make the army his profession for the rest of his life, or not? If he did, he should sit tight. If not, there was no point in making enemies of men who had been his friends, he should go on half-pay for six months or a year, and look round to see if there was something else he would rather do. It was eminently sensible advice, and George took it.

Not only was the Prince civil and sensible, his brother, the Duke of Connaught, offered to put the forthcoming marriage before Queen Victoria in its proper light. Meanwhile Jennie had cabled to both Jack and Winston, telling them the news. She followed the cable to Jack with a letter—Winston was already on his way home.

> 35A, Great Cumberland Place, W.
> June 23rd, 1900

My dearest Jack—I hope this will find you with yr face more or less turned towards home—I dined with Cassel last night—& he said he thought that now all danger was over—you had done yr duty by yr country, & that you ought to come home & attend to yr business—I pointed out to him that you might have to stay with the regt. until it disbanded—But perhaps this will shortly take place. It is rather hard on me never to hear one word from either of you boys. At the same time I understand how difficult it must be to find the time, & perhaps the material when one is on the move like you—My darling boy I wonder if you will have had the cable I sent you telling you that I was going to marry George? I also wrote a long letter to Winston on the subject telling him to forward it to you—I cant think what he is about

—I hear he has not written to Pamela for 8 weeks—Now as regards my marriage I should like to tell you all my plans for you & myself—but it must be in a very concise form as time presses—& I have *such* a lot to do—*The Review*—my book—my marriage! I have much to write—Now listen darling boy—I have thought over everything & have come to the conclusion that for *many* reasons—it would be unwise for either you or Winston to live with us once we are married—Knowing how fond I am of you both you will believe that I have not come to this conclusion hastily—It seems hard—& it gives me a pang every time I think of it—but I *know* it is the wisest plan—I shd like you & Winston to have rooms together, which I would furnish for you, & arrange your life as far as material comfort goes to the best of my ability—I need hardly say how *more* than welcome you will always be here—you cld look upon it as yr home for everything but sleeping—George is help-ing me in every way possible to make my income larger by putting my affairs straight—As I wrote to Winston, I hope to be able to make you both independent of me—by giving you a certain amount of capital—Of course this wld have to be worked out when you come of age next year—Meanwhile if all goes well George and I propose getting married very quietly (but not at the Registry Office) on the 28th of July—I have many things to settle & arrange—We shall go to Paris—& then to Aix—& after that here—God bless you—My *darling* boy—You must stand by me—I have, & will, always by you—

> Your loving Mother
> J.R.C.[6]

Jack felt rather abandoned in South Africa, and this letter cannot have done much to raise the low spirits in which he'd written on 2 June:

I am beginning to feel like the prodigal son who is sent away to these horrible colonies with instructions never to be seen or heard of again. . . .

Winston had failed to forward letters as requested. Jennie felt somewhat guilty about Jack, perhaps. She wrote more regularly now. In her letter of 30 June she said:

Winston will be here in time for my wedding if all goes well—It will be very quiet—no breakfast—except for the family—but I won't do it in a 'hole & corner' fashion as tho' I was ashamed of it—I pray from the bottom of my heart that it won't make you unhappy—You know how dearly I love you both—& the thought that it may hurt you—is the

one cloud on my happiness—But you won't grudge me the latter?—
Nothing could exceed George's goodness & devotion—& I think we
shall be very happy—Everything I can do for you I will—Meanwhile
my real friends are most kind—& have given me charming presents—&
they all like him so much that they are reconciled. . . . Leonie has
had a boy—I do so *long* to hear from you & how you are—you must be
rather short of clothing—Best love—

> Your loving Mother
> J.R.C.

When he got the news, Jack did not exactly put Jennie's mind at ease.
He wrote at the end of a letter only 'Good best love to George'. What he
thought, what he said to Winston, what Winston said to him—they neither of them put on paper.

On the morning of her wedding Jennie wrote to Jack once more:

35A, Great Cumberland Place, W.
My darling Jack   July 28th, 1900

   I am more than distressed to think that my letters with the exception of one have not reached you—You must know that your
'Mommer' would not forget you—I wired you & Winston that I was
going to marry George—& here I am actually at the day—I would give
much if you were here & I could give you a big fat kiss & could assure
you with my own lips what you already know—& that is that I love
you & Winston *dearly* & that *no one* can ever come in between us—I
shall always remain your *best* friend & do everything in the world for
you—You both can count on me—I am glad to think you know & like
George—He has behaved like a brick—By next mail I will write & tell
you all about the wedding—Sunny[7] is giving me away & I am well
supported by the Churchill family. People have been most kind &
given us heaps of presents—I want you to come home as soon as you
decently can—Both Winston & I hate to have you away—I have all
sorts of plans for you & want to make yr life as pleasant as possible.
God bless you *my darling boy ever.*

> your loving Mother
> J.R.C.

The marriage took place at St Paul's, Knightsbridge. Winston was
there, but none of the Cornwallis-Wests, to George's intense regret. For
their honeymoon they went first to Broughton Castle, near Oxford,
home of Lord Saye and Sele. From there George wrote to Winston on 30
July:

My dear Winston,

I would have written to you yesterday only there is only one post out, and that is at 8.45 a.m. so you can understand why you received no letter from me this morning.

This is an ideal place for any couple to come to, honey-moon or otherwise, we are most comfortable the best of food, drink and everything, besides a most delightful old rambling weather-beaten, stone-roofed house of the 14th century.

My dear Winston I cannot impress upon you how much I appreciate the line you have taken as regards my marriage to your mother. I have always liked and admired you, but I do so ten times more now. I only wish, as I wrote and told my father, that my family could have taken a leaf out of your book. Nothing could have exceeded the sympathy and kindness which you, and all the Churchills have shewn me. I hope always, as now, to be a real true friend to you, and never to come in between yourself and your mother. If I ever do, which God forbid, you can always refer me to this letter which is a record of the feelings I have in the bottom of my heart towards you and yours. We arrive tomorrow at 2.15 will you order lunch for 3 unless you have another coming. *A demain* my dear friend.

> Always *your* sincere friend
> George C-W

Winston reported on the wedding to Jack next day:

Mamma was married to George West on Saturday and everything went off very well. The whole of the Churchill family from Sunny downwards was drawn in a solid phalanx and their approval ratified the business. The wedding was very pretty and George looked supremely happy in having at length obtained his heart's desire. As we already know each other's views on the subject, I need not pursue it.

After Broughton the newly-weds went to Paris and Belgium and Scotland: the honeymoon, in fact, lasted a couple of months. Staying, as she had so often in the past, at Guisachan, with the Tweedmouths, Jennie decided to leave George there for a few days, while she went and campaigned again for Winston at Oldham. She had been quarrelling with John Lane, the publisher of *The Anglo-Saxon Review,* from early on, and the magazine's failure to make money was worrying: it needed her attention. But Winston begged her to come, so she went. He invited George, too, but no doubt Jennie thought she would be more effective on her own. George wrote to her on 28 September:

Guisachan,
Beauly, N.B.
My beloved little Wife　　　　　　　　Sept. 28th, 1900

I was glad to hear from you today, that you are comfortable, & none the worse for your tiresome journey. Dont overdo it darling will you, for my sake.

I have read yesterdays *Daily Mail,* poor Winston, I can well understand his feelings, & how exasperated he must be.

My portmanteau has been found, and where do you think at Ballater, it was never put in there, I did not go stalking today but went fishing instead. I caught a salmon 8 lbs the first in my life, I was very excited, but it cant be compared to stalking.

I do implore of you really to make up your mind to get rid of Lane, this is a golden opportunity, which you must really take. You will never make the *Review* pay until you do.

Dearest little Missie you know well that anything that I can do to make things easier, from a pecuniary point of view, is done more than willingly, & is nothing to what I would do for you. Bless you my own, come back safe & well to your loving

Husband

As Winston said, George had obtained his heart's desire. He could call himself 'Husband', and give advice, and help with the bills. The only question was, how long would it be before his heart found some other object of desire? But no cloud marred Jennie's happiness that autumn. Winston was elected on 1 October. The Prince did not use his sanction, indeed he wrote to her as 'My dear Mrs Jennie Cornwallis-West! & *Chère Amie!*' All troubles behind her, Jennie was now ready to face the twentieth century.

NOTES

1. Though leaving later than Jennie, Jack travelled by the much faster mail steamer, and got to Cape Town first.

2. Captain Percy Scott of HMS *Terrible* was supposed to go on the expedition, but was too busy. It was from his ship that the gun named after Jennie came.

3. The Colonel seems to have become over-excited.

4. He did not, in fact, publish them, perhaps because they were not long enough to make a book.

5. The *Maine* did not go on a third voyage to South Africa, instead it went to China, where the European powers were busy suppressing the Boxer Rising.

6. Jennie was now signing herself Jennie Randolph Churchill.

7. Randolph's nephew, the 9th Duke of Marlborough.

13

MRS PAT

Jennie's new life was like her old. George was rather dazed by the splendour of it. As he wrote in his memoirs:

> Those were wonderful days. Taxation and the cost of living were low; money was freely spent and wealth was everywhere in evidence. Moreover it was possessed largely by the nicest people, who entertained both in London and in the country. Dinners were Gargantuan affairs, far too long, but although there were innumerable courses, the foreign fashion of serving innumerable wines had disappeared. It was very seldom that sherry was even offered with the soup. Champagne, port and old brandy were the order of the day, or rather, night. One or two hostesses, notably Lady Hindlip, all the Rothschilds, and Mrs Ronnie Greville, had wonderful cooks, but on the whole the cooking was indifferent and meretricious, though the same could not be said of the wines. The champagne vintages from 'eighty to 'eighty-seven were infinitely superior to anything since produced. They were also considerably more potent.

Wealth was not quite as universal as George suggests. After paying many of Jennie's debts, he himself had only a small income to live on, and it did not begin to suffice for Jennie:

> In money matters she was without any sense of proportion. The value of money meant nothing to her: what counted with her were the things she got for money, not the amount she had to pay for them. If something of beauty attracted her, she just had to have it; it never entered her head to stop and think how she was going to pay for it. During all the years we lived together the only serious misunderstandings which ever took place between us were over money matters. Her extravagance was her only fault, and, with her nature, the most understandable, and therefore the most forgivable.

George resigned from the army, and sought the advice of Sir Ernest Cassel, who told him: 'There are many young men of your class who should never go east of Temple Bar. Perhaps you are one of them.' George, he meant, was not for the City. More or less the same advice came from the millionaire Mr McEwen, father of the hostess with the wonderful cook, Mrs Ronnie Greville. He looked at George and said: 'Some men are born to make money, it just comes natural to them; others never will. Maybe ye're one of the latter.' Both men were right. It was not in George to make money. Cassel arranged for him to become a director of the Potteries Electric Traction Company, which he seems to have enjoyed, but four years later he joined up with a north-countryman named Wheater to found a small issuing house in the City. He did not consult Cassel or any of his City acquaintances before taking this step, which was to prove disastrous. But in the beginning the new firm prospered, making over £23,000 in its first year. Even so, George was swindled by a crooked lawyer in 1906 of £8000, and his brother-in-law the Duke of Westminster had to come secretly to the rescue.

In 1905 Jennie and George moved from London to a beautiful, moated, red-brick, Jacobean house near St Albans, called Salisbury Hall. It was only seventeen miles from Hyde Park Corner, but felt in the depths of the country. There they gave week-end parties for their many friends. The Salisbury Hall visitors' book survives, and the names in it are a roll-call of the high and mighty: Connaught and Curzon, Manchester and Roxburghe, Marlborough, Harcourt, Lennox and Lytton. Frewens and Leslies were frequent visitors, of course, as were Jack and Winston and Winston's faithful secretary, Eddie Marsh. On 27 May 1906 the King came: the ground-floor rooms were rearranged for his convenience. With him that weekend were his current favourite, Mrs Alice Keppel, Mr and Mrs William James, the young American Duchess of Marlborough, Consuelo Vanderbilt, Prince Francis of Teck, and various others. It was Edwardian England at its most full-blown.

On more family occasions, two names stand out: Lady Gwendeline Bertie, always known as Goonie, and Clementine Hozier. Goonie was the daughter of the Earl of Abingdon, and it seems that Winston may have had thoughts of her for himself, but it was the quiet Jack whom she loved. Their engagement in the autumn of 1907 must have inspired Winston, for the following spring he fell in love with Clementine, daughter of Jennie's old friend from the 1880s, Lady Blanche Hozier. Both boys were married in the summer of 1908.

By then the prophets of doom had been proved right about Jennie's marriage to George. An undated note gives some indication of the strain it had undergone:

45 Devonshire Street,
Portland Place, W.

Darling old Puss-Cat

I have got back to bed as I am tired.

I'm awfully worried as I feel you thought I chasséd[1] you. You know I didn't & that I'd sooner see you than all the others.

your loving
Husband

It hardly matters who 'all the others' were, but others there were. George's heart was weak in both senses. In March 1906, only a couple of months before the royal visit to Salisbury Hall, two more notes show that Jennie and George were actually apart for a while:

50 Park Street,
Grosvenor Square, W.
March 8th, 1906

Darling old Puss-Cat

I didn't mean to be beastly last night. But you will admit the events of the last few days have been somewhat disturbing. Just off to hunt. Bless you

yr loving
Husband

50 Park Street,
Grosvenor Square, W.
March 9th, 1906

My Beloved,

I am not going down to the Guthries, who have put me off. So I have written proposing myself to Cassel. I will call & see you this evening about. 8.0. before dinner.

your loving
Husband

The strain was apparent to everyone. George's sister, Daisy, Princess of Pless, wrote in her diary for 14 April 1907 that Jennie still loved George immensely, 'poor dear'. 'She is uncommonly nice and still very handsome, but of course the difference in age is a sad and terrible drawback (no babies possible).' It sounds as though George was beginning to make excuses. Jennie was unhappy, even bitter:

Salisbury Hall,
St Albans
May 15th, 1907

Dearest Leonie

I feel that I was cross & unreasonable the other day when I saw you —I am sorry—The fact is when I go to London—there are only 2 peo-

ple I ever try to see, one is Winston the other you—Both are often sad
disappointments—one on account of work—the other on account of
pleasure. I go away feeling sore at heart—I snatch a few minutes of
Winston's society, by driving him to the Colonial Office,[2] & the most
you can offer me—are a few words uncomfortably (for me) at the
telephone—But I have made up my mind—& shall not risk it any more
—You know I love you & that when you want me I am to be found—I
like to think that you are enjoying yrself & making up for all those
dull years when as you say yrself—your greatest excitement was to see
me dress for a ball—Make the most of it all while it amuses you—You
looked very bright & happy last night Keep so—

Yr loving
Jennie

If ever a letter said 'Nobody loves me', this was it. But if Jennie
showed Leonie her unhappiness, she had her own cure for it. She began
to write her memoirs. She did not find it easy, particularly when Winston was scathing about her political chapters, but when *The Reminiscences of Lady Randolph Churchill* was published in England and
America in 1908, it was quite a success, in spite of being extremely
discreet. Jennie thought she might take a leaf out of Winston's book and
do an American lecture tour. She consulted Henry James, the novelist,
who sent her a most delightful reply:

Reform Club,
Pall Mall, S.W.

Dear Mrs West

Your letter overtakes me in town. I am much thrilled by your idea
of possible Lectures in the U.S., & give you with pleasure the benefit
of my very limited experience upwards of four years ago. I say very
limited because that describes the real *accident* & the particularly
circumscribed nature of my small performance. I went to America
(the 1st time for 24 years) with no such notion & nothing prepared;
but was almost immediately *asked*—promptly written to by the Secre-
taries of those essentially American institutions known as Ladies'
Clubs, & which swarm all over the country. They earnestly proposed
it—my 'addressing them on some literary or other subject', & under
competent advice I responded on trial, 1st, to Philadelphia. I had an
old sketched lecture (a mere beginning) on Balzac (planned & laid
aside ten years before:) this I sent out to England for, & 'worked up' &
finished & this I delivered to about twenty (*only*) of the said Ladies'
Clubs—& only in the big places. It was a bad subject—nevertheless one
had a degree of success, & one saw thereby the place, the people (the

people oh *too* copiously!) the manners etc, as perhaps one wouldn't have done otherwise. A 'personal' subject wd. have had of course much more success—& if I had gone with a plan I should [have] done differently. But I had nothing to do with any bureau or agent or big organisation. *That* I could never have stood—ruin, madness, illness, & perhaps money, would have overwhelmed me on those lines. I simply said Yes to the best & most important of the Ladies Clubs that asked me & absolute no to the others. That selection works best by the clue of fees. When they inquired as to my Fee I said Fifty Pounds & closed with those who wd. give that. (The smaller clubs give less.) But twenty gave me the said $250 for my hour—from New York to Los Angeles California. And I delivered but the one poor literary Lecture —warning them as to exactly what it would be. It was interesting, amusing—& very fatiguing! The meeting the number of *people* involved is the drawback—all very pleasant & kind, but of a terrific monotony & indistinguishability! The being 'run' by a regular Agency or 'Lyceum' must be awful & fatal—though, if done on high terms, likely to be proportionally lucrative—I mean as lucrative as dreadful! However, *you* can't possibly fail, I am sure, to have a huge success & vulgarly speaking, a big harvest. The only thing is to be able to *stand* it—& to be confident of *being* able. Speak to them of your personal experiences & observations (could you have 'Kept back' for the purpose part of the matter of your delightful book, *that* would have been the valuable note:) that is really all they want & to look at you for all they are worth. But don't *tie* yourself too much before getting there. Leave something—much—for the occasion.

Yours most truly

Oct. 5, 1908   Henry James

Jennie abandoned the idea of a lecture tour, though one feels that Henry James was right, and she would have been a great success, even though she never enjoyed speaking in public. Instead, she wrote a play. It was called *His Borrowed Plumes,* and according to George, it was Jennie's own idea to get the celebrated actress and wit Mrs Patrick Campbell to produce it and play the leading role. That winter George and Jennie rented the Prime Minister, Mr Asquith's, house in Cavendish Square. Mrs Pat, as she was known, was a constant visitor, and agreed to do the play at a series of matinees the following summer. Later, Mrs Pat was to be scornful about the play and the great social flutter it caused, and even Jennie had early doubts. She wrote to Leonie in March saying 'Sometimes I feel despondent and doubtful of my being able to make it a really good play. I should hate mediocrity.' But when the play came to be rehearsed, she seems thoroughly to have enjoyed it:

> Polesden Lacey,[3]
> Dorking
> June 27th, '09

Darling Snippy—Yr good news was given to me by Mary[4]—I am *so* glad Norman[5] is improving—What a wretched time you have been having & we want you here so much. The Connaughts are coming to my play on the 8th. I am rather surprised that they have not invited me to tea, or to come & see me. But you know I have always thought that they did not like me over much—one in the family is enough— The rehearsals are getting on & this week there are 2 be two daily— Mrs Pat. has really been an angel & the play wld not exist without her —but we spar something of no consequence—

I can't understand why I feel so calmly about the play—Bernstein[6] tells me he is *dans les trances*[7] weeks beforehand—Perhaps I do not know the horrors before me!—I gave a supper party at the Ritz last Friday—too successful for words. . . . We kept it up till 2.30—even Gladys staying[8]—wild dances—& fandangos—everyone taking the floor—

It was as well that the fandangos took place before the play opened, for there were to be none after. *His Borrowed Plumes* was not exactly a failure, but it was not a success, either, and the fashionable audience and its hats came in for as much appreciative comment as the play itself. It was a comedy about two women writers, one of whom tries to steal the other's husband. Unfortunately, the events on stage were all too closely paralleled by those off, and there was to be no happy ending. As a result of the play, George went off with Mrs Pat. They drove to Burnham Beeches and read plays together. Though the marriage struggled on for a few years, it was really over.

It must have been with very mixed feelings that Jennie had heard of the death of Charles Kinsky's wife earlier in 1909. The Kinskys had been to stay at Salisbury Hall, so presumably Jennie was on friendly terms. It is sad that the only letter of Charles's that Jennie kept should have been this one:

> Wien,
> 1, Freiung 4
> 23/IV. 09

Dearest Jennie,

So many thanks for your kind letter.—Yes you are right I feel it more &—deeper than I could say—but I should feel small before her

indeed & the memory of all that quiet natural—honest pluck & courage
with which she died—if I was to give way.—The peace & pluck thats
left in me I owe to her—the best & last gift of love that she left behind
to me even in her sufferings & her death.—& that is more much more
than most people could imagine. Its as real & honest as she has been in
life & even death.—

Your book I have found here on my return & I shall read it as soon
as I get a little rest of all the tedious business that awaited me here on
my sad return & the hundreds & hundreds letters of condolence that I
have to answer now.—So many thanks for it & above all for your letter
& all the kind thoughts of me.—from all my heart.

Yours ever
Charles

From all his heart, he said. What secret regrets there must have been
both in London and Austria.

II

The best cure for the blues, Jennie thought, was a visit to the couturier
Worth, but the next best was hard work. Her experience in the theatre
had not daunted her—she wrote a second play, in fact, which was put on
briefly in Glasgow in 1913. If she could not make money as a playwright
herself, she could at least raise it for other people. The National Theatre
was then little more than an idea, but Jennie sat on the Committee and
helped put on a successful Shakespearean ball at the Royal Albert Hall
in 1911. (She went as Olivia.) The ball gave her the idea for a whole
Shakespearean exhibition to be held at Earl's Court, with Elizabethan
shops and sideshows, and a special club called The Mermaid Tavern.
Jennie was not entirely altruistic about it: she was to receive a percentage
of the profits: they might be very large: the exhibition might go to
America and Canada.

Shakespeare's England, as it was called, was an excellent idea, which
might today, with modern leisure and modern advertising, have been a
great success with large crowds. Alas, in 1912 it wasn't. The reasons for
its financial failure can be easily guessed from a study of the lavish
programme for the Tournament which was to be the exhibition's climax.
It was the first Tournament to be held since 1839, and it was highly
spectacular, with real jousting by real dukes and earls, and a great parade of horsemen in splendid costume. All Jennie's friends and relations

were made to take part, except Winston, who was now in the Cabinet, and perhaps felt he had enough tilting to be getting on with in the House of Commons. Jack Leslie and Hugh Warrender were among 'The Martiall's Men': Sunny Marlborough and Lords Ashby St Ledgers and Tweedmouth, all nephews of Randolph, were among the jousters: Eddie Marsh was a trumpeter. Claire Frewen, now married to Wilfred Sheridan, was one of the 'Wayting Ladyes' on the Queen of Beauty. Among others in the Queen's train were Muriel Wilson, Lady Diana Manners (later Cooper), and two girls to become notorious sixty years later for their stormy love-affair, Victoria Sackville-West and Violet Keppel. The Princess Errant was played by Daisy Pless: in her escort was Charles Kinsky. Jack Churchill led the parade of Knights: George brought up the rear.

It was all gorgeous and rich and colossally expensive, and the tickets were so dear that almost no one came. There were no profits from the exhibition or from the Mermaid Tavern. *Shakespeare's England* did not go to America, or Canada. Fortunately one of George's rich lady friends, Mrs Leeds, had stumped up a large sum, for which she got her reward in the shape of a husband: Prince Christopher of Greece, who had also been part of Daisy Pless's escort.

Jennie's own marriage, however, was nearing its end. In August 1910 she had written to George's mother about it. Her draft, with its original erasures, survives:

My dear Patsy
    Please don't apologize—I am only too glad that the house can be of use to you—I understand from Walden[9] that George returns tomorrow —It is tiresome for him that the City should require his presence so much—as fresh air and an active life would do so much for his health & incidentally his peace of mind—You know that our relations have become very strained on my part nearly to breaking point. As he is your son—your only son—& I am sure in your own way you love him— I implore of you to think out for him *without any consideration of me* —what is best for *him*—He can have his freedom if he wants it—free to marry Mrs Patrick Campbell or anyone else he thinks would make him happy—I have done my best & have failed—There is much that I could say but I will refrain In respect to money & extravagance of with which he has reproached me there is absolutely nothing to choose between us. In fact if our mutual finances were looked into I think mine would come out the best—I make seek no excuse for my own shortcomings—they are many—we are but human but in many

~~ways I can claim to have done my best but~~ I have loved him more than anyone on earth & have *always* been true & loyal.

Yours affectly
Jennie C-W.

By April 1911 things were so bad that Winston and Jack had to come to the rescue:

10 Talbot Square,
Hyde Park
April 4, 1911

Dear Mama—It was a shock to get your wire this afternoon. I went off to Winston who is much upset on your account—We tried to get hold of G., but he will not be back until tomorrow.

W will see him then, & have a clear understanding with him as to our opinion of affairs. What he can hope to gain by behaving like a blackguard I cannot understand.

Dont be too depressed—when all this is over—you will find yourself more settled & happier than you have been for some time, and you will come back again nearer to W & me whose love is always just the same.

Dont be pessimistic—The post is off, so goodbye—best love from both of us

I have sent £100 to Smith Bank—from both of us—50 is from Winston

Jack

Winston found time from his duties to see George, and Clementine wrote a sympathetic letter:

Wednesday

My Darling B.M.[10]   33, Eccleston Square, S.W.

I am *so* grieved that you should be unhappy—This is just a line to bring you my love & sympathy—I can't bear that you should be sad. I have not seen Winston since he has seen G. but he telephoned to me & said G. seemed much upset—But of course he did not say much on the telephone.

Dearest try not to be too miserable—I am sure it will come right—after a little time—G must love you—You have been so much to each other. I don't know what has happened—Please don't think me indiscreet or impertinent to write to you about your private affairs, but you seem so far away abroad & I want to tell you how much we all love you & how sorry we are. I wish you were not away Darling B.M.

Your loving Bru
Clementine

Winston is at the House all the time this week. No dinner—no time for anything because of the Parliament Bill—He is in charge when the Prime Minister is not in the House.

Goonie wrote, too:

10 Talbot Square,
Hyde Park

My Sweet B.M. 7th April

This is just a line to remind you that Jack and I are always there by you, ready to do anything and everything for you, that we love you & that you ask of us whatever you want or want us to do & it shall be done—dearest B.M. you must never forget that or hesitate a moment—Jacks is most frightfully unhappy about you, & he would give his blood for your happiness—you can trust him and rely upon him, he is the most devoted & loyal of sons—

Bless you my dearest B.M. & I kiss you with my whole heart.

Your devoted
Goonie

Jennie could not ask for two nicer daughters-in-law.

George must have asked to come back this time, for later that month Winston checked a draft of a letter Jennie wrote to him from their home in Norfolk Street, Mayfair:

2, Norfolk Street,
Park Lane,

My dear George April 19th, '11

Certainly come back to your own home—& with God's help we will start afresh—I see no reason why we should not be able to live in peace—I only want of you the respect and *consideration* which is due to me as your wife And on my side I will always try & help you in every way possible—In respect to our financial arrangements—these can be discussed amicably later—I accept your statement in respect to the notices to servants writing to people, etc—I will only add that I want you thoroughly to understand that you return at your own wish

& without any pressure or coercion from me—I do not wish later on to be reproached for not having given you your freedom.

Meanwhile your room is ready for you when you choose to occupy it.

> Yrs affectly
> Jennie

Winston suggested cutting from 'reproached' to the end of the sentence. 'Freedom has more meanings than one,' he commented.

But if George returned, it was not for long. As his business slowly collapsed, he took to travelling. In 1910 he went to Mexico: in 1911 to America. On both occasions he was seriously ill. The end of the marriage came with the end of 1912. Jennie must have written to George that Christmas. He replied from Eaton Hall, the home of the Duke of Westminster:

> Eaton,
> Chester

Dearest Jennie   Dec 29th, 1912

I was glad to get your kind generous letter. I have put off answering it, as I honestly could not bring myself to write the other. However I am certain we neither of us wish to again go through the terrible ordeal of parting, and as after all that has happened we cannot go back, —I have written it—& enclose it. I can honestly say I have never done anything in my life that I so hated doing. I only pray I may not regret it as much. Even now I would not send it did I not feel that in the long run it may be best for both; & moreover if I did not think Dearest Jennie that we could be true friends after it is all over, I would tear it up now.—you are a splendid woman, & if I ever have done or are likely to do anything in the world, it has been & will be through your good influence. So far as the past is concerned it sounds silly to write this, as I have done nothing beyond trying to make an honest living, still I know some of my best endeavours, thoughts & ideals have emanated from you.

My future is in the 'Lap of the Gods' who alone know what fortune or misfortune is in store for me.

So far as you are concerned, it will always be my aim in life to provide for you according to your tastes & to the best of my ability. I am not waiting until the New Year to send the enclosed, as perhaps it will be better as we have made up our minds on the subject, to start afresh in 1913.

Bless you dearest Jennie, if you are ill communicate as I will with you.

> always affectionately
> George

Jennie kept a copy of her reply:

> Coombe Abbey,[11]
> Coventry

Dearest George   December 31st, 1912

I am glad that I was prepared for your letter—the blow falls hard enough as it is—But if the thing is to take place it can't be done too quickly now—& we shall both be happier when it is over—Thank God I have physical & mental strength & courage enough to fight my own battle in life—I only hope that you will have the same—It is not for me to preach but you will be a happier man if you set yourself a higher ideal of life than heretofore—I mean to—& altho' I know it is difficult—still one can but try. *Of course* we shall be friends—and it will not be my fault if we are not the best. My affection help & advice shall always be yours in the future as it has been in the past—When this & our financial difficulties are settled—a new & I hope prosperous life will be open to you—Make use of it in the best sense—& your happiness & prosperity will be my best reward for the sacrifice I am making in giving you up—No one knows better than you what that sacrifice means to me—for I have loved you devotedly for 12 years—You have been ever in my thoughts & this love will only die—with me—Remember this in any dark hour which may come to you—God bless you & keep you from harm & prosper you is the prayer of

> yours ever affectionately
> Jennie

A few days later Jennie wrote again. George had taken rooms in Curzon Street, where he talked by the hour to his dog Beppo: 'Thanks for your nice letter', he wrote. 'I have been on the verge of ringing you up once or twice, but honestly I don't think I could bear to hear the sound of your dear old voice just now.'

Jennie's behaviour during the divorce proceedings the following year was dignified. George went to Brazil with his sister Daisy. Mrs Patrick Campbell was ill, and when she recovered, busy with her mock-affair with Bernard Shaw. Jennie attracted wide sympathy. After an appearance in court, she received this from George's friend Rosamund Greaves, who had predicted the marriage would be such a success:

Quenby Hall,
Leicester
Thursday, July 16th

One little line to tell you how much I have been thinking of you these last days. I know how brave and plucky you are & how deeply you feel. No woman was ever a better wife—& no one knows this better than poor George in his heart—you gave him *so much*. Poor George—

Now rest a bit if you can, you have such interests, so much intellect you will come up all brisk and fresh again. I cant tell you how much I admire you for not letting any bitter thoughts enter into yr *big heart*. Bless you—

If you want to be quiet come here any time after the 24th.

yr affecy R.

I filled up an Insurance paper & returned it.
How am I to address you?

Jennie changed her name back to Spencer-Churchill. Her friends were glad. Lord Curzon, for instance, wrote:

Hackwood,
Basingstoke
My dear Lady Randolph   Jan. 30, 1914

Good to get back to the old name or did we get in our old age to Jenny & George? I cant remember. Anyhow I am ready. This is to say why not come here for a Sat-Monday Feb 21–23? Do if you can.

Yours affec
C.

There was much wrangling between solicitors about bills, as there always is in a divorce case, but George and Jennie remained friendly. Jennie wrote to Leonie in October 1913, 'If you meet him don't be hard on him,' and on New Year's Eve George wrote to Jennie:

I hope you are well and happy. For me I have had a terrible year & shall not be sorry to see the last of 1913. I will drink a silent toast to you tonight dear Jennie for your health, happiness & welfare.

Jennie wrote back saying she was not unsympathetic about his business troubles and lack of money, *but*—To her lawyers she wrote suggesting a compromise. The decree was made absolute on 6 April 1914.

George's sister Daisy sent telegrams urging Jennie not to let it go through, but Jennie knew what she wanted. On the 4th she wrote to George:

>   Ladies Athenaeum Club,
>   31 & 32 Dover Street, W.
> My dear George   April 4th, 1914
>   Mr Wheater brought me your message—The decree nisi will be made absolute on Monday—& I understand that you are going to be married on Tuesday—You need not fear what I may say—For I shall not willingly speak of you—and we are not likely ever to meet—This is the *real* parting of the ways But for the sake of some of the happy days we have had together—should you ever be in trouble & wanted to knock at my door it would not be shut to you—In returning to you my engagement & wedding rings—I say Goodbye—a long long Goodbye—
>   Jennie

George in fact married Mrs Pat a few hours after the divorce was made absolute. Jennie was showered with sympathetic messages:

> JENNIE DEAREST YOU DID YOUR BEST ITS AWFUL AND HE WILL REGRET JUST READ NEWS IN PAPER AM MISERABLE HOPE SEE YOU SOON MUCH LOVE—DAISY

George's other sister Shelagh wrote a letter:

>   Rome
> Dear Jennie   April 15th
>   I must write you a little line as I feel so much for you during this last year and especially by the announcement of last week. George must have been absolutely driven or out of a sense of honour to you and us he would never have acted with the indecent haste he did. Believe me Jenny I knew all the time what you were going through; and I admired what you did for him more than I can say. . . .

From Ireland, Leonie wrote three times:

>   Monday
>   Glaslough,
>   Co. Monaghan
> Darling, I sent you a wire because Moreton wrote that the Decree N. wd be today—and I know what you feel now that George has his

liberty—Dearest—you have done *all* you could—and we can only *deplore* the folly, if he commits it, of marrying Mrs P.C.—I know how generous & noble you have been—and how you made the sacrifice, hoping it wd be for his good—It is not yr fault if he follows his own foolish way—Poor man—what a hash he has made of the whole thing. We, who look on, can only rejoice however, that you are free from him—You wd have been in your grave if that strain of life in Norfolk Street had continued—

I am glad Easter is coming, & you will get away from London again. Leonora[12] is a kind being—and you will feel better at Overstrand— Write to me Darling—I will tear up yr letter—and it will do you good to give vent to yr feelings—

Politics—& art and *joie de vivre*—how much we have to fill our lives—

Yr devoted & loving
Leonie

Two days later it was:

Darling—You take it in the right way—You are very fine—courageous —and human—I did not know it was a *fait accompli* when I wired Monday—just a kind of telepathy made me do so, knowing the Decree was that day—I must say I felt very hateful & revengeful—and look-ing forward to the stony stare I cld give them—& the 'serve you right' to Daisy & Sheelagh. But *yours* is the right spirit—no animosity—no bitterness—just—*Fini*—The only tiresome part, is she is always in the papers with her acting—& one may be occasionally reminded of them —Jack very disgusted. . . .

Three days later:

I won't refer to that beastly marriage—but I must just say this once— that I think it was disgraceful of G. to put such an indignity on you— and that I never want to see either of those two, or speak to them—*Ce n'est pas permis* to be such a weak fool—and to show such ingratitude to you—I resent it for you—altho' you are big & noble enough to forget it—He should never have come in to yr life—And as for Her—Well there is nothing too bad to describe my feelings about her—the only consolation, is that *she* will have a pretty bad time of it, if she cares for him—& serve her right—there. . . .

Mrs Pat *was* served right. Her marriage to George lasted even less time than Jennie's, though there was never a divorce. George and Jennie kept in touch. Winston provided him with a job at the beginning of the war, and George wrote to thank Jennie for having 'seconded the appointment'. When George's mother was involved in an unsavoury scandal about a young soldier, Jennie wrote him a brief note:

> 8 Westbourne Street,
> Hyde Park
> My dear George   Jan. 5th, '17
> I feel I must write to you a few words of sympathy in, what I know is to you a very great trial—Please believe that I feel most deeply for you—But remember that a son should always seek & find extenuating circumstances for his Mother—
> Apart from this sorrow, I hope life is treating you gently
> Yours affectly
> Jennie R.C.

This does not seem to be a copy, and perhaps she had second thoughts and decided not to send it. In 1919 she wrote to him again. By that time his marriage was virtually over.

> 8, Westbourne Street,
> Hyde Park
> My dear George   17.6.19
> I heard all about you from Claire therefore was not surprised at your letter—I am glad you wrote—& in your heart of hearts, you must know that I never could have any but kindly feelings towards you—I never think of you but to remember all the happy days we spent together—I have forgotten everything else—I do wish you all that is best—Peace is an essential of life—& if you have that, you are on the fair way to happiness—Life is frightfully hard. One's only chance is within oneself—I shall hope to see you again soon. Bless you—
> Always your best friend
> Jennie R.C.

Though George and Mrs Pat had separated for ever, she refused to give him a divorce, and he was not able to marry again till after her death in 1940. His third marriage was announced on the day of Mrs Pat's memorial service. He had filled in the years shooting, fishing and writing. His plays were not usually performed, but a novel was published with some success, as well as a biography, two volumes of memoirs and a book called *Us Dogs*. In old age he suffered from depression and then Parkinson's Disease. In April 1951 he shot himself. He was seventy-six.

Thirty years earlier, when Jennie died, he wrote to Winston:

May I be allowed to write & tell you how grieved I am to read of the death of your mother.

I find it difficult to say all I feel: perhaps you would not believe me. But I can truly say I never had anything in my heart for her but affection & admiration. I realize that, from my point of view, the greatest mistake I ever made in my life was in allowing myself to be persuaded into a separation from her. I can assure you that I have lived & am living to bitterly regret it. It is a joy to think that I saw her not much more than 18 months ago, & learnt from her own lips that she bore me no ill will for the hurt I had done her. Thank God I could never have harmed her, her position was far too secure. I wonder how you & Clemmy & Jack & Goonie are? I so often think about you all, & the old days.

Yours ever
G.C-W.

NOTES

1. Sent you away.
2. Winston became Under-Secretary of State for the Colonies in December 1905.
3. Home of Mrs Ronnie Greville.
4. Probably Leonie's sister-in-law, Mary Crawshay.
5. Leonie's second son.
6. Henry Bernstein, popular French playwright.
7. Shivering in his shoes.
8. Probably de Grey, now Marchioness of Ripon.
9. Jennie's long-serving butler.
10. Both daughters-in-law called Jennie B.M., short for *belle mère*.
11. Home of William George Robert, 4th Earl of Craven. He was married to Cornelia Bradley Martin, a New Yorker, whose parents once gave so flamboyantly expensive a fancy-dress party there were popular riots.
12. Leonora Speyer, wife of Sir Edgar Speyer, the banker. Jennie went to stay with the Speyers at Overstrand in Norfolk that week. Their house was called 'Seamarge'.

14

ARMAGEDDON

Jennie hated growing old, and sometimes she could not help saying so. She wrote to Jack from Monte Carlo in the spring of 1914, about the sordid details of her financial arrangements with George. She was sixty and felt low:

> . . . apart from Goonie & perhaps little Johnnie,[1] who cares if I return or not? Not that I do not know that you and Winston love me, & are very good to me—but you lead busy lives, & have your own families to be absorbed in. What am I? Only an old 5th wheel—I am not complaining, only stating facts. . . .
>
> Love to Goonie & keep some for yourself tho' you don't send me any! I suppose I'm a sentimental old goose & don't deserve any for all the ennuis I cause you. My letter seems peevish but I am really not so.

No? She took things out on Leonie, too:

> I wish we could see more of each other. Life is so short and we are both so down the wrong side of the ladder! The fact is that we are 'Marthas' instead of 'Marys' and allow things which do not really count to take up our time and to keep us apart. We pander to the world which is callous and it only wants you if you can smile and be hypocritical. One is for ever throwing away substance for shadows. To live for others sounds all right—you do, darling!—but what is the result? You are a very unhappy woman all round!
>
> As for me every effort I make to get out of my natural selfishness meets with rebuff. My sons love me from afar and give me no companionship even when it comes their way. The fault is undoubtedly with me. Every day I become more solitary and prone to introspection, which is fatal.

Leonie indignantly denied that she was unhappy, and the idea of Jennie as a self-sacrificing Martha must have caused some mirth in the Leslie family. But Jennie did not always feel so low. Not, for instance, when she went to Rome for the wedding of her nephew Hugh Frewen to the daughter of an Italian Duke. Hugh had been in the Colonial Service, and among his friends at the wedding was a small, neat, prematurely white-haired man who had served with him in Nigeria. His name was Montagu Porch. He was thirty-seven, three years younger than Winston, but found Jennie very attractive and on his way back to Nigeria wrote to her:

R.M.S. *Mendi*

Dear Lady Randolph, 16 May 1914

You said I might write to you so here goes!

We are now well on our way to Nigeria for tomorrow all being well we shall reach Sierra Leone. I say 'we' for I am taking out a young soldier servant & a puppy of the Great Dane breed.

In my choice of both I have been lucky the former is a cheerful looking fellow & a keen sportsman. The latter a handsome darling creature black as a nigger already considers herself our protector & tries to bark off all intruders.

We are bound for Kaduna the new capital of the federated Nigerias—There, we aspire to great deeds, that our names may be inscribed with glory in the annals of our country & that I may win your approval, dear friend.

I am greatly looking forward to my sojourn for the prospect is very pleasing.

The weather is glorious—The sun shines from out an azure sky on to an azure sea—a light cool breeze steals in under the awning where stretched on deck chairs we are lazing away the noontide. My thoughts turn towards my loved ones & I think with regret of all the disciplines often self-imposed & the pleasures that I let escape me.

Then I remember you dear kind friend, all the nice things you said of me & I would they were true or at least that you believed what you said.

Have you so soon forgotten that I want your photograph—will you send it to me please—one that can live in my lettercase. The likeness of a dear friend I couldn't bear to expose to the rude gaze of the vulgar.

Your essay, too, on Friendship am I not to have it. I would like it very much & a kind word straight from you would buck me up enormously.

I've heard nothing from my Italian friends save from Paolina Marchesa Rusconi who posted me farewell in the form of a little gold cross & from Card: Merry del Val[2] who sent me an excellent photograph of himself with his very virile autograph—inscription. Of all my Roman friends only Cardinal Merry del Val remembered me.

Tomorrow we stop at Sierra Leone. The Governor Sir Edward Mereweather & his Dame I know, so I shall go ashore & pay them my respects.

Goodbye, dear Lady Randolph—I want your friendship & I mean to get & keep it. *Nil difficile volenti.*

Don't think me conceited will you I am only finding expression.

Montie

Porch's literary expression was rather quaint, but no doubt Jennie was amused and delighted by his presumption. At any rate, she wrote back. She was doing a lot of writing—a series of essays for a magazine, later published as a little book called *Small Talks on Big Subjects*. The essay on Friendships contains the passage already quoted about Pearl Craigie turning a ploughed field into one enamelled with flowers. Jennie was writing to make a little money, for as usual her finances were precarious. Jack felt obliged to read her a little lecture on the subject:

> . . . you have over £2000 a year. . . . We have begged you so often to live within your income—which is not a very severe demand. Your income is larger than mine in most years and you have nothing whatever to keep up. Unless you are able to do so and if you start running up bills again—there is nothing that can save you from a crash & bankruptcy.

'Lots of others whom you know', he added, 'are in much worse positions than you.' The Edwardian world was cracking up. Quite soon, and no one seemed to know why or how, the first world war was destroying everything Jennie had known. Winston, at the Admiralty, was right at the heart of events, and kept Jennie informed. Jack, in the City, was appalled at the panic of late July:

> The world has gone mad—the whole financial system has completely broken down. . . . Be careful with what you have got—Gold will soon be unobtainable. . . .

Jennie hastened to pass this news to Leonie, with other rumours:

72 Brook Street, W.

Darling Sniffy   Aug. 1st

Only a line to tell you that W. tells me Poincarré[3] has written an impassioned letter to the King imploring his aid—The fleet (British)

will be mobilized today probably—Germany is holding up English vessels—& has mobilized & massed troops on the French Frontier—Money is fearfully tight here & one cannot get a cheque cashed—& the Banks will give no gold—But W. says the financial situation will be easier as they are going to issue at once paper pound notes—Paris is in an awful state risings in the streets—The whole world seems to have gone mad. I am depressed beyond words—Ireland seems to have sunk out of sight —for the moment—The Volunteers of both parties are sure to be commandeered. Just off to Ramsey Abbey till Tuesday—

Love
Jennie

War was declared on 4 August. Jennie plunged at once into hospital work again. Clementine and Goonie were staying with their children at Overstrand, and Jennie seems to have complained that they weren't sending her enough news in these exciting times:

Beehive Cottage,
Overstrand

My darling B.M.

Of course I love you and if I have not written to say so, it is because I have been worried and sad about ourselves—Jack & I & the children— as you may have realized we have not a 'bob' left in the world and I do not know what the future holds in store for us—however this is not the moment to lament about ones own private affairs—It is splendid of you to get this hospital scheme going & I am sure it will be an engrossing & congenial work for you—& you will do it with great skill and energy—Jack has gone off to join his Yeomanry, & is at Banbury at this present moment. I am very glad for his sake that he is occupied & busy, for it would have been intolerable for him to have had leisure to brood over the situation—It is very exciting here being on the Coast & in the zone of 'danger'—There is no reason why the Germans should not come along & shell Overstrand—Clemmie & I may qualify for a war medal afterwards! She, Clemmie, is very flourishing & we lead a healthy & quiet life with our children, on the beach—I play a little bad tennis at the Speyers & we go & look at the troops who are now quartered at Cromer & such like innocent pastimes. Father[4] & brother Jimmy[5] are staying with me and are consoling me for Jack's absence— my Jacko—I wish he had not to go, but I am proud that he is serving his Country! It was very dear of you to find time to write to me & I appreciated it very much indeed—Could I get another letter from you?

We hear all the news here, as Clemmie gets on the telephone daily to the Admiralty, but your news I would like to get sometimes—

Your loving bru
Goonie

X from Johnnie
X from Peregrine—and Father sends his love.

When she got back to London, Goonie went to dinner with Jennie, who had a great gift for buying houses, doing them up, and selling them again. It was one of her few really profitable ventures. Goonie's account to Jack not only describes Jennie's latest house, it gives a very good idea of the gloom with which people were approaching the war:

Darling—
41 Cromwell Road
Sept 1st, 1914

On my arrival in London I went to lunch at the Admiralty & Winston told me that Lord Kitchener said that the Yeomanry will train for three or four months at Churn & then go on active service as Divisional Cavalry—I am not happy as you may imagine, as that means you will come face to face with those swines of Germans, who by that time will be more savage & desperate than ever—Everybody, or at least every woman is going to be unhappy this year, so I am no exception, but it is cruel that this is to be so—I want to be with you all the time now till you go—In three or four months lots of things might have happened & there is always a glimmer of hope that you will not be called upon to expose your self to be slaughtered by the Germans—Write to me darling and console me—I do try to be brave—Would you have preferred to have gone to Egypt? Winston did not know who they were going to send to Egypt—Some Territorials I think—Commodore Keyes[6] was at Lunch, just back from Heligoland—He was not very voluble & *he* looked like if he had gone through a tremendous strain—It appears most of the German sailors desert their ships too soon—& in consequence get shot at in the water by their officers—Winston said he might go down to Churn to see you today—but he would not take me, as he said it was all men & I would be in the way in fact? When can I come & where could I stay? . . . who is close?—I dined with B.M. last night at 72 Brook Street—Needless to say we had a seven course dinner beautifully served, Platters of luscious fruits etc. all in a lovely dining-room the walls of which were decorated with lovely pictures—We afterwards sat in a 'pickled' oak room, beautifully lighted in the cornices by invisible electric Lights, & filled with lovely bibelots, furniture, rugs, flowers, in fact it looked very rich & opulent, comfortable & luxurious—I did not go up the thick pile carpeted staircase to the drawing [room] but I hear its quite beautiful, green painted & tapestries & wonderful lighting— Then further up there is a silver bedroom, a white bathroom and a blue dressingroom—but this I have not seen either—Downstairs alone I espied several new pieces of furniture—writing tables, chairs, tables, etc—but perhaps she has exchanged it for some of her old furniture—

The children are well & very pleased to get back to their old nurseries—I am trying to get the House clean and I have a charwoman hard at work scrubbing & washing—We shall get straight I hope soon —What is your telegraph address—The post office says there is no office at Churn—so I have been sending telegrammes to Didcot—Have you received them alright? Love from

yr loving wife
Goonie

Jennie was meanwhile keeping Leonie in touch:

72, Brook Street, W.
Aug 16th, '14

Darling Sniffy—

I telephoned to Marjorie[7] yesterday early to ask for news of you but she knew nothing! My 'poor child' I am sure you are going through bad moments, but we are more or less in the same boat. . . . I saw W. in the afternoon—No fresh news the 2 Armies are not likely to meet for a few days—& until then we shall hear nothing. I am hoping against hope that my Jack won't have to go but W. thinks he will probably volunteer—He is at present at Bury St Edmunds or somewhere near with the Oxfordshire Yeomanry—I have written to Goonie to offer to take her & the children for the winter—or in fact till Jack returns—It will be a squeeze but I think I can manage it—as I write I hear the tramp of the troops going off—The Reveille sounds at 5.30 but I was so tired this morning I heard nothing—Our American War Fund is progressing—but Minnie Paget is a great care—however if anything goes wrong I propose to stick to the Hospital. . . . I wish I had some news to give you—Rest a little & get fit for the strain to come —Let me know if there is anything I can do about yr house.

Fond love
Jennie

Love to Jack

The strain to come was indeed appalling, and an individual's happiness or otherwise seems irrelevant when compared to the general horror of the First World War. But the death of a loved one always counts more than the death of a whole army of strangers. Jennie was to lose many friends and relations in the war: her nephew, Norman Leslie, was killed before the year was out, and Wilfred Sheridan died in 1915. Her own son Jack went all through the war, in France and Gallipoli and France again; Winston, too, served in the trenches after he was forced to resign in 1915, following the failure of the Gallipoli expedition. Jennie defended him tigerishly, and could never forgive Asquith for what she regarded as his disloyalty. As for herself—she did the things she was good at: she organized concerts and matinees for military charities, she took in Goonie and her children for a while, and paid for Johnnie's schooling, she edited a book on *Women's War Work*, she visited the bereaved, and, never forgetting the country of her birth, she worked at American hospitals in Paignton and London. Sometimes she did things she wasn't so good at: she knitted a scarf for Hugh Warrender, who was in the trenches, which was so big that he used it as a blanket instead. In war, she wrote, 'To be dressed in the latest fashion is not to be in the right note.' And: 'the more virile a nation becomes the more she seeks for, and asks for, simplicity and truth. All the shallow, stupid, snobbish habits which were beginning to blot out our horizon are vanishing like mists before the sun.' Doing her bit to help the process, she gave up her footmen, and substituted footmaids in the men's cut-down uniforms. And she let herself go. Her hair became white, and the figure which had once been so slim, and carefully kept to look so, took on its actual ample proportions. She wrote to the troops, too. She kept up a regular correspondence with Hugh Warrender, and with his sister Eleanor, busy nursing the wounded. She had toyed with the idea of marrying Hugh, who was still devoted: things went so far that Jack asked what they wanted for a wedding-present. But that was before the war, and before Jennie met Montagu Porch. She was writing to him in Nigeria and he was writing back:

> Tati river, E. of Takum,
> Nr Anglo German Boundary,
> Muri Province, Nigeria
> 5 Oct. 1914

How sensational—your dear letter written on the eve of 'Armageddon' finds your humble friend at the front beating back the attacks of the covetous Huns.

At the outbreak of hostilities I was sworn in a soldier transferred from Zaria to this Province & shortly afterwards appointed Intelligence Officer to this column.

Jennie writing letters
in the drawing room
at Brook Street

Montagu Porch in Nigeria (above)

Jennie with her children and grand-children (above right)

Jennie in about 1920 (right)

Jennie with her grandson Peregrine, co-author of this book

Takum was attacked on 19th ult when the Germans got more than they bargained for. Their O.C. killed 1 European seriously wounded & a lot of native soldiers killed & wounded—our casualties were a bruised thumb; so cunningly were our block houses arranged.

I send you a relic of the fray the legend explains itself—who was the wounded man one wonders & where is he now?

Many died of wounds in their flight back to Kamerun—a week later I held 2 of their skulls in my hand, chalk-white like museum-exhibits, so well had the vultures done their work.

I will write to you again dear Lady Randolph. Two of my spies have just come in & I am anxious to hear their news.

We are a very happy family here—20 Europeans in the column—I feel v. responsible for these dear souls—our native troops are playing up v. well.

Goodbye, dear friend, I will write again & you must write to me for I am lonely too.

Montie

There was more to Porch than met the eye. He seemed quiet, dapper, nothing very much, but he proved a good soldier in awful conditions:

The Residency,
Zaria, Nigeria
2 October 1915

Forgive you, of course & with all my heart. Your dear letter has touched me deeply. How kind & like you, thank you.

Ohimé this horrible sickening war, will it ever end. Almost all the men one has ever heard of seem to be either killed or wounded. Poor Lady Leslie, I heard of her loss. All my men kith & kin are in the trenches save brother-in-law Gillmore who is with his regiment in India.

It is well for you that you have lots to do, dear friend, you will then have less time for grief and heartache. I am indeed glad you are running the American hospital. History repeats itself. Jan: 15 years ago I, a trooper coming of age on my way to the front, passed a gorgeously equipped American hospital ship run by one of the most brilliant & beautiful women in England. Now you are again taking your part in this bigger & more frightful war.

I too have played my small part all they would let me do. Aug. 8th '14 I was transferred from peaceful Zaria to our Front the Nigerian-Kamerun Border where I was attached as Intelligence Officer to the Nigerian Regt .West African Frontier Force. Our column was a very small one & had to run up & down 200 miles of border & shoo off the Huns whenever they appeared.

Lots of scrapping we had & I lost some gallant comrades. As yet our campaign has received little recognition—Far greater dangers than trench work have been endured by our men who winter and summer have braved swamp and jungle, fever and bush ambuscades, heavy marches & fighting in terrible heat. Tormented by insects, stung by all the creatures of the bush, scorched by unshaded sun in the fiercest heat of an African summer—such has been our lot.

In January I was recalled from the column to resume my duties as Resident in charge of this Province. In May and August I had to take patrols into my Pagan Districts who had revolted against the Native Administration & didn't want to pay their taxes after having heard that the white men of consequence had all gone off to the Great War. However I went & saw—one of the tribes put up a little fight, got well wopped, came to their senses & promised never to do it again.

I am 5 months overdue for leave and sail on October 26th. I shall go straight to Kewstoke Somerset, where a patient old housekeeper & a man await me in a roomy cottage poised on a spur of Mendip which dips into the Bristol Channel. I dread the first few days in Somt. Relations to be visited & tenants seen. Duty done I shall hie me to town. I shall live at the United Empire Club quite near you but won't be a nuisance. I'll only come when I'm called.

Edgarley Lodge my little place near Glastonbury has just been let on a seven years' lease!—Thank goodness.

Think I shall have seven months leave, what *shall* I do—I would go Dardanelles—if Bonar Law[8] will accept my resignation—If I can't get to the front I shall make shells or be guided into doing something else useful.

Au revoir dear Lady Randolph,

> Your devoted friend
> M.P.

Montie Porch must have been visiting London, and Jennie, when an extraordinary telegram appeared in the papers, addressed to His Majesty The German Emperor, Berlin, from New York.

The name of Napoleon fades before the prowess of your mighty deeds, Sir. May 1916 bring to the world that peace which for years we have had the high honour of hearing Your Majesty insist upon and may God guide and bless you, Sir.

> Katherine and Jordan Mott,
> Ritz Hotel.

Kitty Mott was Jennie's cousin, through her mother, and the three Jerome sisters were outraged. Leonie wrote at once to Jennie:

Thursday
Glaslough,
Co. Monaghan.

Darling—

Moreton has just sent me this extraordinary cable of Kitty's to the Emperor—No use asking her to deny it! One recognises her style— Poor Devil, I suppose she thought if she mollified the Emperor with flattery he wd listen to the *Peace* suggestions—Pretty mean of him to publish it, knowing it wd be resented—

I am *really* sorry for Kitty—she is such a d——fool about the war— She adores England & English, does not want ever to see Germany again, but she is persuaded if she could see the Emperor for ½ hour she could get him to make Peace—

She doesn't understand that it *is up to* the Allies to decide when Peace is to be & NOT to the Emperor—Claire is *terribly* upset!—& is returning the little cheque Kitty sent her for Xmas.—

Do write, we've no news.

Aff. L.

Jennie wrote sharply to her cousin:

72, Brook Street, W.
Jan. 10th '16

Dear Kitty,

The enclosed appeared in the *Pall Mall* a few days ago—Needless to ask if you wrote it—The style is too peculiarly yr own—With the views you hold—I don't suppose you care if England is shut to you for ever—for I tell you frankly you can never return here—When I think of the glorious deaths of Norman Leslie and Wilfred Sheridan.—of Hugh Frewen in a hospital, of Oswald at sea[9]—of Jack in Gallipoli & Winston in the trenches in Flanders—When I think of all the horror of this war, conducted by the Kaiser with the most awful cruelty & barbarism ever known since the world began—which a stroke of his pen could have stopped—I feel I cannot write one more word to you. . . .

To Kitty's husband, Jennie wrote:

72 Brook Street, W.
Jan. 10th, '16

My dear Jordan

I can hardly believe that you were a party to Kitty's telegram to the Kaiser—It was intercepted by wireless & published here—I cannot tell you how deeply the family is ashamed of it—If it was done without your knowledge or sanction & your name wrongly used—I should be glad if you would write & deny it.

Yrs ever
J.R.C.

Jennie might have been born in America, but her loyalties were entirely English now. Later that year she wrote to Shane Leslie in America:

. . . How truly magnificent is this country—We promised 160,000 men, & we have given 5 millions, besides keeping the seas & financing every ally—England will be the greatest nation in the world when the war is over—Yes not excepting America—for she missed her chance of coming out as a nation—not that I really blame the U.S. for keeping out of the war—but the consequences will not tend to glorify the States. . . .

From New York Shane reported the result of the infamous telegram:

You are wrong about Kitty Mott! She will simply *have to live in London,* because nobody will speak to her over here. They have begun to insult and avoid her. How one can suffer for one moment of madness!

He added in a P.S.: 'There is a window in Broadway entirely devoted to a "Lady Churchill" cigar with an imaginative portrait of you.' Jennie's fame had long been transatlantic.

How much Jennie actually saw of Montagu Porch that winter is unclear. He was very discreet, doubtless, and so was she. He had brought her a present from Nigeria which she doesn't seem to have appreciated:

The Residency,
Zaria, Nigeria
22 June 1916

Dear Lady Randolph

I have just got here & have taken over charge of the Province. That is I am the Resident in charge of Zaria Province which from its central position brings one much under the limelight. Three Railways in my Province & Kaduna the future *capital of Nigeria.* Hurray. This childs work.

Do please send me a word to inspire me to further effort—I am so lonely.

If you wont wear the Crown Birds crests yourself please burn 'em. That no one else may wear 'em—that would be the most unkindest cut of all.

> Very sincerely yours,
> M.P.

Jennie had another admirer, at a distance of another sort:

My dearest Lady Randolph,

You will perhaps think my presumption amazing, but not if you knew my feelings. I have felt drawn towards you since the time you came to England, even when you were a bonnie bride, you are indeed sweeter to me than at that time, I have always called you my Jennie, I have followed your career, your sweet personality has always been uppermost in my life and foremost in my thoughts. I have always felt that you have a very warm temperament, only fitted to be mated with such a one as mine.

Dearest I have kept pure for you alone, and never until the last few days have I ever thought of letting you know this, it has always been my life's secret, sacred to myself, but love is stronger than, shall I say commonsense and here I stand convicted self confessed, of loving the sweetest woman in the world, my Jennie always my Jennie, I am yours body & soul, to do with me what you will, when I am thinking of you dearest my physical senses make me feel a superman, *your man*, Jennie darling, do you want me, if so, I am yours, one cur I would like to thrash, the one who humiliated my darling.[10] I felt at the time if only I were a friend, God help him, dearest if you can respond will you please answer through *Daily Telegraph* personal column, or *Times*, under the name of Jennie, but if you treat it with contempt, let my great love for the sweetest, on God's earth, be my only excuse.

> Yours for ever & ever.
> Jack

It seems that Jennie did not reply in the manner requested:

My dearest Lady Randolph   13/12/16

I greet you sweet one. After much longing, I saw a personal ad in *Times* Dec 2nd and thought it might be yours, but after reflection wondered if you would condescend to acknowledge my poor epistle, even after writing I half relented having done so, my presumption (in cool moments) I considered to be amazing. I am much afraid that at times the heart overrides the brain, but dearest, one thing stands out, every word was the hearts truth, call it folly or what you will, although, I feel that you have sympathy if nothing more, for one who just craves one single thought from the one whom he worships night & day, from the one always in his thoughts, the sweetest woman in creation, my one wish is for your happiness, if only I could be the one to make you so, that would be my gladness, dearest *do forgive* but I want to be yours your very own, yours only for always. I long for you and you alone, my own sweet Jennie, darling I always think of you as Jennie Jerome, my own sweet love, please do not spurn this, it is life to me, and dearest I am longing to know if you really answered, will it be asking too much, if it was so, to repeat in *Times* on Wednesday next 20 inst, if you will please, indicate as J.J. also if I may write again, then I will write you more fully and disclose my identity. Goodnight my own sweet love fondest wishes from yours most lovingly

Jack

Goodnight my own in thought always.

Jennie's spirits went up and down, put perhaps all this attention cheered her up, for she clashed with the rationing authorities about disclosing her age. She obviously felt younger than her 64 years in January 1918, and she was damned if she could see why any red tape should make her admit to them:

> *Local Food Control Committee,*
> *St Marylebone*   6 Holles Street,
>   Oxford Street, W.1.
> Dear Madam,   18th January, 1918
> Adverting to your letter of the 14th December last enclosed with declaration forms in the envelope which you handed to your Retailers, I am directed by the Ministry of Food to inform you that the particulars of date of birth asked for under the Sugar Distribution Scheme are required for two reasons:—
>
> 1. In case of dispute to afford individuals a simple and more expeditious method of proving their identity than would otherwise be possible.
>
> 2. In order that the particulars of age given may be taken into account in connection with any general scheme of rationing which may

hereafter be established for the purpose of determining the appropriate rate of allowance in each case.

I am to ask you to be so kind as to fill in the particulars on your declaration form which I am returning for the purpose.

Yours faithfully,
R. A. V. Morris
Executive Officer

Jennie seems to have lost that battle. She doesn't seem to have got very far with another, either. The sculptor Jacob Epstein asked her to try to use her influence to get him out of the ranks and into propaganda work where his talents might be more useful. Jennie appealed to Lord Beaverbrook, then Minister of Information.

Jennie was conducting that particular campaign from Castle Leslie, in Ireland, where she was staying with Leonie. With her was Montagu Porch, on leave again. As well as eating legs of lamb—unknown in wartime England—they decided to get married. The wedding took place on 1 June, at Harrow Road Register Office. Jennie told the novelist George Moore: 'He has a future and I have a past so we should be all right.' What the family thought is not recorded. It took everyone by complete surprise. Montie wrote to Winston on the morning of his wedding:

Connaught Hotel
Dear Winston,   1/6/18

I am very glad you are able to come to our Wedding. It seems almost incredible that today, when the world is in anguish, I should be allowed so much happiness.

I would now assure you that this, the most important step in my life, is not taken in the dark. I have carefully considered the position from every point of view—your Mother's financial affairs are understood.

I love your Mother, I can make her happy. Her difficulties & obligations from henceforth will be shared by me—so willingly.

I thank you for your kindness & consideration. We shall be good friends.

Yours very truly
M.P.

Winston went over to France a few days later, and saw Jack. They'd heard the story about Jennie's obligations being undertaken before, of course. Jack's reaction on hearing the news was:

General Headquarters,
British Armies in France
25/5/18

Dear Mamma,

What a surprise! Your letter has just been forwarded to me. Whenever I go to war you do these things! I feel sure that you have thought it all out carefully, and that you are certain that you are acting wisely. I know the last few years must have been lonely for you. With both of us married it was inevitable that you should be alone. I do not remember hearing you talk of him and I have never met him. If he makes you happy we shall soon be friends. I wish I could get over for the day—but it is impossible as I am just taking on a new post and I shall probably be moving on the 1st June.

Now, my dear, you know that no one can make any change in our love for one another, and it will be something to know that you are no longer alone. And so I send you my best love and wishes, and pray that all will be well. . . .

It sounds as though the brothers may have been secretly rather relieved that Jennie was off their hands again. Winston was a witness, as was Jack Leslie. Clara and Goonie and Clementine all signed, too. The family was loyal. Even Lady Sarah Wilson, Randolph's youngest sister, was there. As her past was loyal to her, so was Jennie loyal to her past. She was Mrs Porch in law, but she continued to be known as Lady Randolph Churchill till her death.

NOTES

1. Jennie's eldest grandson, John Spencer-Churchill.
2. Cardinal Rafael Merry del Val had a Spanish father and an English mother, and was born and partly educated in England. A swimmer and mountaineer, he became Secretary of State to Pope Pius X, and a Cardinal, in 1903. 'Physically he was the most artistic sight in the basilica of which he became archpriest, St Peter's.' (Shane Leslie, in *The Catholic Encyclopedia*.)
3. Raymond Poincaré, 1860–1934, French President.
4. The Earl of Abingdon.
5. The Hon. James Willoughby Bertie, 1901–66.
6. Commodore Roger Keyes, who had commanded the British submarines at the Battle of Heligoland Bight on August 28th.
7. Wife of Leonie's eldest son Shane.
8. Andrew Bonar Law had become Colonial Secretary in the Coalition Government formed by Asquith in May 1915.
9. Both sons of Clara.
10. Presumably a reference to George.

15

BLESS YOU AND AU REVOIR

Jennie was very happy with Montie Porch, and after the war was over resumed a busy social life. She danced, she took to flying in aeroplanes, she organized parties in France for rich Americans, she kept up with everything and everyone. Montie did his best about her extravagance, but no one ever succeeded in curbing it for long, so in 1921 he decided he'd better go back to Africa and make some money. He went to Coomassie in the Gold Coast (now Kumasi in Ghana), where he had very high hopes of making a quick fortune. Jennie planned to go out and join him, as soon as he'd got a house properly organized. When he set off in March, Jennie wrote him a little note:

My darling,   March 8, 1921
    Bless you and au revoir and I love you better than anything in the world and shall try and do all those things you want me to in your absence.

                                        Your loving wife,
                                              J.
P.S. Love me and think of me.

Montie found it in the pocket of his coat as he went on board his ship.

While he was away, Jennie went back to Rome, where she had met him, and stayed, as she had stayed that time, too, with Vittoria, Duchess of Sermoneta. She had a lovely time, as she wrote to Leonie from Florence on 20 April:

I shall come home as good and sweet-tempered as a cherubim. How wonderful is this place! and what fun I am having! It seems positively selfish to be having such a good time and you in Ireland. Winston, Clemmie and I stayed with the Laverys[1] at Cap d'Ail and he painted some delightful pictures. Vittoria met me in her car and I found Rome very gay, races, dances, *antiquaires*. Her palazzo charming but not grand like the Colonna palace where I lunched. Such magnificence!

They all play bridge *madly* and for very high stakes. I had to stop, you know how badly I play and the Romans are rapacious to a degree!

Jennie thought of taking a big country place and having the whole family to stay with her. She ordered a great many very expensive antiques. She also bought a pair of shoes. Eddie Marsh said she was the sort of woman for whom life did not begin on a basis of less than forty pairs of shoes. Back in England she went to stay with her friend Lady Horner, at Mells, in Somerset. One of those forty pairs of shoes—perhaps the new one—betrayed her. She slipped on the stairs and broke her ankle.

Communications between Coomassie and England were not good, and it was a few days before Montie heard the news. His letters, for the same reason, were written over several days, there being only a few posts. He was so upset when he heard that he put May for June:

> S. Cyprian's House,
> Coomassie,
> The Gold Coast
> 8 May, 1921

My own Darling—I am so terribly distressed, I can hardly pull myself together to write to you some words of comfort & sympathy. Your poor darling little foot—the cable telling me you had broken it met me this morning on my way to the town early. I am terribly upset. My sweet love you will never be able to dance again—you may be crippled. But I shall love you very very much to make up for all the pain & anguish you have suffered.

Thank God, you are at home in your comfortable house with the good tempered & loyal Etienne to look after you—You have your sons near you your sisters & your many friends around you for all this I am v. thankful.

Darling, I am ready to come to you any day—this I have cabled to you. But my business would suffer v. much—my business that has turned out an amazing success.

10th Friday
The Bishop of Accra arrived this evening, as usual I sent my Agent & car to meet him—I should have met him myself but for my business He understands that so well.

The good man was so sympathetic when I told him of my great trouble.

Sunday 12th

Today has been a repetition of last Bishop's Sunday here. Mass at 8.30 & back in time to hear the Bishop's sermon at S. Cyprian's Church.

On the 13th, before closing his letter, he heard news that distressed him terribly. Jennie's ankle had become gangrenous, and her leg had to be amputated above the knee.

13th

My sweet precious Darling only now that you are maimed & tortured I know how much I love you—You poor Darling are in pain—Terrible suffering you must be going through while I am here powerless to help & comfort you. My head aches, my eyes pain me, my throat is swollen with passion & despair—I am ill.

The Bishop has had a steadying effect on me—I showed him Winston's cable I could not tell him about it. I have managed to pull myself together—somehow.

Saturday night I could not sleep—perfectly well & no worries save the anxiety about your poor little foot—I only got to sleep at Dawn—the time I'm usually awake—I told the Bishop what a wretched night I had—I put it down to telepathy from you to me.

Jennie Darling I will help you to bear all this. How can I ever love you enough—I will be very good to you, considerate & faithful—I could never be disloyal to you now.

Bless you sweet Darling—I send you all my love & kisses & more kisses for the poor little place where the stitches are.

Your devoted husband M.

Jennie made a good recovery at first. Winston was able to cable on 23 June that the danger was over. Montie Porch was deeply relieved, but still, naturally, very worried:

S. Cyprian's House,
Coomassie, The Gold Coast
25 June 1921

My own Darling, I love you very much & I am suffering agonies of anxiety. Winston's last cable that 'Danger was definitely over' was reassuring—still I am often frantic with apprehension & fear. I have no one in the world but You that is no one I love, as I love you. Darling, I implore you for my sake to take care of yourself. You must never attempt to move without assistance. Another fall might kill you. Do be careful sweetheart. I long to be with you—it will be such a joy to look after you. I don't mind what I do or how hard I work to help get the comfort you need & deserve.

Thank goodness I have established this wonderful business—it was an inspiration, before long the railway from Accra the capital of the Gold Coast will reach Coomassie. Trade here will then be doubled (v. map).

I have made S. Cyprian's House so nice for you—I shouldn't have spent so much money on myself. And now perhaps you will never come—I can't bear the thought.

Business in general is bad, mine in particular is doing well.

I am picking up the Ashanti language & am getting the Ashanti custom.

The Bank Manager came to my office yesterday—he thinks I am doing amazingly.

I still need a little capital & have written to Terrington to arrange a mortgage of £2000 on 8 Westbourne St. He will then be able to pay Williams the £1000 the other £1000 he will put to my credit at Parrs Bank, Weston S. Mare.

27th

I have arranged with the Inland Revenue Authorities to pay our 1920–1921 tax by instalments the last instalment in Jan 1921. You will therefore have your own little income—entire.

Strachey's *Queen Victoria* has arrived I know I shall enjoy it v. much. The lavender water & toothpaste has reached me too: thank you ever so much, Darling.

A mail arrived yesterday. I got a v. nice letter from my Mother—she is so happy about me & my business venture. But Darling there was no letter from You—but I'm not angry with you for not writing—I shall never be angry with you again.

Mail closes this afternoon so I'll close this in good time. And I'll just say again what you say I can never tell you too often that I love you & will devote my life to you.

Your loving husband M.

He enclosed a map, showing how the railway would run and make his fortune. Jennie knew how worried he must be, and wrote out a cable on the 28th of June saying she'd got his letters and was much comforted and she was all right and was sending him things. The following morning, she suddenly told her nurse that her hot-water bottle must have burst. The nurse pulled back the bed-clothes to see. Jennie saw, too. It was a haemorrhage. She died almost at once.

Years later Montie Porch wrote to Seymour Leslie, sending that last precious note he'd found in his pocket. 'Our married life was a perfect union of temperament & culture where spirituality had its place,' he said. At the time, of all the hundreds of letters which came to Jack and Winston, one from Violet Bonham Carter said everything: 'Your mother was the most intensely living being I have ever known.' Winston himself wrote to Lloyd-George: 'My mother had the gift of eternal youth of spirit.' But perhaps another great Edwardian beauty, Daisy Warwick, should have the last word: 'Do you remember all the fun we had together in the old days, dear Jennie?' she once wrote. 'But I never *regret* anything, do you? We have both *lived* our lives.'

Jennie had indeed lived her life. Now she lay in the little churchyard at Bladon, near Blenheim, next to Randolph. And there, in 1965, she was joined by her famous son.

NOTES

1. Sir John and Lady Lavery. Winston had taken up painting during the war, and Sir John encouraged him. Sir John was an A.R.A. He was knighted in 1918.

REFERENCES

The following abbreviations are used:
AL=*Jennie*, by Anita Leslie, 1969.
ASR=*The Anglo-Saxon Review*.
B=Marquess of Blandford, later 8th Duke of Marlborough.
Blenheim=Blenheim archives.
CJ=Mrs Jerome.
FM=Frances, wife of 7th Duke of Marlborough.
G=George Cornwallis-West.
J=Jennie.
Jk=Jack.
L=Leonie Leslie.
LJ=Leonard Jerome.
LRC=*Lord Randolph Churchill*, by Winston S. Churchill, 1906.
M=7th Duke of Marlborough.
MP=Montagu Porch.
ND=undated.
PSC=MSS in possession of Peregrine S. Churchill.
R=Randolph.
Rems=*The Reminiscences of Lady Randolph Churchill*, 1907.
W=Winston.
WSC=*Winston S. Churchill*, by Randolph S. Churchill and Martin Gilbert, Vols I–III, and Companion Vols, 1966–72.
Chartwell Trust papers are referred to by their file numbers, beginning 28.
Conjectural dates are in brackets.

CHAPTER ONE

The basis for all accounts of Jennie and Randolph's courtship is a typed document in the Blenheim archives (A IV/II) called *Early Recollections*, which Jennie seems to have written for Winston's benefit when he was writing LRC. There are, however, discrepancies between it, LRC and the account given by Randolph to his father. Jennie says that she invited Randolph back to dinner after the ball on the *Ariadne*, which took place on a Tuesday afternoon, and that Randolph asked her to marry him on the third evening of their acquaintance, i.e. Thursday. Randolph told his father he had proposed on the Friday evening. LRC says that Randolph was invited for the Wednesday evening, and proposed on the Thursday.

page
   3 R to J (16/8/73), 28/2.
   4 J to R (17/8/73), 28/92.
     R to J (18/8/73), 28/2.
   5 R to J (19/8/73), 28/2.
     Dod's *Parliamentary Companion*, 1873.
   6 LRC, I, passim.
     R to M 20/8/73, LRC, I, 40–3.
   8 LRC, I, 35.

8–9 R to J (21/8/73), 28/2.
10 B to R 25/8/73, Blenheim A IV/21.
12 R to J (30/8/73), 28/2.
13 J to R (1/9/73), 28/92.
14 M to R 31/8/73, WSC I, Comp I, 12.
   R to J, 4/9/73, 28/2.
15 R to J, 7/9/73, 28/2.
17 R to J, 10/9/73, 28/2.
   CJ to R, 9/9/73, 28/103.
   B to R, 7/9/73, Blenheim A IV/21.
20–21 Francis Knollys to R, 12 & 19/9/73, Blenheim A IV/23.
   R to J (17/9/73), 28/2.

CHAPTER TWO

25 J to R, 16/9/73, 28/92.
27 *The Court Journal*, 13 & 20/9/73.
   R to J, 18/9/73, 28/2.
29 J to R, 18/9/73, 28/92.
   fn. 4 Elizabeth Eliot, *They All Married Well*, 153ff.
30 R to J, 19/9/73, 28/2.
33 R to J, 20/9/73, 28/2.
34 J to R (19/9/73), 28/92.
35 R to J, 22/9/73, 28/2.
38 J to R, 22/9/73, 28/92.
39 R to J, 23/9/73, 28/2.
41 J to R, 26/9/73, 28/92.
42 LJ to J (8/9/73) & 11/9/73, 28/1.
43 CJ to R, 29/9/73, 28/103.
44 R to CJ, 30/9/73, WSC I, Comp I, 15.
   J to R, 29/9/73, 28/92.
45 R to CJ, ND, WSC I, Comp I, 17.
   J to R (3/10/73), 28/92.
46 LJ to J, 7/10/73, 28/1.
   J to R, 24/10/73, 28/92.
   FM to J, 7/1/74, 28/42.
47 J to R, (28/3/74), 28/94.
   R to J, 30/3/74, 28/4.

CHAPTER THREE

50 Rems, 57ff.
51 FM to CJ, 30/11/74, WSC I, 2.
   R to CJ, 30/11/74, WSC I, 1.
52 FM to CJ, 3/12/74, WSC I, Comp I, 4.
53–54 R to B, 31/10/75, B to FM (2/11/75), M to R, 4/11/75, and R to M,
   4/11/75, are all Blenheim A IV/27.
55–56 J to FM (5/11/75), and FM to J, 5/11/75, both 28/42.
57 B to R (5/11/75), Blenheim A IV/27.
58 R to J, 16/1/76, 28/6.
59 R to J, 17/1/76, 28/5.
   J to R, 18/1/76, 28/95.
60 Hawkins to R, 22/12/75, Blenheim L IV/17.

CHAPTER FOUR

62 Philip Magnus, *Edward VII*, 132ff.

63 *Society in London, By a Foreign Resident* (1885), quoted in Anita Leslie, *Edwardians in Love*, 120ff.

64 The Aylesford affair can be followed in detail in WSC I, Comp I, 23-77. Occasional corrections to the printed text have been made from MSS.

65 J to R, 19/4/76, 28/97.

66 J to R, 20/4/76, 28/102.

67 R to J, 20/4/76, 28/5.

68 J to R, 21/4/76, 28/102.

69 WSC I, 33-4.

70 J to R (30/6/76), 28/97.

71 R to J, 30/6/76, 28/5.

72 J to R (2/7/76), 28/97.

73 R to J, 2/7/76, 28/5.
    R to J, 4/7/76, 28/5.
    R to J, 5/7/76, 28/5.
    J to R, 6/7/76, 28/102.

76 W, *My Early Life*, 18-19.
    J to R, 28/96 passim.

CHAPTER FIVE

79 Rems, 91.
    R to J (1/5/77?), 28/6.

80 J to R, ND, 28/96.
    R to J, 15/8/81, 28/7.
    J's Diary, 28/43.
    fn 2. Anita Leslie, *The Fabulous Leonard Jerome*, 254-5.

81-82 J to CJ, ND, Anita Leslie, *The Fabulous Leonard Jerome*, 220.

82 J to R, 10/1/83, 28/98.

83 J to R, 17/12/82, 28/98.

84 J to R, 19/12/82, 28/98.
    J to R, 29/12/82, 28/98.

85-86 R to J, 1/1/83, 28/7.

87 J to R, 3/1/83, 28/98.

88 R to J, 5/1/83, 28/7.

89 fn. 21 Anita Leslie, *The Fabulous Leonard Jerome*, 16, 254 & 284.
    J to R, 8/1/83, 28/98.
    R to J, 11/1/83, 28/7.

91 J to R, 11 & 12/1/83, 28/98.
    J to R, 16/1/83, 28/98.

92 R to J, 16/1/83, 28/7.
    R to J, 17/1/83, 28/7.

CHAPTER SIX

96 W to R, 5/12/84, 28/99.

97 J to R, 5/12/84, 28/99.

98 Miss Thomson to J, 17/12/84, 28/99.
    J to R, 19/12/84, 28/99.

99 R to J, 9 & 24/1/85, 28/7.

Mr Thomas to FM, 15/1/85, 28/7.

J to R, 13/2/85, 28/99.

100 J to R, 20/3/85, 28/98.

101 Rems, 124–7.

103 Sir Henry James to J, Rems, 127.

Francis Knollys to Sir Henry James, 15/3/84, WSC I, Comp I, 77.

Roose to R, 20/6/85, Blenheim N IV/1 (a).

105 Winston's illness may be followed in detail in WSC I, Comp I, 116–22.

Roose to R, 31/3/86, Blenheim N IV/1 (a).

R to J, 20/4/86, 28/7.

106 R to J, 10/7/86, 28/7.

107 R to J, 13/7/86, 28/7. In LRC, II, 123, this and the preceding letter are run together.

Roose to R, 23/7/86, Blenheim N IV/1 (a).

108 LRC, II, 125–7.

109 CJ to J, 5/8/86, 28/1.

CHAPTER SEVEN

111 FM to J, 8/9/86, 28/42.

112 FM to J, 10/9/86, 28/42.

113 R to J (13/9/86), 28/7.

FM to J (13/9/86), 28/42.

114 Lord George Hamilton, *Parliamentary Reminiscences*, II, 38–40.

R to J, 25/9/86, 28/7.

116 FM to J, 26/9/86, 28/42.

117 FM to J, 3/10/86, 28/42.

118 R to J, 6/10/86, 28/7.

R to J, 8/10/86, 28/7.

119 R to J, 12/10/86, 28/7.

LRC, II, 171–2.

R to J, 18/10/86, 28/7.

121 FM to J, 24/10/86, 28/42.

R to J, 1/11/86, 28/7.

122 FM to J, 19/11/86, 28/42.

The Letters of Queen Victoria, Third Series, I, 223–5.

FM to J, 29/11/86, 28/42.

Lady Gwendolen Cecil, *Life of Robert Marquis of Salisbury*, III, 327.

Rems, 141.

123 Brisbane to J, 14/1/87, Blenheim K IV/23.

124 R to Brisbane, 14/1/87, Blenheim K IV/54.

Brisbane to R, 14/1/87, Blenheim K IV/55.

125 J to R, 6/2/87, 28/100.

126 J to R, 15/2/87, 28/100.

R to J, 21/2/87, 28/8.

127 J to R, 21/2/87, 28/100.

128 J to L, ND, AL, 122.

J to R, 5/3/87, 28/100.

CHAPTER EIGHT

131 R to Edward Hamilton, 20/8/94, PSC.
131-2 J to R, 29/4/91, 3/9/91, 7/12/91 & 2/10/91, all in Blenheim H IV/27, 28 & 29.
133 WSC I, Comp I, passim.
J to L, 4/8/94, 28/115.
J to C, 18/11/94, WSC, Comp I, 535–6.
Jk to R, 30/11/94, 28/30.
134 J to L, December 1894, Anita Leslie MSS.
135 J to L, 3/1/95, WSC I, Comp I, 545.
136 J to Jk, 14/1/95, PSC.

CHAPTER NINE

138 W to J, 24/2/95, WSC I, Comp I, 559.
139 Rems, 278.
For George Cornwallis-West's family and background, see the highly enjoyable biography *Perfect Darling*, by Eileen Quelch.
Edwardian Hey-Days, 101–2.
140 G to J, 3/7/98, 28/34.
141 G to J, ND, 28/34.
G to J, 13/7/98, 28/34.
142 G to J, 19/7/98, 28/38.
G to J, 25/7/98, 28/34.
G to J, 29/7/98, 28/34.
G to J, ND, 28/38.
G to J, 1/8/98, 28/34.
143 G to J, 5/8/98, 28/34.
G to J, 23/8/98, 28/34.
144 G to J, 25/8/98 & 2/9/98, 28/34.
Edwardian Hey-Days, 38–9.
Curzon to J, 7/9/98, WSC I, Comp II, 975.
145 G to J, 12/9/98, 28/34.
J to Jk, 20/9/98, PSC.
AL, 223.
G to J, 7/10/98, 16/10/98 & 2/11/98, 28/34.
146 G to J, 3/11/98 & 9/11/98, 28/34.

CHAPTER TEN

148-9 Rems, 285, & J, *Small Talks on Big Subjects*, 31–2.
149 Oscar Wilde to J, ND, Rems, 217.
150 Rems, 279ff & 285.
W to J, 1/1/99, WSC I, Comp II, 997.
W to J, 2/3/99, WSC I, Comp II, 1012.
151 J to Jk, 24/2/99, PSC.
152 G to J, 6/3/99, 28/35.
G to J, 10/4/99, 28/35.
J to Jk, 24/2/99, PSC.
G to J, 7/6/99, 28/35.
Oldham Daily Standard, 27 & 28/6/99.
G to J, 11/7/99, 28/35.

153 G to J, 15/7/99, 28/35.
   Edwardian Hey-Days, 118.
   Confessions of the marquis de Castellane, 225.
154 G to J, 11/8/99, 28/35.
   G to J, 12/8/99, 28/35.
   G to J, 14/8/99, 28/35.
155 G to J, 19/8/99, 28/35.
   G to J, 20/8/99, 28/35.
   G to J, 22/8/99, 28/35.
156 G to J, 23/8/99, 28/35.
   Lady Curzon to J, 3/11/99, 28/66.
   G to J, 24/8/99, 28/35.
157 G to J, 12/9/99, 28/35.
   G to J, 14/9/99, 28/35.
   G to J, 16/9/99, 28/35.

CHAPTER ELEVEN

158 G to J, 6/10/99, 28/35.
   Prince of Wales to G, 15/10/99, *Edwardian Hey-Days*, 105.
   Edwardian Hey-Days, 105–6.
   G to J, 21/10/99, 28/35.
159 *Edwardian Hey-Days*, 107.
   WSC I, Comp II, 1052.
   W to J, 3/9/99, WSC I, Comp II, 1046.
160 For details of the *Maine*, see *The American Hospital Ship 'Maine' Fund: Reports, List of Subscriptions, Donations, Etc.* N.D.
   For Fanny Ronalds, see Anita Leslie, *The Fabulous Leonard Jerome.*
161 Clara Frewen to L, ND, Seymour Leslie MSS.
   Rems, 316.
   Patsy Cornwallis-West and Kinsky to J, ND, 28/69.
   Rosebery to J, ND, 28/67.
   G to J, 3/12/99, 28/35.
163 *Edwardian Hey-Days*, 114.
   Rems, 322.
   G to J, 23/12/99, 28/35.
164 *Edwardian Hey-Days*, 116.
   G to J, 23/12/99, 28/35.
165 J to L, 24/12/99, Anita Leslie MSS.

CHAPTER TWELVE

167 *Maine* Reports, passim.
168 ASR, V, 218–37.
172 Rems, 329–30.
   W to J, 13/2/1900, WSC I, Comp II, 1149–50.
   J to Jk, ND, PSC.
173 G to J, 16/2/00, 28/36.
   G to J, 18/1/00, 28/36.
174 G to J, 2/2/00, 28/36.
175 G to J, 6/2/00, 28/36.
   J to W, ND, PSC.

176 Colonel Cornwallis-West to L, ND, Seymour Leslie, *The Jerome Connexion*, 54–5.
   G to J, 21/4/00, 28/36.
178 J to W, 24/5/00, PSC.
179 Lord Knutsford, quoted in Anita Leslie, *Edwardians in Love*, 226.
   Edwardian Hey-Days, 120.
   Lansdowne, to J, 20/6/00, WSC I, Comp II, 1181.
   G to J, ND, 28/36.
180 *Edwardian Hey-Days*, 121.
   J to Jk, 23/6/00, PSC.
181 Jk to J, 2/6/00, 28/32.
   J to Jk, 30/6/00, PSC.
   Jk to J, 5/7/00, 28/32.
   J to Jk, 28/7/00, PSC.
183 G to W, 30/7/00, WSC I, Comp II, 1187.
   W to Jk, 31/7/00, WSC I, Comp II, 1188.
   G to J, 28/9/00, 28/36.

CHAPTER THIRTEEN

185 *Edwardian Hey-Days*, 119–22, 128 & 137.
186 WSC II, Comp I, 591–2.
   Eileen Quelch, *Perfect Darling*, passim.
187–8 G to J, ND, 8/3/06, & 9/3/06, 28/38.
187 *From My Private Diary*, by Daisy, Princess of Pless, 206.
   J to L, 15/5/07, Anita Leslie MSS.
188 Henry James to J, 5/10/08, 28/78.
189 J to L, 23/4/09, Seymour Leslie, *The Jerome Connexion*, 56.
190 J to L, 27/6/09, Anita Leslie MSS.
   Kinsky to J, 23/4/09, 28/78.
191 See the programme for the Tournament: *The Triumph holden at Shakespeare's England on the eleventh day of July in the third year of the reign of King George the Fifth.*
192 J to Mrs Cornwallis-West, 14/8/10, PSC.
   Jk to J, 4/4/11, PSC.
193 Clementine Churchill to J, ND, 28/80.
   Gwendeline Churchill to J, 7/4/11, 28/135.
194 J to G, 19/4/11, 28/28.
195 G to J, 29/12/12, 28/39.
196 J to G, 31/12/12, 28/39.
   G to J, 7/1/13, 28/39.
   fn. 11 Elizabeth Eliot, *They All Married Well*, 269.
197 Lady Henry Grosvenor to J, 16/7/13, 28/38.
   Curzon to J, 30/1/14, 28/84.
   J to L, 7/10/13, Anita Leslie MSS.
   G to J, 31/12/13, 28/39.
198 J to G, 5/1/14, 28/39.
   Daisy, Princess of Pless to J, 4/4/14, 28/39.
   J to G, 4/4/14, 28/39.
   Daisy, Princess of Pless to J, 7/4/14, 28/39.
   Shelagh, Duchess of Westminster to J, 15/4/14, 28/39.

199 L to J (6/4/14), 28/136.
   L to J (8/4/14), 28/136.
200 L to J (11/4/14), 28/136.
   G to J, 5/11/14, 28/39.
   J to G, 5/1/17, 28/129.
   J to G, 17/6/19, Anita Leslie MSS.
201 G to W, ND, Chartwell Trust MSS, 1/143.

CHAPTER FOURTEEN

202 J to Jk, 4/3/14, 28/152.
   J to L, 24/7/14, Seymour Leslie, *The Jerome Connexion*, 57.
203 MP to J, 16/5/14, 28/84.
204 fn. 2 Shane Leslie, article on Cardinal Merry del Val in *The Catholic Encyclopaedia*, Supplement II (1951).
   Jk to J, 14/2/14, 28/33.
   Jk to J, 31/7/14, 28/33.
   J to L, 1/8/14, Anita Leslie MSS.
205 Gwendeline Churchill to J, ND, 28/135.
206 Gwendeline Churchill to Jk, 1/9/14, PSC.
207 J to L, 16/8/14, Anita Leslie MSS.
208 J, *Small Talks on Big Subjects*, 109–11.
   Jk to J, 14/2/14, 28/33.
209 MP to J, 5/10/14, 28/84.
   MP to J, 2/10/15, 28/122.
210 Katherine Mott to the Kaiser, 28/127.
   L to J, ND, 28/136.
211 J to Katherine Mott, 10/1/16, 28/127.
   J to Jordan Mott, 10/1/16, 28/127.
212 J to Shane Leslie, 3/9/16, Anita Leslie MSS.
   Shane Leslie to J, 30/1/16, 28/127.
   MP to J, 22/6/16, 28/127.
213 Anon to J, ND, 28/127.
214 Anon to J, 13/12/16, 28/127.
   Local Food Control Committee to J, 18/1/18, 28/130.
215 Letters about Epstein in 28/130.
   MP to W, 1/6/18, Chartwell Trust MSS, 1/129.
216 Jk to J, 25/5/18, 28/121.

CHAPTER FIFTEEN

217 J to MP, 8/3/21, AL, 350.
   J to L, 20/4/21, Seymour Leslie, *The Jerome Connexion*, 88.
218 Edward Marsh, *A Number of People*, 154.
   MP to J, 8/6/21, 28/133.
219 MP to J, 25/6/21, 28/133.
221 MP to Seymour Leslie, Seymour Leslie MSS.
   Violet Bonham-Carter to W, 28/138.
   W to Lloyd-George, 28/138.
   Daisy Warwick to J, ND, 28/136.

THE CHURCHILL FAMILY TREE

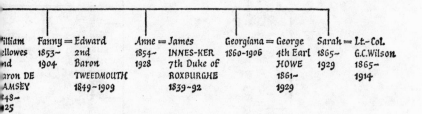

William
ellowes
nd
aron DE
AMSEY
848~
25

Fanny = Edward
1853~   2nd
1904   Baron
         TWEEDMOUTH
         1849~1909

Anne = James
1854~ INNES-KER
1928   7th Duke of
       ROXBURGHE
       1839~92

Georgiana = George
1860~1906   4th Earl
            HOWE
            1861~
            1929

Sarah = Lt.-Col.
1865~   G.C.Wilson
1929   1865~
        1914

John = Gwendeline
1880~ d. of 7th Earl
1947   of Abingdon
       1885~1941

John
1909~

Henry
Winston
(Peregrine)
1913~

Clarissa = Anthony Eden
1920~   1st Earl of Avon
           1897~

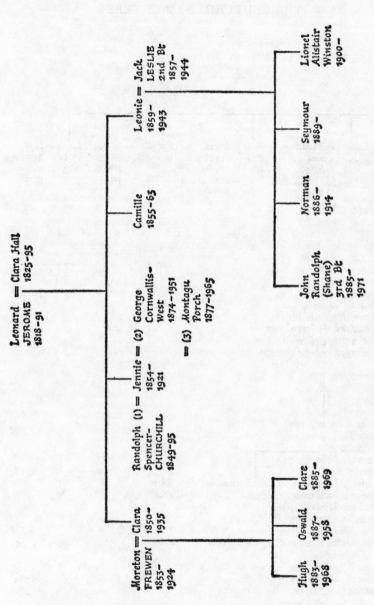

THE JEROME FAMILY TREE

INDEX